Information Technology Education in the New Millennium

Mohammad Dadashzadeh, Ph.D.
Wichita State University, USA

Al Saber, Ph.D.
Friends University, USA

Sherry Saber, M.S.
Friends University, USA

IRM Press
Publisher of innovative scholarly and professional
information technology titles in the cyberage

Hershey • London • Melbourne • Singapore • Beijing

Acquisitions Editor:	Mehdi Khosrowpour
Managing Editor:	Jan Travers
Assistant Managing Editor:	Amanda Appicello
Copy Editor:	Amanda Appicello
Cover Design:	Tedi Wingard
Printed at:	Integrated Book Technology

Published in the United States of America by
  IRM Press
  1331 E. Chocolate Avenue
  Hershey PA 17033-1117
  Tel: 717-533-8845
  Fax: 717-533-8661
  E-mail: cust@idea-group.com
  Web site: http://www.irm-press.com

and in the United Kingdom by
  IRM Press
  3 Henrietta Street
  Covent Garden
  London WC2E 8LU
  Tel: 44 20 7240 0856
  Fax: 44 20 7379 3313
  Web site: http://www.eurospan.co.uk

Library of Congress Cataloging-in-Publication Data

Dadashzadeh, Mohammad.
  Information technology education in the new millennium / Mohammad Dadashzadeh, Al Saber, Sherry Saber.
    p. cm.
  Includes bibliographical references and index.
  ISBN 1-931777-05-5 (paper)
  1. Information technology--Study and teaching (Higher) I. Saber, Al, 1942- II. Saber, Sherry, 1944- III. Title.

  T58.5 .D33 2002
  004'.071--dc21   2001059446

eISBN: 1-931777-24-1

British Cataloguing in Publication Data
A Cataloguing in Publication record for this book is available from the British Library.

Information Technology Education in the New Millennium

Table of Contents

Foreword

How will information technology (IT) education evolve in the new millennium? Brainstorming answers to this question in an era of knowledge management, life-long self-directed learning, distant education, virtual universities, mobile Internet, e-learning, and virtual reality conjures up interesting images. An amusing one is based on the movie, The Matrix, where the protagonist learned kung fu in seconds by having the core skills downloaded directly into his mind. Will we similarly witness our students downloading Java programming skills or the best practices in information systems analysis and design directly into their minds?

The IT sector is expected to continue to face a severe shortage of workers. According to Information Technology Association of America's *When Can You Start: Building Better Information Technology Skills and Careers* study (April 2001), 425,000 IT positions will likely go unfilled this year. To address this "new deficit" in our digital economy, increasing numbers of IT employers are establishing school-to-career partnerships with the goal of developing a reliable IT job pipeline. That is, a labor pool of skilled workers with technical (IT), academic foundation (mathematics, science, general education), and soft skills (problem solving, communication, teamwork, etc.) needed for entry into IT careers. A workforce trained by educators who receive the career awareness and IT training *they* need, when and where they need it, to integrate information age paradigms for learning and working into high quality IT curriculums.

Eager to help fill the IT labor shortage, a growing number of programs have targeted retraining workers from other fields. Paving the way has been the mainstream acceptance of IT certification as a viable method for measuring an employee's skill set. Since 1989, when Novell awarded the first such certificate, the offerings of certificates (Microsoft, Oracle, Cisco, Novell, A+, etc.) and the demand for certification have grown dramatically around the world, reaching an estimated total of 2.5 million certifications (not people) to date. This "parallel universe" of IT education and training, that is competency-based, confers certificates not degrees, and exists beyond government's control, caught higher education off guard and there is no turning back.

The growth of IT certification will continue to come from the supply side. As new developments in IT rise to meet the challenges of exploring new frontiers in a pervasively networked, knowledge-centric world, there will be a greater requirement for specialization in IT tools, methodologies, and processes. Vendors, IT industry associations, and large intermediary "training partners" will continue to formally establish standards for what it takes to perform at an optimal level in different areas of information technology. In turn, other vendors will recognize this public set of educational objectives, students reach for those standards, and employers feel free to require a proxy for their attainment leading to a supply-side opportunity for IT certification and re-certification. Universities and other institutes of higher education have no choice but to join the move towards acknowledging IT certifications as becoming as valuable as college credit and even equivalent to it.

Even with universities joining the IT certification marketplace, the increased numbers of certified graduates will not solve the IT *skills* shortage unless the fundamental problem of learning in isolation from the realities of the workplace, inherent in traditional classroom settings or on the Internet, is also addressed. Structured internships, where the work assigned is closely aligned with the educational curriculum and company supervisors work closely with faculty, can go a long way in improving the situation, just as informal learning or learning on the job can. Moving toward an experiential approach by focusing on intact work groups to build teamwork and classroom exercises based on participants' actual challenges and problems on the job can elevate training to where learning occurs through organizational intervention, and education becomes akin to "edutainment" accelerating the learning process.

Edutaining our youth in IT is an effective long-term strategy to address the growing demand for skilled IT professionals. In the near-term, a promising solution is to send existing employees back to school to be retrained for IT skills and certification. Notwithstanding the promise and the potential benefits, employers justifiably fear that training and certification lead to higher salaries and turnover. Although high turnover is not unusual in any type of job characterized by growing demand and increasing wages, turnover among IT professionals is much higher than among professionals in other occupations. Surveys, however, indicate that IT workers are motivated as much by the opportunity to develop new skills as by compensation. Hence, providing increased opportunities for formal and informal learning on the job will continue to remain a key strategy for retaining skilled IT workers.

As more and more organizations accept IT training as a strategic investment and not a cost center, the adoption of e-learning will accelerate. The initial attraction, of course, will be its cost effectiveness in providing just the right amount of IT training to meet a very specific learning need whenever and wherever it is needed. The indelible attraction, however, will be felt when full advantage is taken of the potential of e-learning for creating an experiential learning program that allows the student to absorb the theory in a highly interactive environment and to take newly acquired IT skills and apply them in a virtually real world. This can only be achieved by allowing the learner to actively experiment with information technology in the real world, or at least a very close simulation of it. Therefore, for example, although the interviewing skills for systems analysis will not be directly downloaded into the mind of the student, the learned skills will be immediately applied in a simulated real world scenario in the virtual classroom.

So, how will IT education evolve in the new millennium? Well, as the research contributions in this volume attest, IT education in an era of knowledge management, life-long self-directed learning, distant education, virtual universities, mobile Internet, e-learning, and virtual reality will look noticeably different. Nevertheless, beneath the new look of IT education a fundamental truth will remain constant:

Tell me, and I forget.
Show me, and I remember.
Involve me, and I learn.

Mohammad Dadashzadeh, Al Saber and Sherry Saber
August 17, 2001

Preface

The field of information technology (IT) education encompasses many areas: educating the IT professional, using IT in the classroom, curriculum issues and the issues associated with distance learning and web-based learning. As information technology is changing rapidly, it is essential for the curriculum being taught to students to keep up with changes. Additionally, rapidly developing technologies can be used to significantly enhance the ways in which students are taught and what they are being taught. The challenges facing IT educators are far more challenging and IT educators need to keep up with these technologies in order to be effective educators. The chapters of this book address the practical experiences of IT educators and those who utilize IT in their teaching. Web-base learning and teaching, accreditation issues, where and how students should be taught and the ethics associated with IT are just some of the issues addressed in the following chapters.

Chapter 1 entitled, "Web-Delivered Education: Shaking the Foundations of the 'Establishment'?" by David A. Banks of University of South Australia suggests that the growth of the new and dynamic educational marketplace, populated by a wide range of education providers will bring with it significant new problems, or rather new incarnations of older problems, that may challenge the existence of some current educational providers. The chapter indicates that these threats are not technical, but are being driven by market related perceptions that may alter provider/student relationships as the web-enabled, client-led learning paradigm develops.

Chapter 2 entitled, "An Advanced Course in Application Programming and Design" by Cecil Schmidt of Washburn University (USA) gives an overview of new course offerings which address the need of the continuing evolution in state-of-the-art business applications such as those that support e-commerce, advancements in programming language such as Java, and the requirements for persistent data access mechanisms. The author suggests that application design should emphasize object-oriented techniques that take full advantage of the most recent enhancements to programming language and that alternative file structures and data access methods should be incorporated into course developments.

Chapter 3 entitled, "Establishing a Telecommunications and Networking Technology B.S. Degree" by Julie Mariga of Purdue University (USA) discusses how a telecommunications and networking bachelor's degree option was established at Purdue University. The chapter discusses why the program started and how it has evolved. Other areas discussed in this chapter include: the curriculum, facilities, faculty and the industrial advisory board. The chapter concludes by examining the future direction for growth of the program.

Chapter 4 entitled, "An Action Learning Approach for the Development of Technology Skills" by Richard L. Peterson and Joan D. Mahoney of Montclair State University (USA) is a case study of the experiences of students in a course that required them to complete action learning technology projects for social services clients. The results discussed in the chapter suggest a generalizable model for improving the relevance of the curriculum within universities in the 21st century.

Chapter 5 entitled, "Real-World Learning of Information Resource Management" by Dusan Lesjak and Miroslav Rebernik of the University of Maribor (Slovenia) describes an Information Resources Management program at the Faculty of Economics and Business at the University of Maribor, Slovenia that is based on a real-world learning principle. The aim of the described course is to provide students with knowledge and experience to deal with information technology systems in small business from a managerial perspective. The theoretical part of the course is conducted in a classroom and the practical part is experienced in mentor firms. Thus students have an opportunity to compare, combine and verify theory and practice instantly and to develop capabilities to transfer the acquired knowledge and skills into practice.

Chapter 6 entitled, "IS Education in the New Millennium: Determining the 'Right' Curriculum" by Sanjeev Phukan of Bemidji State University (USA), Ashok Ranchhod of the Southampton Business School (U.K.) and T. Vasudavan of Edith Cowan University (Australia) presents an exploratory investigation of a specific class in which a case method was taught in both online and face-to-face modes. The study captures some insights on the processes that were seen from a participant observer's perspective. The chapter identifies the changing roles of the instructor and students in an online case discussion. It points out three factors unique to the dynamics of a computer-mediated environment. Finally, the study indicates a number of learning instances that are non-traditional. Most important is the evidence for emancipatory learning as manifested in students' action to be self-determining and self-reflective.

Chapter 8 entitled, "The Place of Homework in an Information Systems Tutorial" by Bill Morgan and Bob Godfrey of the University of Tasmania (Australia) presents findings from a study of Information Systems tutorials. The study presented in the chapter seeks to discover the use of prescribed homework which improves the learning of the students. In addition to regular tests, examinations and assignments, students were given homework to complete. Students are then surveyed using the College and University Classroom Environment Inventory (CUCEI) instrument before and after the experiment. Several components of the study show significant improvement for those students in these tutorials.

Chapter 9 entitled, "Human Learning Models and Data Collection Over the 'Long Haul'" by Kevin Reilly and Norman Bray of the University of Alabama Birmingham (USA) offers solutions and suggestions based on the authors' experiences and theory-based practical approaches. The authors note that modeling human learning and performance that also involved data collection requires teamwork. They further note that when research is of long duration, changes occur in personnel and research areas. The chapter identifies several problems in the "long haul" inter-disciplinary research in which IT plays a key role.

Chapter 10 entitled, "Are Information Systems Students in Their Right Minds?" by Steven Benson and Craig Standing of Edith Cowan University (Australia) examines the fundamental thinking styles and the implications for IS course design and delivery. The authors conducted an initial investigation into the left versus right brain orientation of their students and curriculum. Given the logical and technical biases of information systems, the expectation was to find a high degree of logical left brained orientation in the student sample. Contrary to their expectations, the authors found that the ration of right to left brained students was 3:1. The chapter outlines the left-right brain divide and questions the validity of the division from a neuropsychological perspective. The chapter then discusses the practical implication of the exercise and identifies issues for further research.

Chapter 11 entitled, "The Gender Issue in Information Technology: Collegiate and Corporate Solutions" by Donald Caputo and Frederick Kohun of Robert Morris College (USA) focuses on the ongoing strategies employed for the integration and retention of women in the collegiate and corporate sphere. The chapter recounts the experiences of the authors in revamping the information systems program at Robert Morris College. The program was modified from a one-size-fits all program to a program with tracks that included different options. The chapter reports that the program grew at an astounding rate after the change took place and reports the changes also helped retain women in the program.

Chapter 12 entitled, "A Methodology for Validating Entry Level Value versus Career Value of Courses in an MIS Program" by Earl Chrysler of Quinnipiac College and Stuart Van Auken of Florida Gulf Coast University (USA) reports on a study designed to determine which entry level and career-level course evaluations are drivers of an attitude of approval toward an MIS program, and whether alumni evaluations coincide with the beliefs of faculty who designed the curriculum. The chapter concludes that the extent to which the value of the content of a course is a driver of a graduates overall satisfaction with the course correlates to the graduate's time frame.

Chapter 13 entitled, "A Personalized System of Instruction for Teaching Java" by Henry Emurian of University of Maryland-Baltimore County and Ashley Durham of Health Care Financing Administration (USA) addresses the challenge of how to structure a learning environment to teach object-oriented computer programming to students who may need an introductory course in that discipline, but who lack the experience to use symbol manipulation with confidence. The chapter presents data gathered from self-report and performance in the pedagogical approach which is described.

Chapter 14 entitled, "Places and Processes in Learning Environments" by I.T. Hawryszkiewycz of the University of Technology (Australia) describes ways to create a variety of learning environments. The chapter suggests that good practices require both the definition of places of learning as well as clear definitions of processes to be followed within the learning places. The chapter then presents a metamodel for defining different environments as well as a system called LiveNet which can be used to configure different learning environments to implement the metamodel.

Chapter 15 entitled, "IS Program Issues: From Origin to Accreditation" by Douglas Leif of Bemidji State University (USA) suggests the challenges of academic information systems programs are a product of origin and evolution. Based upon literature and survey results, the author then suggests issues concerning origin, perceptions, solutions and accreditation. The chapter discusses why accreditation is important to industry and how universities can improve.

Chapter 16 entitled, "Educating the Business Information Technologist: Developing a Strategic IT Perspective" by John Mendonca of Purdue University (USA) discusses why a strategic perspective is important for all IT professionals to develop. The chapter then proposes a framework for teaching strategic IT to non-managers. The author explains the need for fostering a strategic information perspective for non-managers and illustrates a practical application of that framework. The chapter indicates that the third-era view of IT as a strategic resource within a fast-paced, fast-changing environment places the burden of strategic thinking on all levels of IT workers. Education and practice for developing this perspective is critical to meet the expectations of corporate leaders, and this chapter explains the crucial steps.

Chapter 17 entitled, "Collaborative Ph.D. Examination" by Mike Metcalfe and Samantha Grant of the University of South Australia argues for an interpretist approach of enriching the learning experience of the examiner, Ph.D. candidate, supervisor and university by requiring the advantages of complex sustained interaction in an oral examination. The chapter provides a literature review in support of the argument that examiners need to be interactively involved with supervisors and examiners, especially in IS which changes rapidly and is experiencing a move from positive to interpretive methodologies.

Chapter 18 entitled, "Information Systems and Computer Science Model Curricula: A Comparative Look" by Anthony Scime of State University of New York College at Brockport (USA) explores the intricacies of the interrelationship between computer science and information systems. The author looks at why universities lack the funding necessary to support two computer-related departments and provides a model for IS and CS curricula. The aim of this chapter is to provide IT departments the ability to develop an information technology curriculum which can effectively meet the needs of its students.

Chapter 19 entitled, "E-Commerce Curriculum Development and Implementation" by Linda Knight and Susy Chan of DePaul University (USA) proposes a conceptual model for the design and development of an e-commerce curriculum and chronicles the experiences of DePaul University's School of Computer Science, Telecommunications and Information Systems in developing a new e-commerce Master's degree. The chapter identifies eight key principles for universities seeking to embark on a new e-commerce curriculum.

Chapter 20 entitled, "The Challenge of Teaching Research Skills to Information Systems and Technology Students" by Beverley Hope of Victoria University of Wellington (New Zealand) and City University of Hong Kong (China) and Mariam Fergusson of PricewaterhouseCoopers (Australia) identifies the core of research skills needed by information technology students. The authors present three pragmatic models for teaching these skills. This research provides a basis for a shared knowledge and discussion based on the lessons learned.

Chapter 21 entitled, "Towards Establishing the Best Ways to Teach and Learn About IT" by Chris Cope, Lorraine Staehr and Pat Horan of La Trobe University (Australia) reports on an ongoing project the ways people teach and learn about information technology (IT). By using a relational perspective on learning, the authors have developed a framework of factors to encourage students to adopt thoughtful approach to learning about IT. This chapter describes the design, implementation, evaluation and refinement of learning contexts and learning activities based on the framework.

Chapter 22 entitled, "Bridging the Industry-University Gap: An Action Research Study of Web-Enabled Course Partnership" by Ned Kock of Temple

University and Camille Auspitz and Brad King of Day & Zimmerman (USA) discusses a course partnership involving Day & Zimmerman, Inc. (DZI), a large engineering and professional services company. The course's primary objective was to teach students business process redesign concepts and techniques. A Web site with bulletin boards, multimedia components and static content was used to support the partnership. The chapter looks at the use of Web-based collaboration technologies used in conjunction with communication behavior and face-to-face meets. The authors evaluate the success of these modes of learning and their effect on the partnership.

Chapter 23 entitled, "Data Modeling: A Vehicle for Teaching Creative Problem Solving and Critical Appraisal Skills" by Clare Atkins of Nelson Marlborough Institute of Technology (New Zealand) looks at the process of learning data modeling techniques. In order to successfully master these techniques, students must understand the problem, be able to create and recognize a number of possible solutions, and then utilize critical thinking skills in choosing between them. This chapter examines these issues and describes various ways in which senior undergraduate students, taking a specific course in data modeling, have been encourage to develop their creative and critical ability to solve problems.

Chapter 24 entitled, "Information Systems Curriculum Development as an Ecological Process" by Arthur Tatnall of Victoria University of Technology and Bill Davey of RMIT University (Australia) argues that in order to understand how and information systems (IS) curriculum is built, and how the human and non-human interactions contribute to the final products, it is essential to utilize an approach that allows the complexity to be traced and not diminished by categorization or assumptions.

Chapter 25 entitled, "Teaching or Technology: Who's Driving the Bandwagon?" by Geoffrey C. Mitchell of Victoria University of Wellington and Beverley Hope of Victoria University of Wellington (Australia) and City University of Hong Kong (China) argues that instead of revolutionizing education, often Web-based education just reinforces poor teaching practices. The authors indicate that this occurs because of a limited understanding of how flexible learning demands an increased focus on constructivism and the sociological aspects of teaching. The chapter presents two frameworks that situate an approach to flexible learning with respect to more traditional education.

Educational theory is constantly changing. The modes and methods of student learning must evolve to keep up with emerging technologies. The IT field is rapidly expanding and universities are facing the daunting task of keeping up with emerging technologies. The chapters in this book represent the best research and practice of information systems curriculum, web-based learning and teaching, educational theory as it applies to the IT field, the ethical issues of IT as well as

x

strategies for teaching emerging technologies. Leading experts in the fields of education and IT share their years of expertise and outline the road to successful technology use and teaching as well as sharing practical tips on how to avoid some of the pitfalls that may lie ahead in the implementation and teaching of IT. This book provides practical guidelines for researchers and practitioners alike. It will be useful to teachers as they strive to improve their teaching, and the research contained herein is an excellent resource for academicians and students.

IRM Press
October 2001

Chapter 1

Web-Delivered Education: Shaking the Foundations of the "Establishment"?

David A. Banks
University of South Australia, Australia

There is a growing emphasis upon the provision of education through web delivery services that will allow universities and other educational providers to reach out to a global audience. The benefits for the learner include the prospect of flexible systems that provide greater consumer choice in terms of subject, times and patterns of study, and choice of institution. The availability of such a diverse, rich and accessible opportunity for learners, combined with the larger market place would seem to offer established educational institutions many advantages and benefits. This chapter suggests, however, that the growth of such a new and dynamic educational marketplace, populated by a wide range of education providers, will bring with it significant new problems, or rather new incarnations of older problems, that may challenge existence of some current educational providers. These threats are not technical, instead being driven by market related perceptions that may alter provider/student relationships as the web-enabled client-led learning paradigm develops.

INTRODUCTION

On the 28th of May, 1968, the students and some of the staff took control of Hornsey College of Art, North London, as part of a revolt against what they saw as an education system that did not support the needs of students. They boldly declared that the college was in the control of the students and that they were demanding a new educational structure that would better meet the needs of the students.

The staff and students were striving to achieve a system where "lecturers" and "students" become partners engaged on the same task, as opposed to the authoritarian models still in use: lecturer as ruler; pupil as subject; lecturer as priest; and student as acolyte (The Hornsey Affair, 1969).

Although that "revolution" was unsuccessful, the core educational structures demanded by the staff and students appear to be sound, and perhaps modern web-based education would applaud, and could quickly address, many of the key ideas. The "revolutionaries" proposed an educational system characterised by the following focal issues:

- An open system whereby all individual demands can be taken into account whether specialised or comprehensive.
- Subjects to be set up in response to the need of individual or group of students at any moment – thus the curricula will be in a constant state of flux.
- Within the operational curricula of any one moment there will be total freedom of choice of options and combinations available to everyone.
- Complete freedom of individual or group research at any time with or without tutorial assistance.
- A system of invited tutors who are engaged for the duration of a project that involves them. Probably only technical staff will be engaged full time.
- Tutors will be determined as suitable according to student evaluation.
- Tutors are those people who have any information that an individual or group want. They can be drawn from any area of involvement.
- The spatial, social materials and equipment organisation should have an equivalent degree of flexibility in use as embodied in the curricula and tutorial structure outlined above.
- All facilities to be open 168 hours a week throughout the year.

This proposal, however educationally attractive at first examination, would appear to have posed several significant problems for the managers of the system that was then in place. Firstly, the process indicated in the student demands would not lend itself to "easy" management of resources (rooms, staff, facilities) as it requires a lack of rigid arrangement of defined subjects. Secondly, the making available of resources on a twenty-four hour basis would have posed practical problems both in terms of finance and management of the security of those resources. Thirdly, the selection of teaching staff by the students would typically raise issues of the validity of the selection process and "credentials" of the appointed "staff," and also of the remuneration of individuals employed on what would be key but, paradoxically, casual contracts. The fundamental problem may well have been that while this would appear to be a truly flexible and student-centred system, a concept to which education frequently pays lip service, its practical application would have had a profoundly threatening impact on existing top-down management systems. Speaking at a meeting with staff and students Sir John Summerson, Chair of the National Council for the Diploma in Art and Design, expressed some of the tensions:

> If you could plan your education for … the type of people who are filling this room at the moment, completely absorbed and dedicated in the problems of art education and their own education, if you could plan education for a body of students who were consistently of that kind, how very much faster you would get along … [but] Education has to be planned on a long-term basis and allow for variations in personality and character that crop up, and for fluctuations year by year … It's got to have some rigid parts to it. It's got to have an Establishment, it's got to have a respectable lid on top of it (The Hornsey Affair).

Conventional educational systems certainly do have to have a measure of rigidity in them, given that they rely heavily on an administrative underpinning to regulate rooms bookings, enrollments, graduations, exams and all of the other structures of typical educational systems. The concept of absolute free choice of study pattern, lecturer and so on can be argued as being totally at odds with a well regulated and managed system in which the student follows prescribed routes at a fixed rate of progress. The availability of web based systems can offer solutions to some of the issues of flexibility of delivery, efficient use of resources etc., but the deeper educational issues of freedom of students to choose staff on the basis of either perceived suitability or on the basis of student reviews may become even more complex and contentious.

As may have been expected, the students and staff did not achieve their idealised learning environment, possibly partly as a result of their overt frontal attack on the establishment. Other writers were also attacking the system, equally strongly, but through the medium of writing rather than direct confrontation.

"DE-SCHOOLING"

Ivan Illich (1971) was a strong critic of the prevailing school system, stating that it tended to confuse process and substance, leading to a position where:

> "The pupil is thereby 'schooled' to confuse teaching with learning, grade advancement with education, a diploma with competence, and fluency with the ability to say something new."

He suggested that a good educational system should have three purposes:

> "… it should provide all who want to learn with access to available resources at any time in their lives; empower all who want to share what they know to find those who want to learn it from them; and, finally, furnish all who want to present an issue to the public with the opportunity to make their challenge known"

This statement echoes some of the key concerns of the Hornsey revolutionaries but also includes an element of public interaction with the educational system. Illich was also stronger in his condemnation of the prevailing educational system, arguing that:

"Learners should not be forced to submit to an obligatory curriculum, or to discrimination based on whether they possess a certificate or a diploma. Nor should the public be forced to support, through a regressive taxation, a huge professional apparatus of educators and buildings which in fact restricts the public's chances for learning to the services the profession is willing to put on the market. It should use modern technology to make free speech, free assembly, and a free press truly universal and, therefore, fully educational."

Here we can see the seeds of an open, technology-based educational system that challenges the notion of "professional apparatus of educators and buildings." He challenges the idea of the educator as the guardian and communicator of knowledge, suggesting that the focus of education should be that of broadening horizons and reducing mystique:

Illich suggested that schools are designed on the assumption that "there is a secret to everything in life; that the quality of life depends on knowing that secret; that secrets can be known only in orderly successions; and that only teachers can properly reveal these secrets." As a consequence of this assumption he believed that "An individual with a schooled mind conceives of the world as a pyramid of classified packages accessible only to those who carry the proper tags." The role of new educational institutions would be to break apart this pyramid and to facilitate access for the learner: "to allow him to look into the windows of the control room or the parliament, if he cannot get in by the door. Moreover, such new institutions should be channels to which the learner would have access without credentials or pedigree—public spaces in which peers and elders outside his immediate horizon would become available."

He also identifies as a key element the freedom of the learner to choose their teacher, again echoing the essential flavour of points five, six and seven of the Hornsey demands:

"In a deschooled society professionals could no longer claim the trust of their clients on the basis of their curricular pedigree, or ensure their standing by simply referring their clients to other professionals who approved of their schooling."

Illich suggested a way in which such a peer-based network could be implemented using the technology of the time:

"The user would identify himself by name and address and describe the activity for which he sought a peer. A computer would send him back the names and addresses of all those who had inserted the same description. … In its most rudimentary form, communication between client and computer could be established by return mail. In big cities typewriter terminals could provide instantaneous responses. The only way to retrieve a name and address from the computer would be to list an activity for which a peer was sought. People using the system would become known only to their potential peers. … A complement to the computer could be a network of bulletin boards and classified newspaper ads, listing the activities for which the computer could not produce a match. No names would have to be given. Interested readers would then introduce their names into the system."

Today the web would enable such a system to be implemented with little difficulty – and Illich seems to have foreseen and partially addressed some of the security and privacy issues that such a system would pose. He also raises an important idea when he repeatedly uses the term "peers" rather than "teachers" and "learners." Rogers and Groombridge (1976) describe the experiments with "learning exchanges" which also build on this peer to peer learning support:

"Apart from its practical value, the idea of a learning exchange is symbolically important. It takes a stage further the implementation of an assumption which runs through adult education, sometimes submerged but often overt and acknowledged - that the human species is not divided into a small group of clever teachers and a large group of not so clever students. Learning exchanges presupposes the client may, if he wishes, change sides or offer both to teach and to learn"

They note that learning exchanges (which Illich described as "learning webs," a prophetic term) could take the form of "loose but strong" links between a variety of participants, and would not need to be built in the traditional education sector. They point to practical examples of learning exchanges in non-traditional settings:

"The first of these was probably the one started at Centreprise, the east London bookshop-come-centre for community action. People saw that the learning exchange was easy to use, like dealing through postcard advertisements in newsagent shops or exchanging goods through swap shop programmes on local radio."

Once again the analogues mentioned here are available in a web environment. Possibly one difference is that the ability of, for example, Amazon.com to add on a for-profit educational structure that could be linked to its other products and services would be easier and faster than in the 1970's. Bring in the idea of them becoming able to confer some kind of qualification and the educational world takes on an interesting aspect that may enable the realisation of the visions of earlier educators.

"TEACHER" CREDIBILITY

Illich suggests that:

"Instead of placing trust in professionals, it should be possible, at any time, for any potential client to consult with other experienced clients of a professional about their satisfaction with him by means of another peer network easily set up by computer, or by a number of other means. Such networks could be seen as public utilities which permitted students to choose their teachers or patients their healers."

Even if peers were proven, through such a register of satisfied clients for example, to be able to demonstrate and communicate their expert knowledge in a way that satisfied the learner, traditional educators may still feel that such an individual lacks "credibility."

Illich also recognises the problem of the "expert" becoming a leader more through charismatic than pedagogic attributes:

"Charlatans, demagogues, proselytizers, corrupt masters, and simoniacal priests, tricksters, miracle workers, and messiahs have proven capable of assuming leadership roles and thus show the dangers of any dependence of a disciple on the master. Different societies have taken different measures to defend themselves against these counterfeit teachers. … Our society relies on certification by schools. It is doubtful that this procedure provides a better screening, but if it should be claimed that it does, then the counterclaim can be made that it does so at the cost of making personal discipleship almost vanish."

Given evidence suggesting that consumers in general are cautious about trusting web based transactions, the idea of placing trust in someone who is outside the formal educational structure and who may also be located anywhere in the world may be problematic. However, a register of satisfied clients, freely available to be consulted, may be one way to reduce this lack of trust. Rogers and Groombridge (1976) highlight the difficulty facing educational "consumers" purchasing education; from a web based provider, remarking that:

"No doubt parts of the solution will stem from a recognition that adults may indeed often be the best judges of whether they are getting what they want. And illiterate adults will not mind whether his tutor is being vouched for and certificated by some validating organisation if in fact he succeeds in learning how to write. On the other hand, people are notoriously unable to tell whether their lack of progress in mastering some skill or body of knowledge is due to poor teaching or their own stupidity and lack of talent."

One solution may be to "police" the activities of those who claim to be educators, possibly by some national or international body as Rogers and Groombridge suggest:

"No doubt those setting up learning exchanges will meet a range of practical problems. Even Illich acknowledges that "public matching devices would be abused for exploitative and immoral purposes". They might also suffer from straight educational imperfections. There are after all incompetent teachers, and how does the learning exchange protect its clients from charlatans? Does it or should it do spot checks on the competence of tutors on offer, rather as a classified advertisement manager has to verify the bona fides of advertisers?" (Rogers and Groombridge, 1976)

If such a mechanism were to be established presumably it would also need to carry out rigorous checks of the formal systems from a 'consumer' perspective, something that may cause problems for the formal system that espouses to be more than a commercial marketing tool for education as a product.

TRUE FLEXIBILITY OF LEARNING

The Hornsey students were seeking twenty-four hour access to learning resources and clearly this is a major feature of web based delivery systems. However the idea that students could join a subject at any time, from their place of work or residence, in any sequence, from any programme of study, using a collection of subjects from providers of their choice, on the basis of recommendation rather than demonstration of formal teaching recognition may prove to be somewhat problematic. If the learner simply wants to learn to satisfy their appetite for learning then they are operating as a normal consumer and would be able to judge the value and quality of the process on their own perceived outcomes. However, problems would probably arise if that learner wishes to translate the collection of "learnings" into a "recognised" qualification. The problems of accreditation of prior learning would surface and lead to difficulties for formal education in terms of equivalence of the various elements of study. This whole situation is an exact parallel to the development of the Extension movement in the UK in the 19th century. Marriott (1981) records that in 1891 an obscure educational magazine, the University Extension Journal, offered a rash prediction:

"Before long some university will seize the unequalled opportunity... will boldly lay down a curriculum of study for degrees on new lines suited to the needs of those who desire to carry on their intellectual culture side by side with a regular business of life."

Between 1884 and 1897 there was a proposal to create a part-time teaching university organised along entirely novel lines that would have embodied some quite remarkable ideas:

- admission of any person likely to benefit, irrespective of age, sex or social status;

- imposition of the fewest possible requirements in the way of entry qualifications or matriculation;
- a programme of part-time study, under university teachers, extending over eight years or more and leading to a degree;
- a curriculum designed to meet the needs of those who were bound to remain in their usual occupations, being a modular structure made up of the smallest educationally viable units;
- examinations based largely on the assessment of each course as it was taken, with little reliance on set-piece tests; and
- courses offered in any place where an acceptable teacher could make himself available, the university to be based on the recognition of teaching and not of formal institutions.

This University of the Future would "not be a chartered body like existing universities but a floating aggregation of voluntary agencies: not so much organised as tending to co-operate." Once again, we see a glimpse of the possible web-enabled educational world we now stand on the edge of.

There was, as may be anticipated, resistance from the established universities of the time, essentially Oxford and Cambridge, who felt that the accreditation of study under such a system could lead to demands for recognition of this external study as part of their own degree provision – "a backstairs to a degree." Practical examples of attacks on the high walls that surrounded early universities in order to grant a diverse group of learners access to education on a full time or part time basis can be found in the last two decades of the 19th century in the UK. Marriott refers to the "missionary Dons," who were:

"College fellows from Oxford and Cambridge and professors from London [who] were taking themselves off into the province's to meet the clients of mechanics institutes, middle-class women's educational associations and societies of working people, trying to give them some better educational fare than the genteel amusements that were commonly available. These were the missionary Dons, men often closely connected with the demand for academic reform but cherishing a conception of university extension more broad and generous than those generally discussed within the university walls."

These are the types of people who would no doubt have greeted the idea of web-enabled education, able to reach a global population and offer a rich learning environment, with huge enthusiasm. It represents not only an exciting learning environment but also has an anarchic element that would allow the testing and development of new forms of education in a somewhat covert and dynamic way.

Marriott notes that Moulton pleaded for elasticity, questioning the wisdom of increasing the numbers of universities and along with them the likelihood of retaining the rigidity that characterised the systems. Moulton suggested that "The true policy is: not to multiply the degree-giving bodies, introducing confusions and impairing the value of degrees (e.g., their antiquity): but, to introduce elasticity into the machinery of testing for degrees." Courses could be provided by a wide range of agencies; the existing universities could control the quality of teaching by scrutiny of syllabuses, and could award their existing degrees on the recommendation of a board of examiners nominated by all those taking part in the scheme. As Marriott comments, "There one finds an imaginative contribution to the theory of academical reform; the essential point was that the university should be identified with teaching of a proper standard and not with fixed institutions carrying the label of higher education." Pursuing this line of thought Moulton once provocatively announced: "University education, as I understand it, has nothing to do with universities. I mean that university education has no necessary connection with universities."

CONCLUSION

True empowerment of learners would require that the conditions demanded by the Hornsey students, along with those explored in the early 19th century, be implemented. Learners would have free choice of where to study and who to lead them along the path of learning; they would want complete freedom to choose the subject and sequence of subjects; they would want to be free to study when and where was most appropriate to them; they would want to be able to select or deselect providers on the basis of evidence freely available to all participants; and they would want to be able to have their studies acknowledged as being of a standard appropriate for recognition in terms of university certification. This empowerment represents a radical change for many current educational systems, but some believe that radical change is the only kind of change that will lead to improvements in the education system. Milton Friedman (1995) commented that "I believe the only way to make major improvement in our educational system is through privatization to the point at which a substantial fraction of all educational services is rendered to individuals by private enterprises. Nothing else will destroy or even greatly weaken the power of the current educational establishment – a necessary pre-condition for radical improvement in our education system."

The total destruction of the formal "Educational Establishment" seems as unlikely now as it was in the 19th century or the 1960's, given the power and vested interests of the traditional universities and their more recent counterparts. However, the continued expansion of the web combined with growth in 'educational consumerism' may well be the vehicle that leads to that weakening of the formal, highly structured and essentially self-serving "Establishment" and to an empowerment of the learner. Growth in third party vocationally oriented providers, responding to profit-making opportunities, and the ability of non-traditional organisations to grant degrees will complicate the scene and may help re-shape the current, essentially monopolistic, educational provision. The pervasive, web-enabled, environment may offer the route to the fulfilment of the dream of true student empowerment – but paradoxically may also lead to the demise of some of those educational providers who currently see it as their future.

REFERENCES

Friedman, M. (1995). *Public Schools: Make Them Private*, Washington Post, February 19th.

Hill, B. V. (1973). *Education and the Endangered Individual*, Dell Publishing.

Illich, I. (1971). *Deschooling Society*, New York: Harper & Row.

Marriott, S. (1981). *A Backstairs To A Degree*, Leeds Studies In Adult And Continuing Education, University of Leeds.

Mee, G. & Wiltshire, H. (1978). *Structure And Performance In Adult Education*, Longman.

Rogers, J., & Groombridge, B. (1976). *Right To Learn*, Arrow books.

Students and Staff of Hornsey College of Art (1969). *The Hornsey Affair*, Penguin books.

Chapter 2

An Advanced Course In Application Programming and Design

Cecil Schmidt
Washburn University, USA

The continuing evolution in state-of-the-art business applications such as those that support e-commerce, advancements in programming language design such as Java™, and the requirements for persistent data access mechanisms have all significantly impacted the required knowledge-base of computer information science graduates. As such these individuals should have a strong background in the design and implementation of client/server applications in both traditional and Web-based environments. Application design should emphasize object-oriented techniques that can take full advantage of the most recent enhancements to programming languages. Also, alternative file structures and data access methods should be explored. This chapter gives an overview of a new course offering which will address these issues.

INTRODUCTION

Knowledge of client-server application alternatives, data access alternatives, and object-oriented design techniques are all requirements of computer information science graduates looking for state-of-the-art job opportunities. Enhancements to traditional programming languages and the development of new ones such as Java™ enable a software developer significant leverage in the creation of a whole new class of applications. Thus, it is important that computer information science (CIS) graduates understand these new types of applications, the software

Previously Published in *Challenges of Information Technology Management in the 21st Century* edited by Mehdi Khosrow-Pour, Copyright © 2000, Idea Group Publishing.

behind them, and the proper design techniques used in developing these applications. Therefore we must develop a curricula, which stresses both these new application alternatives along with a significant emphasis in object-oriented design. "Advanced Application Programming and Design" is a course that has been developed to meet this need. It is a course that has been built as a replacement for both the traditional file structures course and a course that focuses on client-server applications. Students are expected to have mastered topics in logic, structured programming, and introductory material in Java™ before taking this course.

PURPOSE OF COURSE

The purpose of this course is to provide the student with a fundamental understanding of client/server applications utilizing an object-oriented design framework. The following is the catalog description that has been developed for this course:

Advanced topics in application programming and design using state of the art design techniques and implementation language. Topics include design and implementation of alternative file structures and supporting data access methods, user interface design and implementation, and exception handling.

The prerequisites for this course include:
- CM111 Introduction to Structured Programming
- CM245 Contemporary Programming Methods
- PH110 Logic for Computer Programming

It is assumed that the student possess sufficient skills in logic, structured programming, and object oriented programming so that he or she is able to focus appropriately on the advanced topics of this course. By successfully completing the prerequisites listed above, we are confident that the student has the sufficient background.

OBJECTIVES

The following is a list of the high-level objectives of this course:
- Understand and apply HI/PD/DM design framework
- Foundational knowledge of client/server applications with specific applications to the Web
- Identify and utilize alternative file structures including sequential and indexed files, and database tables
- Design and implement advanced GUI interface components
- Understand the alternatives of designing with composition versus inheritance

The HI/PD/DM framework refers to the separation of the human interface (HI), problem domain (PD), and the data manager (DM) classes as described by Coad, et al. (1997).

TEXTBOOKS

Because this course deals with both advanced design topics and with advanced programming issues, a combination of reading materials is necessary. Deitel & Deitel's book, Java™ How To Program (1999) provided the most comprehensive set of reference material for both programming and software engineering concepts. Although it was chosen as the required text book, a good deal of the course will be emphasizing application design issues which are best dealt with by Coad, et.al. (1997,1999). These books will be used as major resources in this course. Additionally lecture material will be provided in the area of advanced data access alternatives. This will be supported by Chang and Harkey (1998).

COURSE OUTLINE

Provided below is a tentative outline of the topics to be covered in this course. Technical readings (Dietel & Dietel, 1999) are listed under the chapter column. Other readings will be assigned throughout the semester along with notes that focus particularly on design issues. The majority of the design topics will come from Coad et al. (1997, 1999).

Week	Chapter	Description
1,2	12	Introduction to Swing and Basic GUI Components
	Notes	User Interface Design Frameworks
3,4	13	Advanced GUI Interface Components (MDI Windows)
	Notes	User Interface Design Frameworks (Continued)
5,6	17	Files and Streams
	Notes	Designing the Data Manager
	Notes	Drill Down Framework
7,8	15	Multithreading
9,10	18	Java™ Database Connectivity (JDBC)
	Notes	Modifications to the Data Manager
11,12	19	Servlets
	Notes	A Web Drill-Down Framework
	Notes	Current Directions in E-Commerce Software
13-15	Project	

PROPOSED ASSIGNMENTS

The following is a list of course assignments, which upon completion will enable the student to meet the specified objectives of the course:

1. Create a master-detail window and a detail-view window that can communicate to each other. Data is created dynamically in order to illustrate the behavior. The dynamic data used in this particular assignment should become persistent in later assignments.
2. Create a detail-view window and a search-by window that can communicate to each other via the passing of objects. Data should be created dynamically in order to illustrate behavior. The dynamic data used should be the same as that used in assignment #1.
3. Create an MDI window along with a startup window that is loaded with the MDI window. The startup window should be able to communicate with the windows implemented in assignments #1 and #2.
4. Implement data managers for the dynamically created data in assignments #1 and #2. Use both sequential and indexed sequential files. This assignment should illustrate the separation of the problem domain (PD), user interface (UI), and the data manager (DM).
5. Implement modifications to the data managers to support JDBC. Add additional search criteria where time allows.
6. Create a simple Web application that utilizes a servelet to automate reporting requirements of the data in the previous assignments. This servlet should be able to perform multiple levels of data explosion.
7. In a team of four create an application which will demonstrate capabilities of the topics covered in this course. This could simply be putting exercises #1 through #6 into an integrated application that is partitioned between the Web and a traditional client-server implementation.

CONCLUDING REMARKS

Because of the continuing evolution in applications which are client/server oriented, advancements in object-oriented programming languages, and the necessity of exploring alternative file structures and access methods it is important that a CIS student be exposed to these items. This course delivers that exposure. Upon completion of this course the student will posses the necessary framework required to undertake development of applications which can range from Web e-commerce applications to traditional client/server applications. It will also provide the background for advanced coursework in systems analysis and design or software engineering. Ultimately, it will better prepare the information systems graduate for the applications he or she will come into contact with in their career.

REFERENCES

Chang, D., & Harkey, D. (1998). *Client/Server Data Access with Java™ and XML*, New York: John Wiley & Sons, Inc.

Coad, P., Mayfield, M., & Kern, J. (1999). *Java™ Design, Building Better Apps and Applets*, 2/E, Upper Saddle River, NJ: Prentice Hall.

Coad, P., North, D., & Mayfield, M. (1997). *Object Models Strategies, Patterns, & Applications*, Upper Saddle River, NJ: Prentice Hall.

Deitel, H. M. & Dietel, P. J. (1999). *Java™ How To Program*, 3/E, Upper Saddle River, NJ: Prentice Hall.

Horstmann, C.S. & Cornell, G. (1998). *Core Java™ 1.1 Volume II*, Advanced Features, Upper Saddle River, NJ: Prentice Hall.

Chapter 3

Establishing a Telecommunications and Networking Technology B.S. Degree

Julie R. Mariga
Purdue University, USA

As distributed computing architectures have increased, the need for technology professionals that are skilled in telecommunications and networking has dramatically increased. Employers are looking for students that not only have conceptual knowledge but also hands-on practical experience when hiring graduates into telecomm and networking related positions. This chapter will discuss how a telecommunications and networking bachelor's degree option was established at Purdue University. The chapter will discuss why the program started and discuss how it has evolved. Other areas discussed include: the curriculum, facilities, faculty, and the industrial advisory board. The paper will conclude with where the program is going to grow.

WHY THE PROGRAM STARTED

As the personal computer emerged companies started networking their computers together. As technology advanced and companies started developing local area networks (LANs) and wide area networks (WANs) the need for skilled professionals in these areas increased. At the same time, many students going through the information systems curriculum at Purdue University wanted more courses in this area and they also wanted hands-on practical experience.

Previously Published in *Challenges of Information Technology Management in the 21st Century* edited by Mehdi Khosrow-Pour, Copyright © 2000, Idea Group Publishing.

EVOLUTION OF THE PROGRAM

The Computer Technology Department (CPT) at Purdue University was established in 1978 and its primary focus was on information systems (IS). In the IS curriculum there was only one lecture-based course on data communications. The students wanted to learn more and also have the opportunity to gain hands-on experience. As a result, the CPT department created a concentration within the IS degree which consisted of four telecomm and networking courses: CPT 176 - Information Technology and Architecture, CPT 230 - Introduction to Data Communications, CPT 330 - PC Connectivity and Local Area Networking, and CPT 430 - Wide Area Networking. After creating these courses and realizing the demand for them from both students and industry in 1997 the department decided to create a bachelor's degree option in Telecommunications and Networking Technology (TNT). There are currently 189 students seeking a bachelor's degree in TNT. The breakdown by class is: 28 freshman, 60 sophomores, 59 juniors, and 42 seniors. There have been 11 graduates from the TNT program and the placement rate is at 100%.

CURRICULUM

In order to earn a degree in TNT a student must complete between 129 and 132 credit hours. The curriculum does differ from the traditional information systems degree in more areas than just the computing courses that a student takes. The TNT curriculum includes three courses in electrical engineering technology, a physics course, two calculus courses, and a more advanced statistic probability course. Additionally, students select one of the following specialization sequences which is made up of three courses: Manufacturing, Information Systems, or Digital Communications. Figure 1 provides an overview of the TNT curriculum architecture.

Figure 1: Overview of TNT curriculum architecture

Advanced Network

Advanced Network	Advanced Network		
TECH 581 Fiber Optic Communications	CPT 343 Systems Administration	CPT 443 Enterprise Network Management	CPT 455 Network Security
CPT 430 Wide Area Networking			

Networking Fundamentals	Work Group Computing	Internet Computing
CPT 330 Local Area Networks	CPT 335 Collaborative Computing (Advanced)	CPT 375 Internet/Intranet Application Development
CPT 230 Data Communications	CPT 235 Collaborative Computing (Intro)	CPT 275 Internet & WWW (Intro)
CPT 176 Information Technology & Architecture		

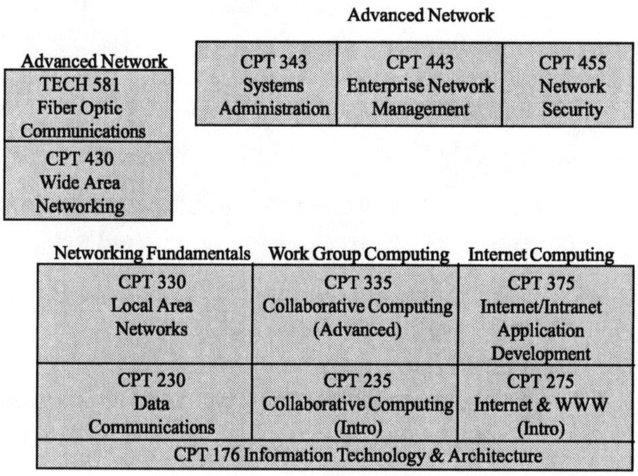

The following are some of the computing courses along with the course descriptions that a TNT major will take:

CPT 176 - Information Technology and Architecture
This course introduces information technology hardware, software, and networks as part of an overall distributed computing environment. Topics include computing platforms of all sizes, operating systems and systems software, peripheral devices and connectivity, client/server architecture, databases, and telecommunications. Lecture only.

CPT 230 - Introduction to Data Communications
This course explores data communications, voice communications, and both local and wide area computer networks; and their proper application to business and industry problems. Topics include vocabulary, hardware, concepts, issues, trends, and business and technical decision making for the telecommunications field. Lecture only.

CPT 330 - PC Connectivity and Local Area Networking
This course explores local area networks and other personal computer connectivity alternatives. Emphasis is placed on problem solving, troubleshooting, and decision making processes for designing and implementing cost effective local area networks and media sharing for client/server business applications. In the laboratory students gain hands on experiences with LAN technology, problem solving development, and troubleshooting techniques. This is not a LAN operating system or system administration course. Lecture/Lab course.

CPT 343 - Systems Administration
This course focuses on the tasks and issues involved in the installation and administration of distributed computing systems. Topics include the administration of network operating systems, UNIX system administration, and network system interoperability. In the laboratory version of the course students implement and maintain local area network and UNIX servers. Lecture/Lab course.

CPT 430 - Wide Area Networking
This course explores the many alternatives available for connecting LANs as well as providing remote access to/from users not connected to LANs. Emphasis is on the effect of telecommunications systems and networking decisions on business performance. Integration of internetworks (LAN to LAN) and micro to mainframe connectivity into client/server and client/host architectures is emphasized. Enterprise networking and interoperability analysis is stressed. Organization and

management of large scale telecommunications projects are investigated. Students construct a wide area network capable of simultaneously carrying multiprotocol data, voice, and video. Lecture/Lab course.

CPT 443 - Enterprise Network Management

This course explores various aspects of enterprise network management with an emphasis on managing faults and optimizing performance to ensure high service availability. Key concepts and technologies explored include basic management functions, standards based management technologies, and the business impact of network management. In the laboratory version of the course, students use standards based platforms to perform on-line monitoring and management of network equipment. Lecture/Lab course.

CPT 455 - Network Security

This course covers conceptual and technological aspects of network security for voice and data networks. The course deals with analysis, design, implementation, and management issues surrounding effective network security. Students are placed in the role of members of a network security task force. Technology research and presentation of research results as well as security technology implementation are required course outcomes. Lecture/Lab course.

FACILITIES

The single most distinguishing factor between the TNT program at Purdue University and any other university is the facilities. By having strong industrial partnerships, the TNT program has been able to secure donations of over $3.5 million

Figure 2: Digital image of the Wide Area Networking Lab

Figure 3: Digital image showing more of the WAN Lab and Network Security Lab

Figure 4: Digital image of the Local Area Networking and Systems Administration Lab

Figure 5: Digital image of the Enterprise Network Management Lab

dollars worth of both hardware and software. Some of the companies that are partners of the TNT program include: GTE Telecom, Tellabs, Caterpillar, Visual Networks, AT&T Paradyne, Amoco, Sun Microsystems, Tivoli, Lotus, Intel, Cargill, and Nortel. The TNT program at Purdue was the first university in the world to be named a university partner with Tivoli. Some examples of the types of technology donated include: $1.0 million in optical transmission equipment (SONET), $.5 million in enterprise network management software, numerous routers, T-1, T-3, frame relay, ISDN, Nortel Meridian PBX, packet switched services, and other software from various vendors. Below are pictures of the various labs and technologies.

Another area that makes the TNT program unique is that the program has its own separate entire network segregated from Purdue's network. This allows students the opportunity to gain very valuable hands-on experience with various technologies in a safe networking environment. Figure 6 provides an overview of how the TNT network is setup. Figure 7 provides a look at the Linux Proxy Firewall that protects the TNT network.

Figure 6

Overview of TNT Network

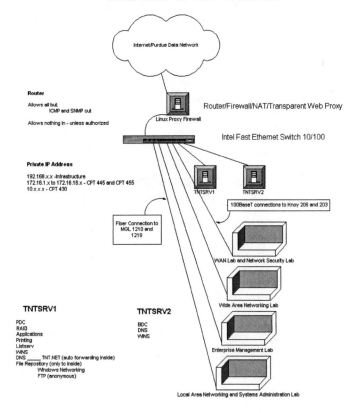

Figure 7

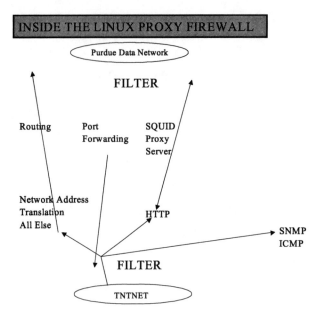

Figure 8: Keyboard/Mouse/Monitor Switch Implementation Results

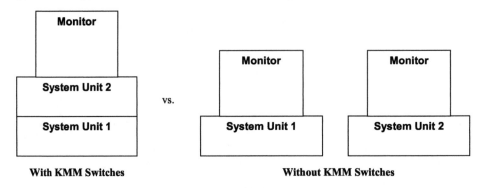

The TNT program has run into some space limitations but by being creative it has been possible to overcome some of those limitations. An example of one way is by using keyboard/mouse/monitor (KMM) switches. There is no reason that each system must have a dedicated keyboard, mouse, monitor, and workspace. As shown in the following figure, installing keyboard/mouse/monitor (KMM) switches allows two system units to be stacked (Figure 8). This approach effectively doubles capacity by allowing two system units to exist in the same footprint as a single system unit. This is called a "cell concept" where each laboratory group is assigned to a cell which consists of two clients and one server. By using the cell concept it has allowed the TNT program flexibility in assigning various courses to the various labs and it has allowed the program to effectively utilize their hardware resources.

FACULTY

The TNT program is housed within the School of Technology at Purdue University. The mission of the School of Technology is to provide career educational opportunities to students whose technological interests and aptitudes are essentially *applications-oriented*. The school's goal is to produce occupationally ready college graduates with marketable skills and potential for growth to meet defined technical work force needs, for business, industry, and service agencies. With that mission statement, the TNT program focuses primarily on teaching and educational scholarship (not basic research). For all positions, candidates must have an *earned* Masters Degree in a relevant field (the doctorate is not a requirement for employment, promotion, or tenure for these positions). All candidates should have at least three years of full-time, relevant, industrial experience in networking and telecommunications. In the past, when a faculty position in TNT was open the skill set that a candidate needed to have was one that would complement the existing TNT faculty. For example, the latest faculty member hired into TNT needed to have the following skills: experience with network operating systems, networking protocols, local area networks, and wireless communications. In addition to the industrial experience, it is preferred that candidates have prior teaching experience.

The TNT program currently has four full-time faculty members. Each faculty member has their own specific area of interest(s). Examples of areas of interest include: local area networks, wide area networks, system administration, network management, messaging infrastructures, network protocols, network security, and wireless communications. Each faculty member within TNT has a common goal of continuing to grow the program and provide a quality education to our students and provide a quality graduate to industry.

INDUSTRIAL ADVISORY BOARD

Another major force within the TNT program is the TNT Industrial Advisory Board. The board was formed prior to TNT becoming a bachelor's degree option and meets formally every 18 to 24 months. The members of the board are all nationally prominent in the telecom and networking field from a variety of industries and provide the faculty with continuing feedback regarding the curriculum and what courses need to start being developed so that the program can continue to improve and enhance. The board has been instrumental in the continuing growth and support that has been received from the school. After the last meeting with the board back in May 1998, the board drafted a resolution and sent it to the Dean of the School of Technology. As a result, the TNT program has seen many exciting things happen. For example, an additional faculty member was hired, both the LAN and WAN labs grew in size, more clients and servers were purchased, and additional courses are being offered in the areas of network security and network design and optimization. As can be seen from the outcome of one meeting with the board, the growth of the TNT program would not happen without their support. Members of the board come from the following companies: IBM, GTE Telecom, Inc., NCR, Exxon, Bristol-Myers Squibb, Caterpillar, Network World, and Cargill.

FUTURE DIRECTION

The TNT program has set many goals for where the program needs to continue to grow and develop. The following areas have been identified by both the TNT faculty and the TNT Industrial Advisory Board:

- Develop a wireless course sequence that would include courses on the business applications of wireless technology as well as a follow-up course that would provide students with hands-on experience in a laboratory environment.
- Develop a graduate program with more emphasis on applied research in the areas of network security and network capacity planning. A graduate course has been developed on network design and optimization. Another graduate course being developed is about Information Technology Economics.
- Increase emphasis on international telecommunications since the Internet, Intranets, and Extranets continue to grow as well as the global nature of business.
- Increase emphasis in the area of network testing and monitoring. As the use of networks continues to grow, it is important to provide students with the knowledge on how to test and monitor networks.

The TNT program has had great success to date with a great mixture of talented, motivated faculty and an Industrial Advisory Board that provides the leadership for the program. The program has also benefited from hard working, motivated students that have gone through the program and provided the faculty with feedback on how to improve the program.

RESULTS

This section is going to provide information from a former student about his experience in the TNT program as well as feedback from two major recruiters of TNT graduates.

A student that graduated in May 1999 is now a network administrator for a technology company in Chicago, IL and he is in charge of 7 remote sites across the Midwest. He supports 300 clients running Microsoft NT Workstation. They use frame relay to communicate between sites and he is responsible for making sure all communication stays up and running. He is also in responsible for a HP

3000 mainframe. He is excited to be in charge of so many things early in his professional career. His advice to improve the program includes: making sure TNT students get a good grasp of routers, HP Jetdirect printing devices, and NT. He also suggested that students get more experience with doing quotes on configurations. He believes the TNT program taught him 3 critical things:

- Discover what you are good at and what you will need assistance with.
- Keeping your knowledge base current and knowing how to avoid information overload.
- Teaching the students what can be done if done correctly.
  He believes the program can improve in the following ways:
- Cover cloning, print server setup in more depth, learn how to specify new equipment, and dealing with users.
- Bring in past students as well as professionals in the industry for guest lectures.

One recruiter stated that the TNT program produces graduates who are knowledgeable about TNT theory and also who have significant hands-on training. He stated TNT graduates are able to step into an ExxonMobil assignment and are able to deliver real results from day one. He stated that he has not found another program that is as thorough as the TNT program and stated that biggest strength of the program is that students have concept knowledge and practical experience with a wide range of technology and solutions which allows them to contribute in industry faster than their peers. He would like to see the graduates have a longer term focus on what they would like to be doing 5 to 10 years into their career. He believes some students only focus on TNT and do not think about more traditional MIS roles. The students they hire have the following responsibilities: Server admin, LAN operations, upgrades, new installations, network design, supporting application projects by performing required infrastructure design and implementation.

Another recruiter stated that the TNT program at Purdue is very unique and beneficial. He stated he is not aware of any other programs that are similar to TNT, especially with the complex and realistic WAN lab environment students have an opportunity to gain hands-on experience with. He also stated that the TNT students have both conceptual knowledge as well as real hands-on practical telecom and I/T experience which allows the graduates to hit the ground running once they are hired. The students hired into this company have the following responsibilities: WAN/LAN networking, LAN admin, Network Operations, WAN/LAN provisioning, telephony/voice work, and vendor management.

Chapter 4

An Action Learning Approach for the Development of Technology Skills

Richard L. Peterson and Joan D. Mahoney
Montclair State University, USA

Information technology provides a unique challenge to universities to maintain the relevance of their offerings as the rate of technical change far out paces curricular reforms. What is needed for students of information technology are opportunities that provide real world, hands-on experiences for developing necessary skills and understandings in a relatively "safe" environments. This article is a case study of the experiences of students in a course that required them to complete action learning technology projects for social services clients. Results suggest a generalizable model for improving relevance within the universities of the 21st century.

INTRODUCTION

In the world of information technology (IT), generational innovations occur, on average, every eighteen months. To leverage innovations, businesses need to employ individuals who are qualified on current technology and who also can build their store of knowledge of subsequent innovations on this solid base. Experience is one of the key qualifications sought by employers of management information systems (MIS) program graduates. But, universities vacillate between a business orientation that might include hands-on experiences and education in basic disciplines where real project work is limited or non-existent. In the midst of this schizophrenic-like struggle, one finds outdated curricula, outdated faculty, and poor instructional resources (e.g., 486-level CPUs used in the maintenance laboratory).

Previously Published in *Challenges of Information Technology Management in the 21st Century* edited by Mehdi Khosrow-Pour, Copyright © 2000, Idea Group Publishing.

Could a course be structured to provide this much-needed project experience while maintaining the integrity of the course? This was the question of a course offered in the spring of the 1999 academic year at a mid-sized, four-year, state-funded institution in the metropolitan New York. City area.

RATIONALE

Traditional classroom teaching approaches such as case analysis, action research through consultancy, field research and observation, and multimedia methods are often insufficient for providing quality, lasting learning (Raelin, 1997). These approaches cannot be depended upon to provide the challenge, reflective growth opportunities, or understanding of the long-term implications of short-term projects. Action learning is a developmental approach that focuses on experience-based learning. The basic philosophy is that students learn more effectively within the reciprocity of a social situation and while engaged in the solution of real problems (Pedler, 1991; Weinstein, 1995). According to Raelin:

"The action referred to in action learning is not temporal or simulated. Students need to take real positions, make moral judgments, and define them under pressure. Action learning, then, as a form of management education elicits managerial behavior, not student behavior. Students derive knowledge not *about* management but rather about their own capacities to take action." (Raelin, 1997: 369)

Action learning views the real world as the appropriate learning arena (Korey & Bogorya, 1985). It has been an effective approach in focused settings such as management development programs (Lawrie, 1989; Margerison, 1988) and is also seen as appropriate in more formal education programs (Lawrie, 1989).

While the typical student at the University works many hours in real-world jobs, few are employed in their MIS discipline and even fewer in decision-making positions. Their opportunities to translate the theories and concepts learned in their academic course work to business problems are very limited. For these students, action learning might prove to be the bridge between skills demonstrated in the classroom and skills demonstrated on-the-job. Real project experience might also solve the student's "Catch 22" of needing a job to gain experience and not being able to get a job because of lack of experience. Further, the application of action learning concepts to information technology education seems particularly appropriate as a means of demonstrating to students that the intent of the application of technology is to solve business problems, not to create technical solutions that are in search of a problem.

OBJECTIVES AND PERFORMANCE CRITERIA

The main objective in undertaking this research was to provide university students with a high-quality, hands-on learning experience that would, in part, prepare them to be better systems analysts. Secondarily, we sought to create a partnership among prospective employers of these students, the university, and other third parties who might be instrumental in the education of the students to ensure effective delivery of action learning.

If this approach proved to be successful, students should exhibit a number of changed attitudes:

- An increase in the sensitivity toward the role of customers in systems projects and appreciation of the need for changes in project scope and requirements;
- A greater desire to meet or exceed stated project objectives as observed in an increase in the quality of their work or increased number of work hours; and
- An increased interest in recruiting these students on the part of employers.

While the nature of the project required that most measures be anecdotal, we believe that a successful "first run" of the action learning approach could lead to the identification of measurable performance indicators under stringent conditions.

DESIGN AND DELIVERY

The plan was to have students working in small teams complete a systems analysis and design project. This model was selected as an extension of the internship or cooperative education experience where a single student works for a company as a part of their project team. While for-profit companies might be reluctant to turn over project responsibilities to a team of students in a class. non-profit institutions in the local community might have similar needs and be willing—even thankful—for the "free" help. To the extent that non-profits represent reasonable proxies for commercial business organizations the experience would be the same.

With the local United Way agency driving the effort, the goal of the projects became access to technology by benefactors of these social agencies. Mostly, the first projects involved making technology available to children between the ages of 1.5-12 years of age. Students who registered for the three-credit, sixteen-week course were required to produce a computer learning center complete with five-seven computers, a small network, audience-appropriate software applications, computer center staff training, documentation, and all other components required to establish and sustain a computer learning center. The tasks extended this project beyond a comparable systems analysis and design project in a commercial business setting because these student team members were required to complete all activities associated with the computer center in lieu of delegating tasks to "experts" such as hardware technicians, trainers and networking engineers who might be in a company environment.

Table 1: Computer Learning Center Development Project Worksteps and Deliverables

SYSTEMS ANALYSIS
  Project Initiation
  Survey Project Feasibility
    Preliminary Investigation
      Determine Who to Interview
      Prepare Interview Questions
      Conduct Interview(s)
    Preliminary Investigation
      Write Report
      Review/Revise Report
      Submit Final Preliminary
        Investigation Report
    Feasibility Study
      Perform Feasibility Tests
      Write, Review/Revise Feasibility
        Study
      Submit Final Feasibility Study
  Study & Analyze the Current System
    Analysis of Environment
      Conduct Hardware/Software
        Inventory
      Determine Training Needs
      Assess Physical Environment
    Problem Statement
      Write Explanation/Analysis of Gap
      State Problem
      Submit Gap Analysis/Problem
        Statement Report
  Define and Prioritize Users Require-
    ments
    Develop New System Objectives
    Determine Requirements
      Specify Hardware/Networking
        Requirements
      Specify Software/Services
        Requirements
      Specify Training/Support Require
        ments
      Specify Operational/Physical
        Requirements
      Define Process Flow
    Requirements Definition
      Document Requirements
      Review/Revise Requirements
        Document
      Submit Requirements Document
  Develop New System Proposal(s)
    Identify/Explain Potential Solution
    Estimate Cost/Timeline of Solution
    Recommend a Solution
    Document New System Proposal
      Document Each Solution
      Review/Revise Proposal
      Submit Proposal Document

SYSTEM DESIGN
  Select a Target Design
  Write Formal Systems Proposal
    List Hardware/Software Required
    List Services
  Acquire Hardware/Software Platforms
    Develop a Request for Quotation
      (RFQ)
    Submit RFQ
    Select Potential Vendors
    Solicit Response for RFQ
    Evaluate Proposals
    Make Purchases
  Design and Integrate the New System
    Install and Test Hardware Compo
      nents
    Install and Test Connectivity

SYSTEMS IMPLEMENTATION
  Load and Configure Applications
    Software
  Load and Configure Systems Software
  Test the Hardware/Software System
  Create User Reference Manuals
  Train Staff
  Conduct Pilot Tests
  Install and Test the New Learning
    Center
    Conduct User Acceptance Testing
  Deliver the New System Into Operation
    Completion of Learning Center
    Write/Deliver Operations Manual
    Write/Deliver Maintenance Manual
  Conduct Post-Implementation Audit
    Conduct Audit Interviews
    Write/Deliver Evaluation Reports

SUBMIT COMPLETED BINDER

The course, Systems Analysis and Design for Business Professionals, is an in-depth, hands-on exploration of the systems development life cycle (SDLC), a methodology typically followed in information systems projects to ensure the on-time and within budget completion of projects that meet, even exceed, their stated objectives. The emphasis of SDLC is ensuring the capture and appropriate response to any and all information that that may impact on the objectives and requirements of the project.

While lecture-based or simulated case-based course approaches present information about managing development efforts and how to contain the "oops factors" that frequently kill projects, these approaches do not provide direct, live, performance-impacted experience. Yet, it is this real experience that makes prospective systems analysts employees so valuable. (A Standish Group project reported that 40% of IT projects ion the U.S. are started, but never completed; 37% are completed, but over-budget; and, 42% are completed after the scheduled delivery data has passed. The consulting company estimates the annual cost of these poor project management practices at $142 billion.)

Because the direct experience of systems development project management is not a function of the type of organization, nonprofit organizations are a reasonable proxy for their profit-driven counterparts. Students who develop SDLC skills in one environment should readily be able to transfer these skills to other environments. The environment is secondary to the hands-on type of experience. The hundreds of "oops factors" that creep into IT development projects need-the same careful treatment by analysts regardless of any organizational demographics.

The project work steps and deliverables are included as Table 1. While each of the three project teams had a slightly different customer and end user audience, the objectives and work steps were quite similar across the projects.

The twenty-four students participated in one of three team projects (a fourth project was completed by the professor and community volunteers as a "model" computer center for the other teams). The teams met as a class for one 2.5-hour session each week. These classes included a project status report from each group, a "how to" lecture on the team's next activities, and time for the individual teams to plan their activities for the upcoming week. Outside of classroom time the instructor met with each team, either at the worksite or at the University, for at least one hour per week. These meetings were used to review project task performance, deliverables, and plans for upcoming tasks. Students were required to submit all work products to the instructor before their use or distribution to the customer or any other stakeholder (e.g., the United Way umbrella organization).

In addition to the interim deliverables of the project, students were required to have a working, fully functional computer learning center at their designated site. Full documentation about the project was required so that subsequent project teams completing similar projects could replicate all associated tasks. Finally, customers were to be "delighted" with the results of the team's efforts. Each of these measures was considered as a part of the individual's overall grade.

DISCUSSION

Despite tens of mitigating factors faced by each team (e.g., an automobile crashed into the building housing one center and the center was temporarily displaced), each team successfully completed their set of deliverables. The computer learning centers were fully operational at the end of the semester with a trained staff, supporting documentation, and end users (children) all in place. The objectives of the customers were met to their satisfaction and each customer signed-off on the project completion. More importantly, each customer requested that the relationship with the University be continued through additional projects in the future.

The subjective impression of the instructor, who has reviewed literally hundreds of systems binders presented by students, was that the binders were not as "clean" as those completed for simulated cases. Rather, these binders reflected the twists and turns of the project, the implicit requirements of the project due to its real nature, and the many unique factors faced by team. For example, in simulated cases, a set number of mock interviews are usually conducted. Students record and report the responses of these interviews, not so much as a means of gaining insights about the project, but more as a necessary work step. In this action learning case, students conducted as many interviews as they needed to understand the requirements; in some instances this meant more in-depth interviews with a single person, but more likely, multiple interviews with multiple individuals to ensure all necessary information was known. In this paradigm, each task required the students to take real positions and make judgments under pressure .

Mixed results were observed with respect to an increase in students' desire to perform at a higher level. It appears that while some students recognize the opportunities afforded by action learning and respond to take full advantage of it, other students demonstrate the same cynicism found in the classroom-based approach. That is, these students never grasp the significance of the experience, treating the action learning experience as just another approach dictated by some crazy professor and looking at the course requirements as the same old hurdles to a grade. This was most acutely observed in the binder development of some students. While it was explained to the students that the systems binder would be part of their job-interviewing portfolio and should be exemplary of their work, some students did not even prepare binders until hours before they were due. Apparently, the traditional educational model has fostered an attitude of passivity that will not easily be overcome.

Eight of the twenty-four students received full-time or internship job offers before the conclusion of the semester. The employers of these students were aware of the nature of this action learning experience and fully supported it. It is not certain whether this was a strong determinant in the hiring decision.

In summary, this first run of an action learning experience showed promise as an improved method for developing required systems analysis and other technical skills in university students. While causal relationships are impossible to determine at this juncture, there is every reason to believe that something important happened to most of the students in this course –some did comment that the experience had "changed their lives." The relationship between the university and the community service agencies also changed as a result of this experience: the university sees the larger community beyond its walls as important partners in the education of students and, similarly, community institutions recognize the opportunity to infuse intellectual advances into their programs. This partnership may be among the university reforms of the next century.

REFERENCES

Korey, G., & Bogorya, Y. (1985). The managerial action learning concept: theory and application. *Management Decision*, 23, 3-11.

Lawrie, J. (1989). Take action to change performance. *Personnel Journal*, 68, 59-59.

Margerison, C.J. (1988). Action learning and excellence in management development. *Journal of Management Development*, 7, 43-53.

Pedler, M. (1991). *Action learning in practice*. Aldership, England: Gower.

Raelin, J.A. (1997). Individual and situational precursors of successful action learning. *Journal of Management Education*, 21, 368-394.

Standish Group International (1995). *Chaos Report*. Boston, MA.

Weinstein, K. (1995). *Action learning: A journey in discovery and development*. London: HarperCollins.

Chapter 5

Real-World Learning of Information Resource Management

Dusan Lesjak and Miroslav Rebernik
University of Maribor, Slovenia

The chapter describes an Information Resources Management course in a Small Business Management program at the Faculty of Economics and Business, University of Maribor, Slovenia that is based on real world learning principle. The aim of the course is to provide students with knowledge and experience to deal with information technology and systems in small business from a managerial perspective. The theoretical part of the course is conducted in a classroom and the practical part is experienced in mentor firms. Thus, students have an opportunity to compare, combine and verify "theory" and "practice" instantly and develop capability to transfer the acquired knowledge and skills into practice.

INTRODUCTION

Although small and medium sized companies form an important part of national economies all over the world, business and management schools don't really consider them as being important enough to tailor curriculums to their needs. Small business is not shrunk big business, and individual managing functions in smaller companies cannot be specialized to the same extent as those of large companies. In general, the education process at university institutions is still fo-

Previously Published in *Challenges of Information Technology Management in the 21st Century* edited by Mehdi Khosrow-Pour, Copyright © 2000, Idea Group Publishing.

cused on big companies and educates specialists in different fields such as marketing, finance, accounting, etc. But small business can not afford specialists; it
needs highly competent, practically oriented individuals capable of handling a broad
array of business problems.

The other problem is that the majority of university programs still train people
only to be employed by somebody and to work for somebody, and does not train
them to be self-reliant owners and entrepreneurs, or to be able to take care of
their own professional career. In the majority of business programs all over the
world, students get first hand experience in managing a company after their graduation when they start their business careers. This change from academia to business environment causes quite some problems, frustrations and takes time which
could be spend more efficiently.

To avoid the above-mentioned problems we designed and developed a Small
Business Management program based on action-learning and real-world learning
principles. To illustrate how this real-world learning takes place an Information
Resource Management course will be presented and discussed in the chapter.

The need and idea for effective Small Business Management program

The number of Slovene small business has increased six folds since 1990,
when the transformation of Slovenia's economy began (Bulletin…, 1997).

Until 1993, none of the institutions of higher education in Slovenia offered
education and training programs for management of small business. Representing
one of only two Slovene universities, University of Maribor's Faculty of Economics and Business started and runs an undergraduate Small Business Management
program.

Figure 1: Number of Small Firms in Slovenia

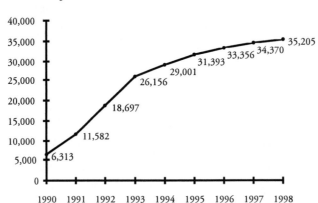

The underlying philosophy of the innovative management program is that education and training for people who are to be either independent entrepreneurs or employed in a smaller company, or who are to own and run it, has to be different from the education and training for big companies. It has to take into account at least three elements that differ a small business: de-specialization of job tasks, resource poverty, and self-employment.

SMALL BUSINESS MANAGEMENT PROGRAM
The Aims and Curriculum of the program

The basic aim of the program is to produce graduates who are able to run and manage small firms or undertake other entrepreneurial jobs immediately after graduation without requiring a lengthy time to get into the business and to get acquainted with actual enterprise life.

The program has been designed to allow students to spend two days a week at the University and two days a week in companies, during four semesters, i.e., about 1000 hours during two years. Entrepreneurs and small business managers train students, and students (with the help of academics) solve real business problems. The program tries to unite academics and managers to the same task: effective management education and training that matches changing business environment.

After successfully completing the first two years of basic business economics studies, students can apply for admission to the small business management program. For each qualified student, a small firm is provided that meets the pre-set criteria, and is capable and willing to cooperate with the Faculty in management education and training. Under mentorship of the entrepreneur or the top manager of such a company during their course of study, the students verify their theoretical knowledge in these companies and obtain practical managerial skills.

The program that continues after successfully completed first two years study (18 general business, management and economics courses) consists of 14 courses in total.

The program was designed and implemented through the cooperation of the following institutions of higher education: University College of Boras (Sweden), School of Economics and Commercial Law, University of Gothenburg (Sweden), De Vlerick School of Management, University of Gent (Belgium), Faculty of Economics and Banking, University of Udine (Italy), and Faculty of Economics and Business, University of Maribor (Slovenia). Needed financial sources were obtained from funds of European Union (PHARE - TEMPUS), the Swedish Government, Maribor Commune, and with tuition paid by mentoring firms.

INFORMATION RESOURCE MANAGEMENT COURSE

Small Business from an IT/IS Perspective

The number of information technology (IT) and information systems (IS) applications used in small business has grown rapidly since the beginning of the nineties. They have been applied both to the office environment (Dwyer, 1990) and other administrative tasks on one hand and to the production line, warehousing, and shipping on the other. But, we can hardly find managerial IT tools such as executive information systems, decision support systems, or expert systems in small firms (Lesjak and Lynn, 1999, Park, 1990, Heikkila et al., 1991).

The person responsible for information resources in a small firm carries a heavy burden of responsibility. It is very easy to make a wrong decision when considering computers and applications for the business. If a wrong set of decisions is taken, usually too quickly, the cost can be incalculable. The installation of computers can consume vast amounts of staff time, which might otherwise be spent on more productive aspects of the business (Aziz, 1990). It is therefore vital that we are sure we will get the best from the system once it is up running.

The secret is not to computerize everything at once, but instead to take a cool look at the business and decide what parts of it really need computers and applications. In many cases, it is rather unlikely that they will need to computerize all of their activities or operations.

The mentioned facts support the notion that entrepreneurs, managers and employees in small firms must resolve (with little specialized assistance) the following groups of questions:

- *Information Management*: What information problems can be found in small firms? How are firm problems identified and solved? Who should and could solve information problems?
- *IT Management*: What is the appropriate information (and communication) technology for small firms? How do managers select, acquire, introduce, implement, and maintain appropriate information and communication technology?
- *IS Management*: What are the type, the size and allocation of information resources? What architecture and characteristics of an appropriate information system are expedient? How do firm managers (arrange) design, develop, "run" and manage (and maintain) such an information system?

Information resources are therefore not a minor problem for small businesses but a crucial one, not only because of IT's rapid growth, which unfortunately causes many additional problems. Yet despite the potential downside risk associated with information resources, there can be huge benefits if we get it right. These days a well thought out, efficient computer operation could make all the difference to the competitiveness of a business, a "make or break" difference. Small business leaders who utilize information resources to improve performance will definitely increase their chances for survival and success.

Content of the IRM Course

Because there were no IT/IS and related managerial issues for small business taught in Slovenia we wanted to cover that area within the SBM program; therefore the Information Resource Management (IRM) course was introduced.

The aim of the course is to provide students with knowledge and experience to deal with "information" problems of small firms and to find or propose solutions or means for solving them. These goals are reflected in the structure and content of the course:

- information and communication technology for small business;
- information development (process) of a small firm;
- the analysis of a firm from strategic, business, and especially IT/IS perspectives;
- strategic IS planning;
- acquiring and implementing information resources; and
- estimating the impact of information resources on firms.

The first part describes which information and communication technology is suitable for small business and the characteristics of small business information resources and systems.

The second part of the course deals with development of small firms from an informational perspective. First, questions and problems concerning information development in firms are discussed. Second, the process of information development is described, also from a general perspective.

The third part presents different tools for analyzing a firm from strategic, business, and information perspectives. The strategic aspect deals with the business strategy of a firm. The business aspect deals with the production and sales program of a firm in terms of its' products life cycles. The main aim of the IT component is to analyze the available information resources and evaluate the opportunities for their usage and implementation.

The fourth part teaches strategic IS planning. First, the vision of the use of information resources is discussed; then the strategy of information development of a firm is introduced; later strategic information needs and the strategic entity-relation model are explained; and finally, a firm's IT architecture and a program of IS's implementation.

The fifth part introduces activities and processes for acquiring and introducing information resources - the development of an IS. First, the purchase of standard application packages, the development of special application packages, and the purchase of hardware and communication tools are illustrated. Second, the introductions and implementation of information resources are explored. Finally, the maintenance and further development of specific systems are discussed.

In the final or sixth part, the economic impact of information resources usage on firms and the challenges of assessing that are discussed. Tangible and intangible economic results are discussed.

With such a structure and content, the course provides students with insight into capabilities and limitations of information resources within a small firm. Emphasis is not on exploring and exploiting the capabilities of information resources but on the business opportunities of a particular firm, which can be addressed with the assistance of information resources.

Teaching Methods

The IRM course is conducted within a two-month period in two different environments: The theoretical and methodological part of the course takes place in a classroom and the practical part is experienced within the host firms.

On Mondays during the first six weeks, one part of the course is given in the form of lectures. Students get familiar with the theoretical and methodological foundations, issues, and trends from the six parts of the course described above. On Tuesdays they try to "use" the gained knowledge on a case, which was developed specially for the course. The issues, problems and solutions of the case, as well as the topics related to the particular part of the course are discussed thoroughly.

Mondays and Tuesdays prepare students for Wednesdays' and Thursdays' practical part, working at their mentor firms. It is important that mentor firms provide a climate that is open to learning and, together with their different activities, offer students a wide scope of tasks. Students must be taken as a resource available to firms; they are expected to play an active role and not just be observers. Thus, students can contribute to firm performance, what is also important with regards to the projects and reports made and results achieved by the students.

Students have to determine information needs and/or problems in their firm and propose or even develop solutions with real data (proposals, offers, etc.) which they obtain from different vendors (as well as via the Internet). In the last two weeks of the two-month period each student has to prepare a project on information development of its mentor firm. The project is presented to other students and representatives from their mentor firms are invited to participate in the presentation.

The student projects have similar structure as the course, so the following topics have to be elaborated:
• Firm's vision and strategy;

- Analysis of a firm's current information resources and assessment of their business impact;
- Analysis of a firm from strategic and business perspective;
- Survey of information needs and information problems of the firm;
- Strategic planning of information systems;
- Projects of acquiring and introducing the needed information resources; and
- Estimation of impacts of current and especially future information resources usage.

Experience with the Course

Because the program is designed to allow students to spend 2 days a week in a classroom and 2 days a week in their mentor firms, we decided to accept no more than 20 students in a program each year. That was necessary to ensure the desired quality of teaching, to find suitable mentor firms for the students and especially to monitor and control students' work in mentor firms. The actual number of enrolled students in a particular year varied from 15 to 20.

In the first 6 weeks of conducting the IRM course, students got the necessary theoretical and practical knowledge. After that, they had 14 days to prepare their projects: to gather all the needed information, design mentor firms' new information systems, and to receive hardware or software offers from various vendors, etc. In that period an information engineering consultant was available to discuss with them their solutions and proposals for further development of mentor firms' information systems.

Students' performance was evaluated through their work and the results of their work. In brief the evaluating system is as follows:

- 40% of their grade consists of their work, achievements, and cooperativness in first 6 weeks;
- 40 % of their grade consists of projects in written form (if all the topics are covered, what are the proposed solutions, how solutions reflect firms' problems, etc.); and
- 20% of their grade consists of their presentations of projects and discussion.

The way that the course is designed and taught brings a lot of advantages and of course some disadvantages. The advantages are:

- SBM students (who are not studying to be IT/IS experts) become aware of characteristics and potentials of IT/IS for small business;
- the theory and practice combination within a week worked very well and students had an opportunity to check and verify theory with practice instantly and by that, got practical experiences sooner that students do from other programs; and

- students' workload during the teaching process (2-month period) is higher but they do not have any other course lectured within that period.
  The disadvantages of a course are as follows:
- since the students ordinarily are not IT/IS experts sometimes more time is needed for a particular IT/IS topic than is appropriate;
- it might happen that a student has a mentor firm, which does not easily accommodate IT/IS intervention. A mentor firm for instance could have data processing and IS development outsourced, their process/products could not be suitable for modern computer support, etc.; and
- if their work and the project are not good enough, they must enhance the work and that requires additional time and effort for them (and the professor).

ACTION LEARNING AND REAL-WORLD LEARNING
Action learning

Action learning as originally developed by Reg Revans in the forties proved to be a good way for education of managers particularly those with high levels of responsibility but long absence from higher education. (O'Hara, Weber and Reeve, 1996) It is also suitable for MBA programs where can be quite successful (Dilworth, 1996). Many examples of successful corporate education in companies such as Phillips, Dutch Royal, Shell Group, Motorola, Unilever, Daimler-Benz AG (Ready, 1995) show the effectiveness of an action learning approach regardless of its use in original or adapted form.

The Revans Center for Action Learning and Research at the University of Salford defines action learning as "a process of inquiry, beginning with the experience of not knowing what to do next, and finding that an answer is not available from current expertise" (Powell, 1999).

The very core of the action learning approach is the Revan's formula $L = P + Q$. Experience is translated to learning through seminar projects where students have to use the programmed knowledge (P) and while working on a company's problems mix it with questions (Q) needed to be answered for the problem to be solved. In this educational model the main role of the faculty is in delivering the programmed knowledge, and in helping the students to adequately solve the company's problem selected for seminar work. The company mentor enable students to freely ask questions and pave the way for them to get all information needed for fulfilling their assigned tasks. The majority of action learning projects are authentic followers of Revan's generic idea of the education of management (Parkes, 1998), but the actual one in the company not the future one, as we do in our SBM program and IRM course.

Action learning components in IRM course

Our SBM program was never been designed as an action learning process, although we can find some action learning components in it. Because at the beginning students receive detailed instructions on how to undertake questioning in the company we could transform formula a little: $L = P + Q + PQ$. Learning (L) is equal to programmed knowledge (P) plus spontaneous questioning (Q) plus programmed questioning (PQ). But that is mainly all about action learning in the program and IRM course.

Why SBM program and by that IRM course as well is not really an action learning model but more a real-world learning approach?

- Firstly, when we form teams we do not form learning teams as "sets."
- Secondly, students do not have the right to take actions, at least not during the first half of their stay in the company. Later on during their cooperation with firm they do get some authority to make minor decisions, but not while IRM course is on the track, i.e. in the first quarter of their cooperation.
- Thirdly, there is no tutorial session in the company, etc. There are also other elements missing that are "prescribed" in an action learning model of education, such as peer evaluation of one's performance, reciprocation of advice and criticism, analysis of learning results, feedback of participants, etc. (Revans, 1983, 1984).
- Our IRM course is definitely more than an experiential learning. We do not put students in simulated, fictitious organizations but into real living companies with all their complexities and with all the small and big problems that are to be solved on a daily basis.

Accepting the dichotomy of management education on the (a) professional education model and (b) the action learning model, our IRM course and SBM program as a whole falls somewhere in between. We think it is more appropriate that it is named a real-world learning model (Bilimoria, 1998).

INSTEAD OF CONCLUSION

Last but not least let us discuss briefly as well as the feedback about the IRM course and the real-world learning approach, which we obtain from our market – i.e., mentor firms' managers and owners.

On average they are very positive about the course and the program on one hand and the students, their efforts and achievements. They say that students are bringing new or needed knowledge to their firms to a great extent. That is very important for managers because although small firms need leaders who are generalists, sometimes they need specialists too.

So fare more than 20 students are offered full-time jobs following graduation by their mentor firm (and 15 of them here accepted offers). That is something what makes this program and its students really different compared to other programs and students who usually do not get offered jobs.

Of course, they also mentioned that the biggest problem regarding SBM program they have is their time needed to be spent with the students and their work. Especially at the beginning when students do not know firms well enough, students need to interview and dialogue with their mentor (who are usually owners or managers).

To share some experience with others as a professor there are some lessons learned from designing and conducting such a course:

- It is far easier (and maybe better) to start with no more that ten firms, because we had many problems and we needed a lot of time for finding suitable mentor firms. Occasionally, we have to substitute one or two mentor firms each year after couple of months;
- You need a very good formal and informal information system to find suitable mentor firms and very good connections to involve all the needed mentor firms into the project; and
- There are some limitations for student projects. If in a mentor firm certain business functional area (e.g., production) is not present, then it is better not to start with a student's project in that area.

And finally our experience show that such programs and courses are justified (and needed), because of the fact that they combine consulting and teaching with objectives of training students to make and implement the key (info related) decisions in their future business.

REFERENCES

Aziz, K. (1990). *The Barclays Guide to Computing for the Small Businesses*. Great Britain, Barclays Published by Blackwell.

Bilimoria, D. (1998). From Classroom Experience to Real-World Learning: A Diasporic Shift in Management Education, *Journal of Management Education*, 22(3).

Bulletin on the Business Results within the Economy of the Republic of Slovenia (1997). Ljubljana, Agency for Payment System of the Republic of Slovenia.

Dilworth, R. (1996). Action Learning: Bridging Academic and Workplace Domains. *Employee Cunselling Today, The Journal of Workplace Learning*, 8(6), pp.45-53.

Dwyer, E. (1990). *The Personal Computer in the Small Business*. Efficient Office Practice, Great Britain, NCC Blackwell Limited.

Heikkila, J., Saarinen, T., & Assksjavri, M. (1991). Success of Software Packages in Small Business; an Exploratory Study, *European Journal of Information Systems*, 1, pp.159-162.

Ibrahim, A.B., & Goodwin, J.R. (1986). Perceived Causes of Success in Small Business, *American Journal of Small Business*, 1, pp. 41-52.

Lesjak, D., & Lynn, M.L. (1999). Are Slovene Small Firms Using IT Strategically? *The next Century... Effectively managing Information technology*, IACIS Refereed Proceedings, San Antonio, Texas, pp. 141-147.

O'Hara, S., Webber, T., & Reeve, S. (1996). Action Learning in Management Education. *Education + Learning*, 38(8), pp. 16-21.

Park, S.W. (1990). *The Characteristics and Usage of Computerized Information Systems in Small Apparel in Textile Industry*. Unpublished dissertation, Georgia State University.

Parkes, D. (1998). Action Learning: Business Applications in North America. *Journal of Workplace Learning*. 10(3), pp. 165-168.

Powell, J. et al. (1999). Action Learning for Innovation and Construction. *Problems of Participation and Connection Conference*. Amsterdam, April 6-9.

Ready, D. (1995). Educating the Survivors. *The Journal of Business Strategy*, 16(2), Mar/Apr.

Rebernik, M. (1994). Mental Models as the Pivot of the West-East Knowledge Transfer. In A. Gibb and M. Rebernik (Eds.), *Small Business Management in the New Europe*, Maribor: EIM.

Revans, R. (1983). Action Learning: Its Terms and Character. *Management Decision*, 21(1), pp. 39-51.

Revans, R. (1984). Action Learning: Are We Getting There? *Management Decision*, 22(1), pp. 45-53.

Chapter 6

IS Education in the New Millennium: Determining the 'Right' Curriculum

Sanjeev Phukan
Bemidji State University, USA

Ashok Ranchhod
Southampton Business School, UK

T. Vasudavan
Edith Cowan University, Australia

INTRODUCTION

The last quarter of this century has seen a sea change in Information Systems (IS) and Information Technology (IT), including computers, communications, and office automation. The effects of these changes have been widespread and as a result, have caused major transformations n the way we live and work. One major effect has been the creation of a global marketplace on an unprecedented scale. This marketplace, in turn, has shrunk the world in such a way as to create tremendous opportunities as well as threats for even relatively small organizations. As a consequence, many organizations today have discovered that their profitability and perhaps even their survival, now depend on their ability to successfully play the game in a new, complex, and often unfamiliar, global arena.

IS and IT have played crucial, pivotal roles in the creation of this global market, and will, we firmly believe, have an enormous impact on its future. The management of organizations that must and will operate in this environment now and in the future will demand a comprehensive array of attributes and skills from their personnel. IS professionals particularly will be subject to an increasing list of de-

Previously Published in *Challenges of Information Technology Management in the 21st Century* edited by Mehdi Khosrow-Pour, Copyright © 2000, Idea Group Publishing.

mands. As is already often the case, in many instances IS personnel, much more so than their counterparts in other functional areas, will be truly "global" personnel, living and working in places that are often far removed from where they were born or educated.

One obvious reason for this is the tremendous shortage of qualified IS personnel the world over and the demand for skilled services. In fact, the tremendous shortage of IT professionals has resulted in a worldwide "head-hunt," or as one recruiter uncharitably put it, "nerd-hunt" for qualified professionals. Obviously, teams of professionals assembled from all over the world are going to present rather unique management challenges. And even though companies today are scrambling to hire almost anyone who even vaguely resembles an IS professional, maturity in the market will place increasingly complex demands on these personnel.

THE NEW IT PROFESSIONALS: WHO ARE THEY?

In many ways, today's global economy is reminiscent of the age of empires. During that period, professionals had to have a working knowledge of other areas of the world, notably the various colonies of the mother country. Toward this end, there was the grand tour, an education strongly based in the liberal education traditions of history, geography, languages, and the arts, and the somewhat dubious distinction of always having the upper hand as a citizen of the ruling country. Circumstances today are vastly different; nevertheless, certain lessons are still valid. The imperial powers, from Rome to Britain, ensured that their professionals had a thorough understanding of the cultures and values of the areas to which they were sent. Those who did not possess this understanding proved to be incapable of operating effectively.

Today's business professionals operate in an increasingly global arena, and as such, must possess global skills. The authors would submit that this is true of IS personnel as well, and that the IS professional of today and tomorrow will need to be a globally oriented. These IS personnel may face a host of issues that may range from technical telecommunications issues to global corporate management (Deans et al., 1991). In addition, they must be familiar with other, non-technical issues as well, such as culture and tradition.

The management of a global IS thus poses special challenges for IS managers (Deans and Ricks, 1993) and the global IS professional will need a far greater depth and breadth of knowledge in comparison to his or her domestic counterpart (Cheney and Kasper, 1993), although professionals that operate solely in the domestic arena are declining in numbers. Global IS professionals will also need to have international experience in interactions with global competitors and global customers (Nelson, 1996). It goes without saying that the successful global IS professional will need be familiar with IS standards and practices in other areas of the world and will have to deal with a variety of additional transnational problems, including those of inadequate infrastructure, sketchy technical support, language problems, geographic separation, differing time zones, and greatly different labor technology cost tradeoffs. Surely one of the most daunting aspects of the task faced by any global IS professional is what can only be described as the simultaneous management of several learning curves. He or she must be well versed in the IS organization, the different national organizations, the corporation as a whole, and the country management. This is above and beyond any technical skills, which must be taken for granted.

Many authors have attempted to define the characteristics that a successful global IS professional must possess. For example, in his examination of the role of a global Chief Information Officer (CIO), Roche (1992) suggests that the CIO's task must include the construction of short term infrastructure requirements with the flexibility to meet the longer-term needs of the global organization. This is a tall order.

Kanter and Kesner (1992) also attempt to define the role of what they define as a Global Information Officer (GIO). They conclude that the GIO must possess capabilities above and beyond the attributes considered necessary for a successful CIO. Aside from a thorough understanding of all aspects of IT and an appropriate IT skill base, the authors believe that a successful GIO must possess a flexible management style, superior organizational skills, a thorough understanding of the national and international environments, and an ability to successfully manage and implement technology transfer.

McFarlan (1992) points out that much of the research that has been carried out concerning the nature of the CIO's job has assumed an almost totally domestic orientation, whereas the reality is quite different. He points out that the CIO that is responsible for international operations must contend with all the domestic issues as well as many additional problems. Even when authors do address the necessity of a global perspective among IS professionals, their focus often falls short of the reality. For example, Flynn (1994) makes a strong case for education to address the requirements of a global market. However, he focuses almost exclusively on interactions between the United States and the European markets. When one considers that in all likelihood, it is the developing nations that offer the greatest potential for market growth, (Cheney and Kasper, 1993) such a perspective is ill-advised and short sighted.

Perhaps, it is not possible to arrive at a comprehensive list of the skills and attributes that a global IS professional must possess. And, maybe this is not entirely a disadvantage. A contingency approach could then be used, where a global IS professional is gradually eased into the global arena during his or her career.

This would still necessitate, however, a certain broad based background that would have to be provided by the educational process.

THE ROLE OF EDUCATION

IS education across the world would thus have to provide a "base foundation" of skills and knowledge that is easily transportable across nation and regions. We believe that IS graduates the world over will require specific skills to succeed in a fast moving marketplace that will be characterized by a culturally and ethnically diverse work force and a significant dependence on IT to cut across many barriers. In addition, for IS graduates to address the needs of developed, developing, and under-developed markets, they will require an expanded IS curriculum as well as a focus that supports the global IS manager's technical needs.

Thus, all over the world, universities and institutions of higher learning are faced with the problem of creating curricula that will meet these requirements of a dynamic and rapidly changing world market. The problem has several dimensions. For instance, as the worldwide demand for IS professionals has grown, educational institutions have been scrambling to try and produce enough graduates to satisfy the burgeoning market. However, concurrent rapid changes in the IT environment and explosive growth and change rates in technology have made the development of a viable IS curriculum extremely difficult. Adding a global element to an already difficult task seems to be akin to adding the last straw to the aching camel's back, and many curriculum initiatives seem to be only too relieved to shove it onto a remote back burner.

The real problem, we believe, lies in determining exactly what the content of these curricula should be. It appears, at least at first glance, that curricula in many regions of the world, while attempting to provide an increasing number of IT skill sets, have done little to address the real problems inherent in creating a global IS professional. The authors believe that even many of the latest curriculum proposals for IS in the United States fall short of addressing these needs (Davis et al., 1997).

The purpose of this chapter is to examine the environment and suggest some changes in the way we educate the IS professionals of today and tomorrow. Initial research will focus on the authors' home countries, namely Australia, the United Kingdom, and the United States.

REFERENCES

Cheney, P. H., & Kasper, G. M. (1993). Responding to World Competition: Developing the Global IS Professional, *Journal of Global Information Management*, 1(1), 21-31.

Davis, G. B., Gorgone, J. T., Couger, J. D., Feinstein, D. L., & Longnecker, H. E. (1997). *Model Curriculum and Guidelines for Undergraduate Degree Programs in Information Systems*, AITP.

Deans, P.C., Karwan, K. R., Goslar, M. D., Ricks, D. A., & Toyne, B. (1991). Identification of Key International Information Systems Issues in U.S.-Based Multinational Corporations, *Journal of Management Information Systems*, 7(4), 27-50.

Deans, P. C. & Ricks, D. A. (1993). An Agenda for Research Linking Information Systems and International Business: Theory, Methodology and Application, *Journal of Global Information Management*, 1(1), 6-19.

Flynn, J. A. (1994). Global Information Systems: Problems, Solutions, and How to Manage Them, *Journal of Information Systems Education*, 6(3), 142-147.

Kanter, J., & Kesner, R. (1992). The CIO/GIO as Catalyst and Facilitator: Building the Information Utility to Meet Global Challenges. In S. Palvia, P. Palvia and R.M. Zigli (Eds.), *The Global Issues of Information Technology Management*, Hershey, PA: Idea Group Publishing.

McFarlan, F. W. (1992). Multinational CIO Challenge for the 1990s. In S. Palvia, P. Palvia and R.M. Zigli (Eds.), *The Global Issues of Information Technology Management*, Hershey, PA: Idea Group Publishing.

Nelson, K. (1996). Global Information Systems Quality: Key Issues and Challenges, *Journal of Global Information Management*, 4(4), 4-14.

Roche, E. M. (1992). *Managing Information Technology in Multinational Corporations*. New York: Macmillan.

Chapter 7

Measurement of a College Computer Literacy Course

Nancy Tsai and Thomas E. Hebert
California State University, Sacramento, USA

INTRODUCTION

A college graduate has to be computer literate in order to gain competitive edge in today's business world since information technology, ranging from the basic word processing software to the complex data base management systems, is used constantly to prepare, present, and exchange information for management decision making. Consequently, it is the responsibility of the education institution to offer a computer literacy class or series of classes for preparing its students with proper computer knowledge in a suitable learning environment before they enter the business world. Therefore, the purpose of this paper is to discuss and present some issues of the college computer literacy classes offered by the Management Information Science Department (MIS) of College of Business Administration (CBA) at the California State University, Sacramento. These issues include the objectives of the classes, the contents of the classes, the classroom environment, and the measurement of class objectives.

COMPUTER LITERACY REQUIREMENT GOAL

The CBA's Computer Literacy Requirement has the overall goal to promote a high level of computer literacy for all students in the education processes of the College and in student's subsequent personal and professional life.

This overall goal can be further classified into four elements:
- It is the goal of the computer literacy requirement that the CBA provide equal learning and working environment for all students, regardless of their financial

Previously Published in *Challenges of Information Technology Management in the 21st Century* edited by Mehdi Khosrow-Pour, Copyright © 2000, Idea Group Publishing.

resources. To achieve this goal the CBA will provide open access to computer technology and ensure that students have the knowledge and ability to use that technology.

- It is the goal of the computer literacy requirement that students be able to independently use computer technology in their courses. For example, a student should be able to use computers to write a paper or prepare a presentation without explicit direction from an instructor.
- It is the goal of the computer literacy requirement that faculty can give computer related assignments that extend or enhance student's basic computer literacy skills without detailed instructions on computer basics. For example, a professor should be able to assign a student to access a Web site and download a file to a spreadsheet for analysis without explaining the basics of the Internet, browsers, hyperlinks, file management, or spreadsheet use.
- It is the goal of the computer literacy requirement that students be prepared for a lifetime of learning new computer technology and software.

MEASURABLE ELEMENTS OF COMPUTER LITERACY REQUIREMENT

In order to assess these overall goals and it is necessary to specify specific objectives with measurable elements. The top-level objective is to achieve these goals. Using top down structured approach, this top-level objective can be classified into three specific areas:

- **Technology:** Adequate facilities, software, and support must be available.
  1. *Open computing labs*
     a. Up-to-date computer hardware
     b. Up-to-date software
     c. Adequate numbers of computers
     d. Adequate hours of operation
     e. Adequate supervision, support, and assistance
     f. Adequate workspace
  2. *Teaching and testing labs*
     a. Up-to-date computer and presentation hardware
     b. Up-to-date software
     c. Adequate numbers of computers
     d. Adequate hours of operation
     e. Adequate supervision, support, and assistance
     f. Adequate workspace
  3. *Classrooms*
     a. Up-to-date computer and presentation hardware
     b. Up-to-date software

    c. Adequate security

    d. Adequatesupport

    e. Physical safety

    f. Adequate lighting

    g. Comfortable viewing

    h. Reliability

4. Faculty Offices

    a. Up-to-date computer hardware

    b. Up-to-date software

    c. Adequate office hours

    d. Adequate, support and assistance

- **Knowledge:** Students must be knowledgeable about appropriate and common hardware and software.

1. Operating Systems

    a. File Management such as copy, save, move, delete, rename, change attributes, find, display, run, and use wildcards

    b. Folder Management such as create, copy, move, rename, delete, find, display, and organize

    c. Configuration including common control panel functions

    d. Desktop Operations including use of common windows features (menu's, dialog boxes, windows, and scroll bars)

2. Internet

    a. Terminology and Concepts

    b. Browser Usage

    c. Search engine usage

3. Hardware terms and concepts

4. Spreadsheets

    a. Create and save a workbook

    b. Format a spreadsheet

    c. Print a spreadsheet

    d. Write correct formulas using operators, functions and relative and absolute addresses

    e. Create graphics

    f. Database operations

    g. Link and embed objects

5. Word Processing

    a. Create and save a document

    b. Format a document

    c. Print a document

    d. Edit a document

    e. Use tools such as spelling and grammar checkers

    f. Create and use columns and tables

    g. Link and embed objects

    h. Create Web page

  6. *Presentations*

    a. Create and save a presentation

    b. Format a presentation

    c. Edit a presentation

    d. Link and embed objects

    e. Use tools such as spelling and style checkers

    f. Printing a presentation

    g. Running a slideshow

- **Usage:** True computer literacy and a lifelong ability to learn and use new computer technology and software require continued computer use and exposure to business application of computers.

  1. Students are expected to use computer technology and software in written assignments, presentations, and information gathering

  2. Students are exposed to new computer technology, software, and applications where appropriate in the functional areas of the CBA curriculum

  3. Students are expected to learn appropriate new software and new releases of software in the functional areas of the CBA curriculum

MEASUREMENT OF COMPUTER LITERACY REQUIREMENT

The final element of assessment is to specify the measurements of these objectives.

- **Technology:** Basically the measurements for these elements will be counts and percentages. For example, the measurement of classrooms is a seven criteria (zero or one) count for each classroom and summarized for the MIS 1ABC classrooms. The specific criteria for each of the classifications listed above will have to be specified and counted each semester.

- **Knowledge:** Our common MIS IABC testing procedures will enable the tabulation of statistics on the specific elements listed above. The common exam tasks will have to be classified according to the above categories and reported each semester.

- **Usage:** This will have to be measured by examination of course outlines and counting.

CONCLUSION

There are more than one thousand students taking these computer literacy requirement courses each year. These courses are taught by part time teaching assistants. There are three major functions can be achieved by the above assessment criteria. The first one is to assure that every student will receive the same computer literacy concepts and working skills regardless of the instructor of the course. The second one is to examine the accomplishment of computer literacy course in terms of its stated goals or objectives. The last one is to improve the computer literacy requirement based on the findings of the assessment.

REFERENCES

Hebert, T. E. & Tsai, N. (1997). An Electronic Classroom for the Teaching and Testing of Computer Literacy. In *Proceeding of International Association for Computer Information System Conference*, October.

Hebert, T. E., Tsai, N., & Barnes, J. (1998). Computer Literacy Issues: Challenge Examinations. In *Proceeding of Twenty—Seventh Annual Meeting of the Western Decision Sciences Institute*, April.

Tsai, N. & Hebert, T. E. (1998). Teaching/Learning Methods for Computer Literacy Courses. In *Proceeding of ₉th International Conference of Information Resources Management Association*, May.

Tsai, N., Hebert, T., & Christenson, A. (1999). Avoiding Mistakes in the Design of Electronic Lecture Classrooms. In *Proceeding of Twenty—Eight Annual Meeting of the Western Decision Sciences Institute* April.

Chapter 8

The Place of Homework in an Information Systems Tutorials

Bill Morgan and Bob Godfrey
University of Tasmania, Australia

This chapter presents findings from a study of Information Systems tutorials. The study sought to discover if the use of prescribed homework improved the learning of the students. In addition to their regular tests, examinations and assignments, students were given homework to complete. Students were surveyed using the College and University Classroom Environment Inventory (CUCEI) instrument before and after the experiment and several components of the study showed significant improvement for those students in these tutorials.

INTRODUCTION

Many universities share a common teaching pattern of lectures and tutorials. By tutorials we mean here small group "teaching" (of up to 20) students. These tutorials are usually based on problems (often drawn from the set text) intended to clarify and reinforce the concepts covered in the lecture, on the assumption that:
- the problems set in the tutorial are relevant to the lecture concepts and interesting in their approach;
- as the concepts being studied are difficult and important, they need the reinforcement offered by a successful problem solving tutorial; and
- the students are interested in the work (being at least sufficiently motivated to attend the tutorial session which is not compulsory).

Previously Published in *Challenges of Information Technology Management in the 21st Century* edited by Mehdi Khosrow-Pour, Copyright © 2000, Idea Group Publishing.

However the students do not usually gain as much as they should from these tutorials because they do not:

- review the lecture material;
- complete pre-tutorial exercises handed out in advance; and
- participate fully in tutorial discussions.

Accordingly, an action research exercise was carried out to see whether, as a result of undertaking a programme of prescribed homework study, students would:

- participate more readily and with greater learning achievement in tutorial activities;
- achieve more effective learning outcomes in the long term.

CONTEXT OF THE STUDY
Action research

Action research in education may be described as a collaborative and participatory approach to improving effectiveness by changing methods and learning from the consequences of these changes. It consists of critically examining the action of individual group members as a means of increasing knowledge about the process, and develops through a spiral of planning, acting, observing and reflecting. It was felt that action research with its assumptions of active participation in the process by the teacher was more appropriate than passive experimentation.

Tutorial/small group work

There are a number of possible approaches to tutorial or small group teaching. Those of relevance in this context are:

- The post-lecture tutorial that seeks to resolve any problems and reinforce the learning generated by the lecture. Strategies include the setting of discussion questions and problems, initially simple and becoming more complex; and the revision of lecture notes in the tutorial.
- Step by step discussion of the topic which follows a repeated pattern of *problem - tutor input - problem - tutor input*. This approach is particularly suitable for handling complex topics.
- Problem solving sessions where the thrust is on developing those problem-solving skills rather than reinforcing factual information. The approach here is to set out the problems in advance and have the students then discuss the solution or have it presented. Tutor-marked submissions are appropriate in this scenario.
- Case studies and simulations where the students work through stage-managed, structured action. These case studies and simulations may extend over several sessions.

Tutorial teaching of the type used in tertiary education is a well-established teaching method, dating back at least to Socrates and Plato. Nevertheless, we still have little precise information on what approaches are most effective, with many (perhaps most) studies being impressionistic rather than analytical. While wanting students to think and participate, small group teaching tends to be dominated by the tutor and students exhibit low levels of thinking. (Brown & Atkins, 1988).

Luker (1987) found that the average time spent by the tutor talking (even in problem solving groups) is about 64% of the total available, and it may reach 80%. She also reported on the difficulties and dislikes found by small group participants which were borne out in the findings of this study; For tutors, the most important difficulties were: (1) 'keeping my mouth shut'; (2) 'getting discussion going'; and (3) 'directing discussion in fruitful directions'. For students, the three most common problems were: (1) domination by a single person; (2) group members not talking; and (3) long silences.

Brown and Atkins (1988) suggest several strategies for the improvement of small group teaching: improvement in the communication and cognitive skills of participants; establishing clear ground rules; building a feeling of safety; subgroup work; and alternative seating patterns. They also suggest ways of controlling and guiding discussion. But there still remains the issue of motivating or persuading students to take part, which issue they do not touch on.

Theoretical basis for homework

The assumption being made in this research is that achievement of identified behavioural objectives is predicated on the design and management of an instructional process. In this study the process comprised three main elements: the lecture, homework, and the tutorial, in that order; plus of course summative assessment through examinations, tests and assignments. The lecture and the tutorial are accepted teaching strategies in the context of tertiary teaching. Formative assessment through regular homework is more commonly used at the secondary level, where the tertiary course might use an assignment (with summative assessment). It is the view of this paper that homework can be a useful addition to the traditional teaching process. Homework in this context is perceived to be an independent teaching/learning strategy appropriate for adult learning intended that it be assessed for formative purposes.

The place of homework in this sequence "lecture, homework, tutorial" is deliberate. It is a conscious attempt to ensure that the learning tasks with which the students are involved are in such a sequence as to permit, with a high level of success, "the learner to develop his capabilities to the point where he can perform the behaviour specified by the objective" (Verner & Davison, 1971).

To that end, homework in this sequence has a dual function: it is a means of generating feedback for both student and tutor, while at the same time operating as an advance organiser.

In his discussion of the process of learning, Gagne (1975, pp. 42-3) points out that many learning theorists see feedback as reinforcement, closely related to expectancy and motivation.

Success in satisfying needs and reaching established objectives becomes a reinforcer for the changes already made and provides a motive for further learning.

In that sense, homework, both as a teaching/learning activity, and in its place in the sequence "lecture, homework, tutorial" of this action research exercise, should achieve the objective of improving the learning effectiveness of students in tutorials. The homework, when reviewed by the tutor, tells the tutor where students are. The tutor's comments tell the students what they have achieved and are a vehicle for encouragement for further success. If the homework phase works effectively, it should be expected that students would as a consequence have greater success in tutorial work, and therefore be motivated and anticipate more effective learning in the future.

Evaluation of homework

In a comparison of fifteen studies of the effect of homework, the most statistically significant result was that:

"Larger effects on achievement were found for homework that bears teachers' comments and grades. Assigned homework produced more learning than no homework; and traditional homework was superior to non-traditional" (Paschal, Weinstein & Walberg, 1984, p103).

In a further study, Walberg elaborated on the value of graded homework.

"When homework is merely assigned without feedback from teachers it appears to raise, on average, the typical student at the 50th percentile to the 60th percentile. But when it is graded or commented upon, homework appears to raise learning from the 50th to the 79th percentile" (Walberg et al., 1985, p76).

Holmes and Croll (1989) did a longitudinal study of a cohort of 79 boys at an English grammar school from 1981 to 1986. The "homework" part of the study took place in their third year of study and compared self-reported time spent in study with performance at the end of the year and at the end of 1986. They found that time spent on homework correlated with immediate and future success, and was a better predictor of success than had been the entry scores for the first year. Students who spent more time than required on homework performed better (and equally well, whatever their parents' background). For those who spent little time on homework, social class was still a predictor of success.

RESEARCH STUDY
Objectives of the action research

Getting the students to talk and think is an objective of tutorials (Brown and Atkins, 1988). Much of the literature on the effects of homework relate to secondary eductation, where homework is more common than in the tertiary sector. Nevertheless, the Walberg group findings on homework seemed worth investigating for university-level Information Systems tutorials to see whether it increased talking and thinking level. It was felt that small exercises, handed out at one tutorial class, to be completed and handed in by the next tutorial session, might prove a kind of catalyst, or might act as an advance organiser, which would prepare students for the tutorial.

Some ways by which such advance organisers might improve the tutorial participation and thinking were believed to be:
- the performance of the task would cause students to review the lecture material and reinforce their learning;
- execution of these tasks would act in the form of an advance organiser in the sense suggested by Ausubel (Dubin and Okun, 1973);
- the feedback provided by grading of the assigned work would act to improve the self esteem and confidence of the students, encouraging them to participate; and
- with increased confidence, the students would feel a more free tutorial climate, leading to more enjoyment and learning.

Method

The thrust of the action research was to establish initial base levels for the opinions of participants, then to change things by incorporating homework exercises for 4 weeks and then re-surveying the participants to gauge the immediate effects of the exercises. A later measure of performance and climate, was applied 4 weeks later, to indicate whether any changes to group performance and climate lasted. The detailed plan of the study is given below.

Research Environment

The study sample was four tutorial groups of a first year, first semester Business Computing course. The total number of students in the study was 34 (more students started but dropped out along the way). Two of the tutorial groups were given by one of the authors and two by an independent tutor.

CUCEI Instrument

The College and University Classroom Environment Inventory (CUCEI) Instrument is intended to measure the actual and preferred classroom environment.

and has been used and evaluated at the university level (Fraser, 1987). By asking a series of overlapping questions and asking for responses on a 5-point Lickert scale, the instrument seeks to measure seven categories:

- **Personalisation:** Emphasis on the opportunities for individual students to interact with the tutor and on concern for students' personal welfare;
- **Involvement:** The extent to which students participate actively and attentively in tutorial discussions and activities;
- **Student Cohesiveness:** The extents to which students know, help and are friendly towards each other;
- **Satisfaction:** Extent to enjoyment of tutorials;
- **Task Orientation:** Extent to which tutorial activities are clear and well organised;
- **Innovation:** Extent to which the tutor plans new, unusual tutorial activities, teaching techniques and assignments; and
- **Individualisation:** Extent to which students are allowed to make decisions and are treated differentially according to ability, interest or rate of working

In asking the questions, there are two versions of the instrument. One asks students what they see happening (called the actual form), and the other what they would wish to happen (called the preferred form).

Steps in the action research

Because in any class there is a settling down period, and because at the end of the semester the students focus shifts to end of semester examinations; the study was conducted over a four week period in the middle of the semester in order to remove these influences as far as possible.

- During the first four to five weeks the group dynamics and climate of the tutorial group was allowed to stabilise. No changes to the normal tutorial programme was applied in this period.
- Just prior to the action changes, a detailed observation was made of the groups to which the study was applied. The CUCEI instrument was used to evaluate the tutorial group climate and the student preferences at that time was applied. Both the actual and preferred forms were applied.
- Over the following four weeks, homework exercises were assigned to the students at the end of the tutorial. The exercises were designed to take about 20-30 minutes to complete. The completed exercises were handed in by the students at the start of the following tutorial. The exercises were corrected and graded by the tutor and returned to the students a week later. Reasonably detailed comments on the assigned exercises were provided to the student.
- Following the action period, detailed observation of the group was again undertaken, using the actual form of the CUCEI instrument.

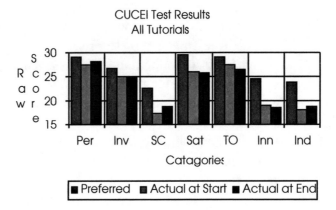

CUCEI Test Results
All Tutorials

■ Preferred   ■ Actual at Start   ■ Actual at End

RESULTS

The CUCUI instrument takes each Lickert-scale response and applies various weights to these values, which are then accumulated to produce measures on each of seven category scales. The average measurement (raw score) is graphed below, for the *preferred* form, and for the *actual* form both at the *start* and at the *end* of the study period.

The graph shows then the relative change in these seven measures. A "t-test" was used in comparing the change in scores for each CUCEI category. The probability level used was p=.05.

Looking at each CUCEI category:

- **Per** (Personalisation): Over the testing period, this category increased for every tutorial as well as in the aggregate of all tutorials. A "t-test" result of 2.181 shows the difference to be statistically significant;

- **Inv** (Involvement): Although the aggregate average was almost the same over the period, when we look at the individual tutorials we find that for one tutor (Tutorials 1 and 2) the score has increased and for the other tutor (Tutorials 3 and 4) the score has decreased. However the differences according to the "t-test" are not statistically significant. The sample was too small to make any valid comment as to the tutor's style being significant however there is that possibility;

- **SC** (Student Cohesiveness): This category showed the greatest increase over the testing period and this increase was statistically significant ("t-test" result of 2.601);

- **Sat** (Satisfaction): This category showed a slight drop over the period of testing, again not statistically significant;

- **TO** (Task Orientation): As for the "Sat" category, this showed a slight drop. Again, for one tutor we see an increase (slight) and for the other tutor, a decrease (in one tutorial this was statistically significant). This drop might be explained by having one more task to worry about;

- **Inn** (Innovation): In the aggregate, the score was the same at the end as at the beginning and there is no obvious pattern of results when we look at the individual tutorials. The point should be made that there is little scope for innovation in this tutorial setting; and
- **Ind** (Individualisation): In the aggregate, this category shows an increase over the period which is below (but verging on) the statistical significant level. As for the Innovation category, there was little scope for Individualisation within the framework of the subject matter being discussed.

CONCLUSIONS

As a general comment, the point must be made that the final number of students studied was not large enough for more detailed statistical analysis. However, it was evident that general trends could be perceived and that some tentative conclusions made from the study.

It would have been more satisfying if all the categories were clearly shown to trend upwards over the testing period but this was obviously not the case. For instance, the "Satisfaction" category was initially thought to be a key figure in indicating that the students were happy with having homework set. The CUCEI results did not bear this assumption out but in informal discussions with the students the general feeling was that homework was a good thing. It must also be said that the end-period testing came at a later and more generally stressful time in the semester, which may have been an outside influence on the test results (especially in the "Satisfaction" category.)

"Personalisation" was shown to significantly increase over the period. This could be interpreted as being a result of the positive influence of the marking of the homework. Equally it may also (in part at least) be the result of the greater familiarity within the tutorial group at a later period. The same could be said for "Student Cohesiveness," which had the greatest increase of all the categories.

Another general point to be made is that the CUCEI scores are high to begin with and therefore there is little room for improvement. It is interesting to note that in several instances within individual tutorial groups, the final score in the personalisation category was higher than the Preferred score for the "ideal" tutorial at the beginning of the testing period.

Further research

The results from this study are constrained in their application by the initial assumptions and by limitations imposed on the researchers. Attendance at tutorials was not mandatory. How this affected the study has not been considered. Nevertheless, the results and interpretations are sufficiently interesting to warrant some further investigation with a much larger sample at a later date. This further study should be able to control for the effect of tutor and other variables on the measurements. It could also include an analysis of examination results of the participants compared with those who were not set homework

In their discussion of Ausubel's use of the adjective "potential" in relation to advance organisers, Lawton and Wanska (1977, p240) point out that pre-testing should be undertaken to establish the presence or absence of relevant subsumers. Students may use previously acquired information in place of advance organisers. The possibility of such advance knowledge should be taken into account. In this study, very little pre-testing was carried out to reveal the existence of prior acquired knowledge which students may utilise, because it was assumed that a very significant majority of the students involved were being exposed to the information to be learned for the first time in their first year of tertiary study.

Walberg et al. (1985) found that daily homework had a much greater effect than less frequent homework. In this study homework of necessity had to be assigned on a weekly rather than a daily basis.

The time spent on the homework exercises by the students, for this action research, was set at about 15-20 minutes. This may be too little, as Holmes and Croll (1989) found a positive relationship between time spent on homework and success at year end.

REFERENCES

Brown, G. & Atkins, M. (1988). *Effective Teaching in Higher Education*, Methuen, London, chapter 4.

Brundage, D.H. & MacKeracher, D. (1980). Summary of learning principles with implications for facilitating learning and planning programs, *Adult Learning Principles and their Application to Program Planning*, Ontario Institute for Studies in Education, Toronto.

Dubin, S. S. & Okun, M. (1973). Implications of learning theories for adult instruction, *Adult Learning*, 24(1), pp 3-19.

Fraser, B. J., Treagust, D. F., Williamson, J. C. & Tobin, K. G. (1987). Validation and Application of the College and University Classroom Environment Inventory (CUCEI). *The Study of learning Environments*, vol 2, Curtin University, Western Australia, chapter 2.

Gagne, R. M. (1975). The process of learning, *Essentials of Learning for Instruction*, Dryden, Chicago.

Holmes, M. & Croll, P. (1989). Time spent on homework and academic achievement, *Educational Research,* 31(1), pp. 36-45.

Lawton, T. T. & Wanska, S. K. (1977). Advance organizers as a teaching strategy: a reply to Barnes and Clawson, *Review of Educational Research*, 47(1), (Winter) pp. 233-244.

Luker, P. A. (1987). *Some Case Studies of Small Group Teaching*, unpublished Ph.D. Thesis of University of Nottingham, cited by Brown, G. & Atkins, M. 1988, *Effective Teaching in Higher Education*, Methuen, London, chapter 4.

Paschal, R. A., Weinstein, T., & Walberg, H. J. (1984). The effects of homework on learning: a quantitative synthesis, *Journal of Educational Research,* 78(2), (Nov.-Dec.) pp. 97-104.

Verner, C. & Davison, C. V. (1971). Psychological factors in adult learning and instruction, *Occasional Papers of the Research Information Processing Center,* Dept. of Adult Education, Florida State University.

Walberg, H. J., Paschal, R. A. & Weinstein, T. (1985). Homework's powerful effects on learning, *Educational Leadership,* 42(7), (April) pp. 76-79.

Walberg, H. J., Paschal, R. A. & Weinstein, T. (1986). Walberg and colleagues reply: Effective schools use homework effectively, *Educational Leadership,* 43(8), (May) p.58.

Chapter 9

Human Learning Models and Data Collection Over the "Long Haul"

Kevin D. Reilly and Norman W. Bray
University of Alabama in Birmingham, USA

Modeling human learning and performance that also involves data collection requires teamwork, most often inter-disciplinary. When research is of long duration, changes occur in personnel and even in the research areas. When computing is a core component, technology change presents additional issues, in how to best exploit new technology and to preserve already successful work. This chapter offers solutions and suggestions based on our experience and ranging from theory-based to practical approaches.

INTRODUCTION

A programmatic research program spanning several years encounters many challenges, increasing when the research is interdisciplinary and affected by rapid change in information technology (IT).

Our research meets these criteria: in progress for several years; inter-disciplinary faculty and students, in computing sciences and psychology; and extensive and varied computing, in the form of multiple simulation models, animations, and distributed data and information. Simulations model memory strategies used by children with and without mental retardation (Anumolu et al., 1997; Bray, Reilly, Huffman et al., 1998; Bray, Reilly, Fletcher et al., 1998).

Previously Published in *Challenges of Information Technology Management in the 21st Century* edited by Mehdi Khosrow-Pour, Copyright © 2000, Idea Group Publishing.

Diversification in our research starts from the machine context, i.e., (networked) workstations and PCs, with different configurations for behavior and computer science participants. Core modeling and general software extends over: PDP and MATLAB neural network packages; MATLAB fuzzy systems package; C, Java, GPSS-H, Prolog for complementary functionality; Tcl/Tk, Proof Animation, and OpenGL for animation; and CGI and Java for networking. Despite this variety, pressures arise for more!

Rapidly changing IT helps and hinders. On the positive side, there are improvements in machines and communications. Unfortunately, the opportunities demand time, and the problem becomes "Can we appropriately exploit them, given the learning curve and the many constraints imposed by maintaining and expanding current applications."

SOLUTIONS AND SUGGESTIONS

The above discourse deals with problems, mainly, some identifiable in increased opportunity! Our solutions and suggestions fall under these categories, each having IT education implications:

- A theoretical view of the overall modeling project in terms of a model (M) and a modeling framework (MF), with practical realization (case studies);
- Animation, promoting communications and defining requirements for models admitted into the modeling framework;
- Networked solutions, speeding data and simulation results between computing and empirical studies lab settings;
- Attention to modeling tools and their relationships, and their roles in the project, e.g., prototyping, executable specifications, and model abstractions; and
- Educational interventions: course modules, seminar materials, etc.

THEORY SCOPING

We mentioned "multiple" simulation models above. These are deemed necessary for the studied phenomena, i.e., the general knowledge gaps on human information processing. Casually viewed, our effort may appear as a collection of (about six) models. An integrating view "sees" a model (M) and a modeling framework (MF). The model (M) is an almost fixed entity, changes being allowed only to fit data statistically. The modeling framework (MF), while not eschewing statistical fits, is open to (and seeks) alternative modules, limited only by usual scientific criteria, e.g., parsimony, precedence in the literature, etc. M builds on Anumolu et al. (1997) and MF emerges first in Bray et al. (1997) and in more detail in Reilly, Bray et al. (1998). The duo, M and MF, create a modeling "style," some aspects of which emerge as we proceed.

The model and the framework have a similar overall structure, partly due to the input-process-output nature of human (and machine) processing. Having similar structures contributes, e.g., to descriptive parsimony and easier model (feature) comparisons.

This modeling style appears in an intriguing manner in a case study: a learning module from M is "borrowed" and, with adjustment, used within MF. The "cooperation" proves productive in producing a statistical fit in MF and suggesting how M may overcome its fitting difficulty.

Another case study shows how MF's openness accommodates modeling flexibility and diversity. Neural networks (NN) have priority in our research, but a NN is not always best achieved from scratch. Thus, we sometimes act indirectly as we now see. The setting is this: a child has gained experience with the physical situation (moving toy objects on a table top, under batched instructions that requires remembering for a (short) duration). Hints (prompts) are given to help children improve performance through exploiting environmental features. M fits the empirical data for most individuals, but its parsimony is sorely tested for remaining cases. The problem seemed more readily solvable in the MF: a fuzzy expert/information system (a FIS in MATLAB terminology) was built over performance statistics (for before-prompt behavior) developed in a stochastic, non-NN simulator (GPSS-H). (Actually competing FIS styles, one partially NN (Reilly, Buckley et al., 1998), were explored.) Later, we developed a NN solution for the FIS. This NN solution, and assessments of fuzzy mechanisms for our problems, would be difficult to obtain without this "prototyping."

ANIMATIONS

Animation serves as a means of cross-disciplinary communication: if computer-science generated simulations produce animations corresponding to observed behavioral events, common ground across the "cultures" is established. A constraint that any proposed model variant must produce screen depictions that are faithful to the task being modeled is most useful.

One of our (Tcl/Tk) animations was presented in a 1 1/2-hour session to a psychology graduate student actively involved in data collection. It had a GUI permitting the user to re-visit a (simulated) trial with altered problem solving strategy, e.g., the user's choice. The experience was deemed a success in that the model covered required options and exhibited no wrong or unusual responses. Since then, interest has grown in more formal measures of success, e.g., correlation between (strategy-based) preliminary movement of objects and final object placements.

Another approach uses an "expert system with confidence factors." With access to model internals and (external) behavior values, it acts as an advanced, independent observer/experimenter, adjusting encoding strategies and correlating internal and external features. This research tact carries over to Turner's (1999) "coordinated animations," one for physical object movements and the other for NN internals giving the "orders."

Animations present opportunity for *subjects,* useful, e.g., in transfer of knowledge. Empirical data exists on two such tasks in the "real" world. The animations suggest transfer studies between real and "screen" worlds, e.g., the subject first experiences the animation and then the real world on the same or related situation, or vice versa.

NETWORKING

Networking models and data sharing are increasingly being employed. We used Java networking to connect models running on SUN machines to animations on PCs (Reilly...Pan, 1997). This work started as a small effort. To join in the "long haul," it will need additional human attention, e.g., to meet changes in machines (even a video card issue!) and software.

A second networking project is a CGI-based server running a MF example. Output currently is tabular, animations being a future possibility (perhaps after a shift to Java servelets).

Several results and other information (participants) are available on the web, some being restricted in access to participants. WWW overtures have been among minimal "growing pains" changes.

TOOL MONITORING

Changing IT has benefits but also forces action neither contemplated nor desired (as changes in personnel, foci on the experimental side, etc. rage). We have used "stable" systems, e.g., PDP, GPSS-H, PROLOG, and C, as much as possible. But even these are undergoing change: embeddings, e.g., C in C++, PDP in PDP++, and (partially) GPSS-H in SLX, are perhaps a good hope. Also, we have experienced difficulties with, e.g., PDP, Java, Tcl/Tk with version changes or moving applications from Unix to Windows.

In Barrett et al. (1995) and Reilly et al. (1995), we embed programming "styles" in a general programming context, describing how this promotes model abstractions, runnable specifications, reverse engineering and other software engineering principles. Ideas inherent have been applied in mimicking logic processing styles for our problem range. Overhead is high for a processor like this, fully dependent on us.

A possibly analogous approach uses an expert system-based logic processing (with confidence factors, mentioned above). Linking with SLX is an exciting extension. Unfortunately, like the previous paragraph's system, this approach needs further NN. Hitt (1998) shows Object Oriented (OO) facilitation in merging OO-NN and OO-simulator systems.

Finally, there are good project management reasons for reengineering solutions. For example, M's "PDP + C-augmentations" solution appears re-doable as "PDP only."

EDUCATIONAL INTERVENTIONS

We can be brief on this subject since it's the main topic of a companion paper (Reilly and Bray, 2000). Interdisciplinary work depends on overlap of fields and can be more or less difficult, accordingly. Acquiring the skills needed for our kind of collaboration currently requires considerable individual effort. Interdisciplinary needs are usually outside regular departmental course structures, so a combination of approaches spreading over every legitimate opening academia has to offer must be evaluated.

CONCLUSIONS

We have identified several problems in "long-haul" inter-disciplinary research in which IT plays a key role. IT is "friendly" in offering new and better methods, but it also introduces changes that provide additional challenges for current work. We outlined our responses, which range from rather abstract moves, such as developing an underlying theory of modeling practice, to more prosaic steps of using the internet and monitoring modeling software. Generalizing to other situations occurs with varying degrees of ease, benefiting perhaps from software engineering or simulation theory insights, a subject needing a full paper to develop, analogous, e.g., to Reilly et al. (1995). For the present, our remarks are "experiential."

ACKNOWLEDGEMENT

This research was supported by research grant HD33041-01A3 from the National Institutes of Health.

REFERENCES

Anumolu, V., Bray, N. W., & Reilly, K. D. (1997). Neural network models of strategy development in children. *Neural Networks,* 10, 7-24.

Barrett, J., Reilly, K. D., Tarng, J. & Hyatt, R. (1995). A computerized formal means to reason about components in simulation models and environments, Part II: System Development Methodology, *Trans. Soc. Comp. Sim.,* 12, 3, 191-244.

Bray, N. W., Reilly, K. D., Fletcher, K. L., Huffman, L. F., Grupe, L. A., Villa, M. F., & Anumolu, V. (1998). Memory competencies and deficiencies: A conceptual framework and the potential of connectionist models. In S. Soraci & W. McIlvane (Eds.), *Perspectives on Fundamental Processes in Intellectual Functioning. Vol. 1: A Survey of Research Approaches*, Stamford, CT: Ablex, 3-44.

Bray, N. W., Reilly, K. D., Huffman, L. F., Grupe, L. A., Villa, M. F., Fletcher, K. L., & Anumolu, V. (1998). Cognitive competencies in children with mental retardation. In W. Bechtel & G. Graham (Eds.) *The Companion to Cognitive Science*. Oxford: Basil Blackwell, 734-743.

Bray, N. W., Reilly, K. D., Villa, M. F. & Grupe, L. A. (1997). Neural network models and mechanisms of strategy development. *Developmental Review,* 17, 525-566.

Hitt, T. (1998). *OBSRV: An Evolution in Simulation Systems Development through Object Oriented Methodologies*. PhD dissertation, University of Alabama in Birmingham.

Reilly, K. D., Barrett, J., Tarng, J. & Hyatt, R. (1995). A computerized formal means to reason about components in simulation models and environments, Part I: A logic based approach. *Trans. Soc. Comp. Sim,* 12 (2), 101-178.

Reilly, K. D. & Bray, N. W. (2000). Prolegomenon to Computer-Based Great Epistemologies Education. *Proc. 2000 IRMA (Information Resources Management Association) Int'l Conference*, (This proceedings).

Reilly, K. D., Bray, N. W., Drake, J. W., Golding, E., Chen, D. & W. Pan. (1997). Intelligent system modeling using neural networks and animation within a distributed programming context. *Proc. Summer Simulation Conf.,* San Diego, CA.

Reilly, K. D., Bray, N. W., Drake, J. W., & Villa, M. (1998). Modular solutions to strategy selection problems in man and machine. *Proc. Systems, Cybernetics and Informatics Conference – 1998*, Vol. 4, 405-412.

Reilly, K. D., Buckley, J. J., Bray, N. W., & Drake, J. M. (1998). The Fuzzy Teaching Machine, Rule Processing and RoboKid Strategy Change, *Proc. SCI (Systemics, Cybernetics and Informatics) Conf. 1998*, Vol. 3, Int'l Inst. of Informatics and Systemics, Orlando, FL, 533-540.

Turner, B. D. (1999). *Coordinated Animations of a Neural Network Model and its Modeled Domain*. Masters thesis, University of Alabama in Birmingham.

Chapter 10

Are Information Systems Students in Their Right Minds?

Steve Benson and Craig Standing
Edith Cowan University, Australia

The "IS skills debate" still persists in being a commonly researched area. In this paper we examine the related issue of fundamental thinking styles and the implications for IS course design and delivery. In recent decades Sperry's work on "split brain"[1] patients has been hijacked by popular psychology. [2] The underlying thesis of many of the publications we surveyed reduces to "find out whether you are right or left brained and learn to draw on your whole brain". We decided that it would be interesting to carry out an initial investigation into the left-right brain orientation of our students and curriculum. Given the technical biases and associations of the Information Systems discipline, our initial expectation was to find a high degree of logical, left brained orientation in our student sample. We were surprised to find the contrary result in that right brained oriented students outnumbered left brained oriented students by 3:1, especially in view of the fact that our curriculum had a definite left brain bias. Our chapter outlines the left-right brain divide and questions the validity of this division from neurophysiological perspectives. We discuss the practical implications of the exercise; i.e. is it worthwhile trying to get student to change their mode of operation or is it more productive to have them control their own learning in an adaptive manner? Finally, we identify several areas for future research.

Previously Published in *Managing Information Technology in a Global Economy* edited by Mehdi Khosrow-Pour, Copyright © 2001, Idea Group Publishing.

INTRODUCTION

The skills required by Information Systems (IS) graduates has been a frequently studied topic (Latham, 2000; Snoke & Underwood, 1999, Standing & Standing, 1999). The debate usually centers on the relative importance, of technical skills, interpersonal and communication skills, and the depth of business knowledge and skills. The debate is complicated by the expectations of employers and how these differ from recent IS graduates (Latham, 2000). Additionally the fragmented nature of the IS profession contributes to this complication (Lee, Trauth & Farwell, 1995). The topic is of ongoing importance to IS Schools in universities which are trying to develop a more relevant curriculum so that their graduates will be highly rated by prospective employers.

This chapter, whilst recognising the value of the work in the IS skills area, investigates the "IS skills issue" from an alternative perspective. Many past studies have assumed that universities can respond to the changing requirements of employers by re-shaping the IS curriculum and teaching methods and thus significantly changing the nature of the end-product – the IS graduate! By examining the fundamental thinking styles of IS undergraduates we aim to address and make recommendations in relation to the appropriateness of IS course content and delivery styles and explain the major issues for IS education and practice.

The first section of the chapter provides a brief coverage of the thinking styles paradigm. This is followed by the description of a survey on the thinking styles of IS undergraduates. These are then related to the IS undergraduate major programme at our own university to determine any clashes between dominant thinking styles of undergraduates and thinking styles required by IS subject areas. Finally, we highlight issues that result from our study and make recommendations for IS course designers.

LEFT AND RIGHT BRAIN THINKING

In 1963, neurosurgeons Joseph Bogen and Philip Vogel carried out a radical surgical procedure to control epilepsy in severely afflicted patients. This treatment was based upon work carried out by Roger Sperry and involved completely severing the corpus callosum, a cord of 300 million nerve fibres which connects the right and left hemispheres of the brain. Breaking the communication, which integrates brain operation, allowed virtually independent testing of brain hemispheres with a view to ascribing perceptual functions and thought processes to one hemisphere or the other.[3] Although severing the corpus callosum as a treatment fell out of favour due to the severe mental effects and advances in drug treatment (Ornstein, R., 1997, pp.65) it is still performed and patients may develop "split brain" syndrome as the result of illness. Sperry's view was that there were "two spheres of

Table 1: Brain Functions By Left/Right Hemisphere (After Ornstein, 1997)

Left Hemisphere	Sequential Analysis: systematic, logical interpretation of information. Interpretation and production of symbolic information: language, mathematics, bstraction and reasoning. Memory stored in a language format.
Right Hemisphere	Holistic Functioning: processing provide "holistic" picture of one's environment. Visual spatial skills. Holistic functions such as dancing and gymnastics are coordinated by the right hemisphere. Memory is stored in auditory, visual and spatial modalities.

consciousness" in the same brain, the left hemisphere housing speech, rationality, and intellect, while the right hemisphere was inarticulate housing creativity and spatial abilities. (Sperry, 1969). Bergland (1985) elaborates "You have two brains: a left and a right. Modern brain scientists now know that your left brain is your verbal and rational brain; it thinks serially and reduces its thoughts to numbers, letters and words; Your right brain is your nonverbal and intuitive brain; it thinks in patterns, or pictures, composed of whole things and does not comprehend reductions, either numbers, letters, or words". A simple summary of brain function allocation is given in Table 1.

Despite a seemingly rigorous scientific foundation, the left-right brain debate moved into the "popular" domain and seemingly gained from the translation. It was argued by many (e.g., Edwards, 1989) that Western education neglected the right hemisphere and by implication disadvantaged many people. The truth is that Sperry's allocation of brain functions was a simplification, language is predominantly located in the left hemisphere but not exclusively so. There are cases of patients who have a single hemisphere and yet function normally (Ornstein, 1997, pp.52.53). The redundancy of connections in the brain allows some (in some cases total) recovery of lost function. (Sacks, 1985, pp. 73). It is proven that images are memorised in the right side of the brain and language in the left in the majority of cases (Kelly et al., 1998). The simple view that the right brain provides contextual setting for perception seemed confirmed when Marshall & Fink's 1997 research (in McCrone, 1999) used brain imaging techniques that allowed the time line for visual processing to be monitored with precision. However when faced with Navons (a large picture made up of smaller pictures, e.g., a letter S made up from letter F's) this processing allocation was reversed with the left hemisphere concentrating on context while the right handled detail. Evidence that both hemispheres have an individual mind is reasonably sound (McLean, 1998), though many regard the right hemisphere as intrinsically inferior to the left, principally on the basis that it has no language capability and hence diminished consciousness (Gazzaniga, in Ornstein pp 6-7, 90-91).

To conclude, it would seem that while there is some neurophysiological evidence to support the simple left-right brain divide as proposed by Sperry (1961), the situation is far more complicated than originally thought. Ornstein (1997, pp.82,83) found subjects with language activity located in either or both hemispheres though with greater frequency in the left). However the validity of the left and right division brain as thinking styles still remains and there are many consultants and agencies making use of it (e.g., Intelegen, 2000). While most people are able to switch between thinking styles, they have a preferred mode. Ornstein (1997, pp. 15) argues that the superiority of one hemisphere over the other does not have to be very great for preference to develop. Using the example of two TV channels showing the same program, the first is 100% reliable, the second 95% reliable he suggests that the small difference would give 100% selection for the better channel. In short partial dominance implies total dominance.

RESEARCH METHODOLOGY

We selected a group of students who were in their second year of study in an information systems major and provided an online, self assessment test to determine the preferred thinking style (left, right or both hemispheres). The test consisted of 20 questions which required students to indicate a preferred modality. Example questions included:

Do you prefer courses which have:
a) one assignment at a time
b) allow students to work on several things concurrently as they see fit
c) either or both

Are you:
a) not very good at reading people's body language, you prefer to listen to what people say.
b) Good at understanding people's body language
c) Sometimes good, sometimes bad at understanding body language

When you are given instructions do you prefer to have them presented to you:
a) in written or verbal form
b) by demonstration (being shown how to do something)
c) either or both

When it comes to planning for study and/or work are you:
a) Well organised and use time management to help plan your activities
b) Not very well organised
c) Sometimes organised, sometimes not

Are you better at remembering:
a) names
b) faces
c) both with similar ease

A) answers denote left brain modality.
B) answers denote right brain modality.
C) answers denote wholebrain modality.

RESEARCH FINDINGS

Our sample size (N) was 28 (corresponding to over 50% of the students enrolled in our information systems major) and we used 20 questions in our test. The raw data are in Table 2.

As may be seen the responses show a high degree of whole brain dominance with a tendency to favour the right hemisphere. The averages of student responses may be found in Table 3.

As may be seen, the modality is whole brained with a marked tendency to

Table 2: Brain modality in information systems students

Total Left Brain Responses	145
Total Right Brain Responses	185
Total Whole Brain Responses	230

Table 3: Average Student Brain Modality

Sample size N=28	Average value	Standard Deviation
Average left brain responses x/20	5.2	2.1
Average right brain responses x/20	6.6	2.3
Average whole brain responses x/20	8.2	2.2

prefer the right hemisphere. The standard deviation shows a slightly wider spread than we would have expected.

Analysing on an individual basis we found that 6 students had a marked left hemisphere preference (Number of right - Number of left responses <-1), 15 had a marked right hemisphere preference (Number of right - Number of left responses >1) the remainder showing a whole brained preference.

THINKING STYLES REQUIRED FOR THE STUDY OF INFORMATION SYSTEMS

Having examined the students and determined their principal thinking styles, we then examined the subject areas which comprised the information systems major and tried to classify them in terms of the thinking style that the presentation

Table 4: 10 Suggested Critical Dimensions For Left-Right Brain Orientation In University IS Education.

	A -Left Brain Focus	B - Right Brain Focus
1	Very clearly defined objectives	Loosely defined, overarching objectives
2	Very clearly defined schedule	Schedule has "milestones" but is flexible
3	Assignments are sequential	Assignments are concurrent
4	Relatively few but large assignments (1,2 or 3) & assessment is periodic	Several Assignments (4,5 or more) and assessment tends to be more continuous in nature
5	Assignments are precise in nature, based on given scenarios, specifications etc. sequential and/or logical in nature	Assignments are essay and discussion type requiring a scenario or specification to be constructed
6	Students are expected to learn and ask questions to clarify concepts or assessment	Students participate fully in class discussions
7	Examinations/assessments make substantial use of multiple choice questions	Examinations are mainly essay based
8	Students make minimal contribution to the course content	Students make some contribution to the course content
9	The lecturer usually explains the subject matter to the students	The lecturer usually demonstrates or shows the subject matter to the students
10	Teaching approach is lecturer centered, pedagogical, objectivist	Teaching approach is student centered, androgogical, constructivist

Table 5: Left Right Brain Orientation In Information Systems Curriculum, Delivery And Assessment Methods (Raw Data).

Criterion	1	2	3	4	5	6	7	8	9	10
Database	1	1	1	1	1	1	3	1	3	1
Networks	1	2	2	1	2	3	2	1	1	1
Systems	3	2	1	1	1	3	2	1	1	1
Software	1	1	1	2	1	1	3	1	1	1
Management	2	2	1	2	2	2	2	2	1	3

Table 6: Left Right Brain Orientation In Information Systems Curriculum, Delivery And Assessment Methods (Summary). A Negative Final Score Denotes Left Bias, A Positive Final Score Denotes Right Bias

	Left Total	Right Total	Whole Total	Final Score
Database	8	0	2	-16
Networks	5	4	1	-2
Systems	6	2	2	-8
Software	8	1	1	-14
Management	2	7	1	10

and assessment of the unit most favoured. Our literature review failed to find a suitable instrument and so we propose the following simple model. A review of unit outlines, assignments and examination, together with questions directed to the lecturer enabled us to establish ten critical dimensions for evaluation. We allocated 1 whenever a left brained focus was encountered, 2 for a right brain focus and 3 for a whole brained focus. We acknowledge the element of subjectivity in our assessment but believed it to be justifiable for a pilot exercise such as this. The evaluation criteria are shown in table 4 and the results of applying these criteria to our curriculum are shown in tables 5 and 6.

NB. Since we used only 10 criteria as opposed to the 20 questions that comprised the student test we subtracted the-Left response total from the Right response total and multiplied the result by 2. While this is not entirely valid in statistical terms it allows a more meaningful comparison to be made.

With the exception of management it is obvious that there is a pronounced left brain bias (in our university the network area is taught from a management perspective and this accounts for the reduced left brain bias). When considered with the results from the student test it is apparent that there is a mismatch between average student brain orientation and the information systems curriculum, delivery and assessment methods.

DISCUSSION

Our pilot survey indicates that the majority of our students are right brained. However, we note the disparity between the modality of student thinking and the orientation of our subject matter, teaching and assessment methods. Our initial expectation was that we would find our students to be relatively whole brained in their thinking. This was based upon our own view of information systems as a very diverse discipline with a firm technological foundation, i.e., requiring both logical and creative thinking styles. In retrospect, it have been useful to survey the respondents to see what their views of the IS discipline were and what had attracted them to its study.

We suggest that the left-right brained model has applicability for IS course development and teaching styles and offer the following observations:

- The model explains why a significant percentage of IS students find the IS discipline difficult:

Basically, the right brained students are ill-equipped in terms of thinking style to deal with the more precise and detailed technical programming and development modeling found within most IS programmes. However, these students may perform particularly well in the management components of the course.

- There are implications for teaching styles:

For students with a right-brained focus it is important to provide the context for understanding, provide visual walkthroughs and examples of solutions to problems rather than a purely syntactical approach. In other words, attempt to teach left brained skills from a right brained perspective!

- The model accounts for the difficulties involved in the career path transition from technical to managerial (mainly left to mainly right brained work emphasis):

The transition for left brained graduates and practitioners from a technical focus to a managerial focus should not be underestimated. Hence, the need for postgraduate courses in IS which focus on the managerial skills.

- Thinking style is relatively immutable:

There is a prevailing view that fundamental thinking approaches are unlikely to change radically (Stenning, Cox, & Oberlander, 1995). It is important therefore to steer students to appropriate occupations within the profession that are aligned with their thinking styles. It is unlikely that right brained students will ever make excellent "techies" even with lots of training.

- The lucky few:

We suggest that students with a whole brain orientation (and there are relatively few of those 20% in our survey, and fewer in the population at large (Ornstein, 1997 pp.80-86) are perhaps best positioned (maybe not to enter the IS profession as programmers) to liaise with users, deal with uncertainty and join the management ranks of the profession whilst at the same time cope with a reasonable amount of technical detail.

To elaborate on point 4 above, switching hemispheres and thinking styles is difficult (more so than switching from right to left handedness) (Stenning, Cox, & Oberlander, 1995). Certainly left brained people can employ techniques on a neo-algorithmic basis that can engender creative thinking, this has been the basic thesis for many books on thinking (DeBono,1994). There were movements in the 19th century which attempted to maximise brain use by encouraging ambidextrousness[4] (Ornstein, 1997 pp 54) but it is doubtful that using the least preferred hand will encourage left or right brained thinking. Laterality (handedness) has only a weak linkage with dominant thinking styles, neurologically functions may be distributed in either or both hemispheres (McCrone, 1999, Kelley et al., 1998). There is some evidence that the discipline of Information Systems requires both left and right brained thinking styles. The right hemisphere handles spatial concepts and usually contextualises perception (see McCrone, 1999), however it is apparent that the attention of the right hemisphere may be directed consciously, this may account for the aberrant processing distribution when perceiving Navons. Sein et al. (1993) used visualisation ability as a predictor for learning outcomes in hierarchical database use and complex file/directory structures. Garavan and McCracken (1993) noted that abstract (left brained) learners performed better than concrete learners in certain circumstances, most notably when the subjects have no prior experience of the subject area.

Based upon our literature survey and conversations with practitioners, we believe that the conscious mind has plenty to occupy it without trying to change its own fundamental mode of operation. On efficiency grounds alone, it does not make sense to seek to change the students but rather educate them in meta-learning techniques would allowing them to adapt the teaching materials and processes to suit their own preferred mode of operation. The implications for curriculum development and delivery are that a whole brained (holistic) approach should be adopted using both conceptual frameworks and concrete examples. While Meyers-Briggs Indicators would allow for greater customisation of teaching and assessment, we believe that assessing each student would be time consuming and the level of diversity too great to allow it to be used advantageously. The simple left-right view has the advantage of being relatively easy to comprehend and implement.

Figure 1 shows our suggested framework relating brain orientation to IS careers. This may be of use to students planning their future careers.

Figure 1: Occupations and skills in the IS/IT industry with left-right brain orientation (adapted from Standing, C. & Standing, S.,1999).

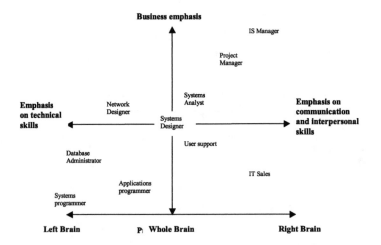

FUTURE WORK

Our initial intention was to carry out a pilot study to establish the preferred thinking styles of our students. While acknowledging the element of subjectivity, the results are sufficiently convincing to highlight a misalignment between our courses and our students. From our pilot study and consideration, we have identified areas for further investigation. Changing teaching and assessment methods in selected areas would allow comparison of normalised marks to be made across subject areas. If as we believe, adaptive teaching and assessment strategies are conducive to better student outcomes then average grades in those subject areas should be higher. We will be allowing students to have access to our simple self diagnostic test and providing them with information on memory, teaching and learning processes suited to each mode of thinking. These will be provided as part of our foundation course and average assessment and examination grades together with attrition data will be compared with similar periods in the past. We suspect that students who are aware of their preferred thinking styles will be able to adjust their work patterns to improve their performance. We are considering a longitudinal study, tracking students who make use of the materials, reviewing their progress and interviewing a selection of respondents to ascertain their beliefs as to the usefulness of the test and associated materials. Finally it would an interesting exercise to assess the brain orientation of IS practitioners since there is potential to reopen the IS skills debate from a very different perspective.

ENDNOTES

- The term "split brain" is not to be confused with schizophrenia in which the patient is split from reality while the brain remains whole.
- An investigation by the authors shows some 112 in print and available from Amazon.com and we estimate at least that number to be out of print.
- Severance of the corpus callosum may not completely isolate the hemispheres, it possible for some residual connections to remain.
- Sir James Crichton-Browne, the Lord Chancellor's "Visitor in Lunacy" noted periodic outbreaks of ambidexterity and associated them with addiction to "vegetarianism, hatlessness or anti-vaccination and other aberrant forms of belief".

REFERENCES

Bergland, R.(1985) *The Fabric of Mind*. Viking Penguin, Inc., New York, pg.1.

DeBono, E. (1994) *Parallel Thinking*, Pub Viking.

Dennett, D.C. & Kinsbourne, M. (1995). *Time and the observer: The where and when of consciousness in the brain*. Behavioral and Brain Sciences 15 (2): 183-247.

Edwards, B. (1989). Drawing on the Right Side of the Brain. NY: Tarcher/Putnam.

Itelegen, Inc. (2000) *Online brain portal* http://www.intelegen.com/.

Kelley, W. M., Miezin, F. M., McDermott, K. B., Buckner, R. L., Raichle, M. E., Cohen, N. J., Ollinger, J. M., Akbudak, E., Conturo, T. E., Snyder, A. Z., and Petersen, S. E. (1998). *Hemispheric specialization in human dorsal frontal cortex and medial temporal lobe for verbal and nonverbal memory encoding.* Neuron 20, 927-936, May 22.

Latham, A. (2000). Information Systems Graduates: the Challenge for Course Designers. *Proceedings of the European Conference on Information Systems*, Vienna, p. 1432-1438.

Lee, D. M., Trauth, E. M., & Farwell, D. (1995). Critical Skills and Knowledge Requirements of IS professionals: a Joint Academic/Industry Investigation. *MIS Quarterly* 19(3), p. 313-340.

Marshall & Fink (1997). paper (*Proceedings of the Royal Society B, vol 264*, p 487).

McCrone, J. (1999). *Left Brain, Right Brain*, New Scientist, 3 July.

McLean (1998). press release on line http://www.mcleanhospital.org/PublicAffairs/2brain.htm.

Miller, G.A. (1956). The Magical Number Seven, Plus Or Minus Two, *Psychological Review* 63, pp. 81-87 Also online at http://www.well.com/user/smalin/miller.html.

Nørretranders, T. (1991). *The User Illusion, Cutting Consciousness Down to Size* Pub. Viking Penguin (translated by Sydenham, J. 1998).

Ornstein, R. (1997). *The Right Mind - Making Sense Of Hemispheres*.

Pierce, J.R. (1961). *Signals, Symbols and Noise*, Pub. New York Harper.

Sacks, O. (1985). *The Man Who Mistook His Wife For a Hat*, pub. Picador.

Snoke, R., & Underwood, A. (1999). Generic Attributes of IS Graduates: An Australian IS Academic Study. *Proceedings of the tenth Australian Conference on Information Systems (ACIS)*, Wellington, New Zealand, pp. 817-824.

Sperry, R.W. (1969). A Modified Concept of Consciousness, *Psychological Review*, 76(6), p. 532-536.

Standing, C. & Standing, S. (1999). The role of Politics in IS Career progression. *Systems Research and Behavioural Science*, 16, 519-531.

Stenning, K., Cox,, R. & Oberlander, J. (1995). Contrasting the cognitive effects of graphical and sentential logic teaching: Reasoning, representation and individual differences. *Language and Cognitive Processes*, 10(3), 333-345.

Chapter 11

The Gender Issue in Information Technology: Collegiate and Corporate Solutions

Donald J. Caputo and Frederick J. Kohun
Robert Morris College, USA

A paradox is occurring today in the Information Technology (IT) field. At the very moment that a large unmet demand for IT workers exists, approximately one-half of our work force is largely declining the offer. The Information Technology Association of America estimates the number of IT jobs languishing at a staggering 840,000 (eWeek, 2000). Though women in IT earn 60 percent more than women in other occupations, their numbers have dropped from 40 percent in 1986 to 29 percent today (CIO, 2000). The White House Council of Economic Advisors (CIO, 2000) estimates that women are leaving the IT job market at twice the rate of men.

This report focuses on the ongoing strategies employed for the integration and retention of women in the collegiate and the corporate sphere (Frenkel, 1991).

Inequality of computing does not start at the corporate level. The U.S. Department of Education reports that the number of women computer science graduates declined from 37% in 1984 to 28% in 1994. Robert Morris College developed a program to remedy this problem.

The first element C and nucleus C of the program took the form of a far-reaching and expansive curricular innovation. Simply stated, the previous Information Systems offering was a one-dimensional Above it or leave it @ affair that

Previously Published in *Managing Information Technology in a Global Economy* edited by Mehdi Khosrow-Pour, Copyright © 2001, Idea Group Publishing.

concentrated mainly on the development of competent computer programmers. It was replaced by a track system that was more responsive to student needs. Five tracks became available to the student:

- Computer Information Systems,
- Health Care Information Systems,
- Network Administration,
- Accounting Information Systems, and
- Office Information Systems.

Prior to the curricular change, only the programming-oriented Computer Information Systems option was available.

The five-track option quickly became the catalyst for the entire program. Previously, students who were unhappy with the narrowly defined major had but two choices: drop out of college or transfer to a new major. With the introduction of the track system, students could concentrate on the specific niche within the discipline that energized and rekindled the learning process. While the rate of retention increased for both men and women students since the program took hold in the fall of 1993, the retention rate for women advanced from 60.11% to 79.35% by 1997. The corresponding data for men show an advance from 69% to 83% over the same time frame. Thus, the retention improvement factor for women was 32%, while the male factor improved by 20%. The rationale, as voiced by the women students, was that health care, accounting and office information systems were more traditional areas of female interest.

We believe that the rapid growth of our department from less than 400 students in 1991 to 915 students in 1998, while somewhat a reflection of the steady rise in the vitality and prominence of the computing marketplace, is also a result of innovative collegiate and departmental policies. The remarkable improvement in the retention of women in computer system studies indicates that it is a stubborn but solvable problem.

CORPORATE STRATEGIES

As part of their cooperative education job responsibilities, the authors make approximately one hundred on-site visits each year to the 47 corporate workplaces where our students are employed. Along with reviews of student performance, information is gathered from various levels of information systems management concerning the corporate environment, employee job duties, salaries, mobility, hardware, software, employment criteria, legacy systems, subcontracting and myriad other subjects. These corporations and institutions range from large multi-national corporations to health care institutions, government facilities and small businesses with less than 15 employees.

Pittsburgh, as the fifth largest U.S. commercial software center in the United States, would seem to be an ideal city for the rapid assimilation of women into the computing field. A small-city ambience, combined with a low cost-of-living ratio, a lessened incidence of crime and highly concentrated health-care and research facilities are advantages that seem to indicate equality in cyberspace. There is some encouragement in the fact that 36% of computer science workers in the area are women (Pittsburgh Post Gazette, 1997).

The survey of 47 corporations in the Pittsburgh metropolitan area has attempted to determine the corporate response to the recruitment, retention and promotion of women in the Information Sciences. Specifically, the following questions have been posed:

- What specific strategies are employed by corporations to capitalize on the resources provided by women in Information Technology?
- Has the A glass ceiling @ been shattered at the middle and upper levels of the corporate technology world?
- What are the three specific barriers, according to highly placed Information Technology managers, that are most often raised to suggest the reason for the absence (if such absence exists) of women at the highest levels of Information Technology?

It is interesting to note that some inconsistencies exist in the Pittsburgh metropolitan area. The Report of the Progressive Policy Institute stated that Pittsburgh, in concert with the state of Pennsylvania, scored 19% above the national average for the extent in which it used information technology to deliver services, an indicator of the area's ability to fully utilize its resources (UPCSUR Report, 1999).

However, according to the University of Pittsburgh Center for Social and Urban Research 6th Annual Report, women with college degrees in the area earn less than 50% of the wages of their male counterparts, and were 50% less likely than men to be employed in executive or managerial capacities, a considerable notch below that of other American cities (Pittsburgh Post Gazette, 1999).

Most corporate managers of information technology have suggested various reasons for unequal treatment of male and female technology workers. Few believe that a formal Aglass ceiling @ exists.

In fact, the U.S. Department of Labor, in conducting Aglass ceiling @ reviews since 1992 in the Pittsburgh (Mid-Atlantic) area, has verified that nearly 40% of reviewed corporations have been identified as Anon-compliant @ practitioners of subtle practices that discriminate against women (CIO, 1999).

The corporate failings most often noted by female IT employees (eWeek, 2000) were the dearth of female role models, the lack of respect and consideration by fellow employees, and the refusal of managers to recognize the people-oriented skills of the IT women.

The most difficult task of this study was to determine what, if any, strategies existed to retain and promote women. Nearly every manager felt that the corporation had in place a number of initiatives to further the careers of women, but it was difficult to nail down exactly what they were, how they worked, and how formally they were integrated into actual company policy. It was felt that mentoring, for example, was always available to the Information Technology employees of the company. Yet, little was known concerning the implementation of the plan, and whether it was available to (and used by) women as well as men. In fact, most studies have shown that mentoring is arguably the most important factor affecting the female corporate progression. A recent survey by CIO Magazine found that 70% of upper-level Information Technology women considered that the lack of a mentor was the greatest barrier to corporate advancement (Pittsburgh Post Gazette, 2000). The following statistics display the most often-mentioned strategies, and the percentage of companies that employed them in a somewhat structured or formal manner.

Strategies for women in Information Technology:

Recruitment and retention	23%
Career development	17%
Identification of high-potential women	47%
Mentoring by upper-echelon employees	6%
Providing internal support	17%
Establishing training programs	6%
Providing Clear paths of responsibility	53%

The majority of managers did agree, however, that the relatively smaller number of women with computer-related degrees, the corporate inflexibility on family issues, and the simple fact that women have not been in the information technology pipeline long enough to become fully integrated into the corporate design for career advancement, were the deciding factors resulting in the less-than-satisfactory use of the female technology resource in the corporate sphere.

Rationale of information technology managers:

Family/flexibility issues	64%
Not in pipeline long enough	55%
Fewer women with IT degrees	19%

A critical factor in determining the viability of women at various corporate Information Technology levels is the percentage of workers at the entry and lower managerial level, and the percentage at the senior managerial levels. This information is derived from the 47 corporations surveyed in the Pittsburgh area.

Percentage of women technology workers.

Entry/lower managerial	38%
Senior managerial	8%

In light of these statistics, it would appear that there is no significant lack of job potential for women at the corporate hiring level. At the upper strata of the Information Technology hierarchy, however, it is apparent that women are in a distinct minority.

THE DOCTORAL PROGRAM IN INFORMATION TECHNOLOGY

The responses of the local corporate community, as well as national statistics, served as input into phases of the doctoral program. As an example, consider that only 18.8 percent of those seeking doctorates in computer science in the United States are women (Information Week, 2000). Certainly, this became a program priority issue to be addressed. Because technology allows for mobility and remote accessibility, women are empowered by taking advantage of flexible work schedules, telecommuting facilities and job-sharing. The doctoral program attempts to incorporate similar flexibility into its structure.

Additionally, a survey of 252 students at Robert Morris College was initiated. The purpose of the survey was to find the mentoring preference of male and female IT students at the undergraduate, master's, and doctoral level.

At the undergraduate level, 87 percent of the women would accept either gender, 13 percent preferred female mentors, and no respondent chose male mentors only.

At the master's level, 96 percent of the women would accept either gender, 40 percent preferred female mentors, and no respondent chose male mentors only.

At the doctoral level, 67 percent of the women would accept either gender, 8 percent preferred female mentors, and 25 percent preferred male mentors.

It is interesting to note that women at the highest educational level leaned more towards acceptance of the male mentor than either of the lower educational levels.

The Doctor of Science in Information Systems and Communications (D.Sc.) degree program was debuted in the Fall of 1999. This doctorate was conceived as a professional degree to meet the needs of industry for "specialized generalists" who are capable of performing rigorous applied research and problem solving. Specifically, the program was designed to address the expanding needs of professionals who manage information resources, and solve information, communication and technology-related problems in businesses and other organizations. The program has three distinct characteristics: it is a full-time program in an executive format (three year program with one seven day residency and three weekend residencies in each of the six terms), it is cohort based, and it is interdisciplinary. An endorsement and qualified commitment, often financial, from the applicant's employer or sponsoring organization merges the educational experience of the student to his/her ongoing professional practice.

After the admission review process was completed, fourteen applicants were admitted. Of these, ten were women. These ten women included three CEO's, the Chief Information Officer of a major urban metropolitan police department, a technology section leader of a large international corporation, and two executives in the steel industry.

When the admitted women were informally asked why they were attracted to this program, they all stated the three unique characteristics cited previously: executive format, cohort-based study, and interdisciplinary composition within a team concept. The most interesting comment, however, was that they perceived that the cohort support and administration of the program with a faculty member assigned to each student to be the mentoring ideal that was essential to their success.

During the student's final term, a comprehensive critical technology infusion project will be designed and implemented in conjunction with local corporations and their key information technology managers, who will function as facilitators, consultants and knowledge experts, thus completing the mentoring cycle.

Three rationales were reported in this study to explain the lack of upward mobility of women in corporate information technology. Two of those rationales—the time-in-the-pipeline issue and the family/flexibility issue can not be properly addressed in this study. The third rationale, which underscores the relatively low number of women with information technology degrees, is a pervasive but solvable problem that we have begun to address. In tandem with this rationale, more effort needs to be directed to the closely-related problems of retaining women and promoting them into the upper echelons of the corporate world, lowering the barriers of discriminatory practices, and effectively deploying the unique qualities of the female IT practitioner.

REFERENCES

CIO (September 1, 2000). Why women hate IT.

CIO On-line Magazine (September 1999). A Self-assessment survey.

eWeek (September 11, 2000). eBiz Strategies.

Frenkel, K. (1990). Women and Computing. *Communications of the ACM*, November.

Frenkel, K. (1991). Women and Computing. *Communications of the ACM*, April.

Information Week (April 24, 2000). IT talent shortage renews interest in mentoring.

Pittsburgh Post Gazette (September 8, 1997). Jobs beckon to women in computer science.

Pittsburgh Post Gazette (September 30, 1999). Denying bias, corporation to pay women.

Pittsburgh Post Gazette (March 19, 2000). Female Exec pushes for more women.

Report of the Progressive Policy Institute (June 23, 1999).

University of Pittsburgh Center for Social and Urban Research 6th Annual Report (1999).

Chapter 12

A Methodology for Validating Entry Level Value versus Career Value of Courses in an MIS Program

Earl Chrysler
Quinnipiac College, USA

Stuart Van Auken
Florida Gulf Coast University, USA

The purpose of this study was to determine which entry-level course evaluations are drivers of an attitude of approval toward an MIS program, which career-level course evaluations are drivers of an attitude of approval toward an MIS program and whether alumni evaluations coincide with the beliefs of faculty who designed the curriculum. Alumni were asked to indicate the value of the content of each required course of the program during their first year on the job, then in their current position and then asked to evaluate the entire MIS program yielding a factor score for one's overall attitude toward the MIS program. The resulting factor score for each alumnus was related to the scores for the value of courses during one's first year on the job and the scores for the value of courses in one's current position. The plans of the faculty who designed the MIS curriculum as to what point in time, entry-level position, later in one's career, or a combination of the two, each course would be of value is reviewed. The perceptions of the alumni are compared to the beliefs of the faculty.

Previously Published in *Managing Information Technology in a Global Economy* edited by Mehdi Khosrow-Pour, Copyright © 2001, Idea Group Publishing.

BACKGROUND

When the faculty of an MIS area design a curriculum they consider providing their students with courses that provide entry-level skills and knowledge and courses that provide skills and knowledge that will be more applicable at points later in their careers.

There are various methods of determining the extent to which the courses in an MIS program are providing students with an education that is valuable both initially and at a later time in one's MIS career. One method would be to survey firms recruiting graduates of an Information Systems program as to how well graduates are performing, as suggested by Van Auken (1991). Still another method of assessing the effectiveness of an educational program is to have the program evaluated by the graduate, another approach mentioned by Van Auken (1991). A survey approach used by Gasen et al. (1991-92) asked students to evaluate various aspects of an MIS program. This study focused only on the satisfaction students perceived with the entire MIS program and not the content value of individual courses. A questionnaire proposed by Hanchey (1995-96) asks the graduate to indicate the value of specific MIS topics in addition to the quality of preparation in several areas such as analytical skills, values and ethics, etc. rather than specific course content.

THE PURPOSE OF THE STUDY

The objectives of this research were to determine:
- The perceived content value of each required course in an MIS program during a graduate's first year on the job;
- The perceived content value of each required course in an MIS program in a graduate's current position;
- A graduate's overall satisfaction index with an MIS curriculum;
- The relationship between one's overall satisfaction index score and one's evaluation of each of the curriculum's required courses during the first year on the job and in one's current position;
- The differences between the relationships between one's overall satisfaction index scores and course evaluation scores in the two frames of reference in number 4 above; and
- Whether the differences found are consistent with the objectives of the faculty when they designed the required courses.

METHODOLOGY

- Course Evaluations

A questionnaire asked the respondent to evaluate the content value of each required course using a six-point Likert scale.

- Frame of Reference
  The graduates were asked to evaluated the content of a course at graduation versus one's current position.
- Overall Satisfaction Index
  Graduates were asked, again using six-point Likert scale, to indicate their feelings toward the MIS program on several sets of bipolar semantic differential adjectives. This method is based upon the technique of Mitchell and Olson (1981) as applied to research in the field of Marketing.
- Subjects
  A questionnaire was sent to students who graduated between 1986 and 1994 from an MIS program of an AACSB accredited College of Business in California.

FINDINGS

Required Course Content Evaluations - First Year On The Job
The mean and rank for each of the required courses are shown in Table 1.

Required Course Content Values - In One's Current Position
The next phase yielded the alumni evaluations in Table 2 for the same set of courses with their current position as the frame of reference.

Table 1: Mean Scores for Required Courses During First Year on the Job

Course Title	Mean	Rank
Business Information Systems and Organizations	3.86	6
COBOL Language Programming	4.56	4
Accounting Information Systems	3.20	8
Structured Systems Analysis	4.67	3
Software Project Management	4.89	2
Data Base Concepts	4.92	1
Information Center Administration	3.65	7
Systems Development Practicum	4.47	5

Table 2: Mean Scores for Required Courses in One's Current Position

Course Title	Mean	Rank
Business Information Systems and Organizations	4.05	5
COBOL Language Programming	3.13	7
Accounting Information Systems	3.09	8
Structured Systems Analysis	4.89	3
Software Project Management	5.37	1
Data Base Concepts	5.22	2
Information Center Administration	3.74	6
Systems Development Practicum	4.85	4

Table 3: Semantic Differentials and Their Factor Loadings

Scale Item	Factor Loading
Good Experience-Bad Experience	.67448
Good Use of My Time-Bad Use of My Time	.82859
Valueless-Valuable	.78144
Useless-Useful	.77598
Desirable-Undesirable	.80548
Ineffective-Effective	.81820

Table 4: Correlation of Program Satisfaction Index Score With Value of Course Content During First Year on the Job

Course Title	Correlation Coefficient	N
Business Information Systems and Organizations	.4528*	31
COBOL Language Programming	.1643	57
Accounting Information Systems	-.0159	56
Structured Systems Analysis	.3898**	58
Software Project Management	.3358*	58
Data Base Concepts	.2917	58
Information Center Administration	.2833	54
Systems Development Practicum	.4088**	55

* $P < .01$
** $P < .001$

Development of Overall Program Satisfaction Index

The graduates were asked to indicate their feelings toward the entire MIS program on several sets of bipolar semantic differential adjectives. A principal components factor analysis revealed that only one factor was present. The items shown in Table 3 had high factor loadings. The Cronbach alpha for the items was .9245, showing a very high level of internal consistency of the responses to the items.

Analysis of First Year On The Job Course Content Scores

The overall program satisfaction index score for each graduate was then matched to the graduate's evaluation of the content of each required course during the first year on the job. The Pearson product moment correlation values are shown in Table 4.

Analysis of Current Position Course Content Scores

The overall program satisfaction index score for each graduate was then matched to the graduate's evaluation of the content of each required course in

Table 5: Correlation of Program Satisfaction Index Score With Value of Course Content in One's Current Position

Course Title	Correlation Coefficient	N
Business Information Systems and Organizations	.5598**	30
COBOL Language Programming	.1902	57
Accounting Information Systems	.0484	56
Structured Systems Analysis	.4339**	58
Software Project Management	.3536*	59
Data Base Concepts	.2250	59
Information Center Administration	.3370*	54
Systems Development Practicum	.5235**	54

* P <.01
** P <.001

one's current position. The Pearson product moment correlation values are shown in Table 5.

ANALYSIS

When the faculty designed the MIS curriculum, they planned that the content of the following courses would have primarily entry-level value:
- COBOL Language Programming,
- Accounting Information Systems,
- Structured Systems Analysis, and
- Data Base Concepts.

It was also planned that the content of some courses would have major applicability later in one's career. Those courses were:
- Software Project Management, and
- Information Center Administration.

Some courses were designed in such a manner that the course content would have applicability not only in an entry-level position but as one progressed in the MIS field. The courses of this type were:
- Business Information Systems and Organizations,
- Structured Systems Analysis,
- Software Project Management, and
- Systems Development Practicum.

The following findings are consistent with the faculty plans. The Business Information Systems and Organizations course showed a high correlation between the value of the course in the first year on the job and the graduates' overall measure of satisfaction with the MIS program. The correlation was even higher and much more significant statistically when the graduates related the course value in one's current position to overall satisfaction with the MIS program.

The Structured Systems Analysis course content both during one's first year on the job and in one's current position was very highly correlated with one's overall satisfaction with the MIS program. The Software Project Management course exhibited the same relationship as the Structured Systems Analysis course.

The Information Center Administration course content value during one's first year on the job was not significantly correlated with a graduate's overall satisfaction with the MIS program. However, there was a significant correlation between the perceived value of the content of the course in one's current position and one's overall satisfaction with the MIS program.

As to the Systems Development Practicum course, the score for the value of the course content during the first year on the job was significantly correlated with one's overall attitude toward the MIS program. Additionally, the value of the content of the course in one's current position was correlated even more strongly with a graduate's attitude toward the entire MIS program.

Some other findings were worthy of note. The Data Base Concepts course content value during one's first year on the job was more highly correlated with a graduate's overall satisfaction with the MIS program than in one's current position, but was not significantly correlated in either case. Also, the COBOL Programming course had a high perceived value during one's first year on the job. However, its content either during the first year on the job or in one's current position was not correlated with graduates' overall satisfaction with the MIS program. Since this course was offered by the Computer Science Department rather than the MIS area, it is possible that the students did not relate this course as part of their MIS program. Similarly, the Accounting Information Systems course showed low correlation, whether viewed during one's first year on the job or in one's current position, with overall satisfaction with the MIS program. Once again, this course was offered by the Accounting Department rather than the MIS area. As a consequence, the students may have perceived the course as a peripheral rather than core member of the MIS program.

SUMMARY AND CONCLUSIONS
Summary

The extent to which the value of the content of a course is a driver of, i.e., correlated to, a graduate's overall attitude toward, or satisfaction index for, the entire MIS program differs as a function of the graduate's frame of reference, i.e., first year on the job or one's current position.

Conclusions

It is suggested that if an MIS faculty wishes to validate the extent to which its beliefs as to the entry-level versus career value of course content are consistent with the perceptions of its graduates, they can do so by using the method described in this paper.

REFERENCES

Gasen, J. B., Weistroffer, H. R., & Haynes, K. (1991-92). Development of an Instrument for Assessing MIS Majors. *Journal of Computer Information Systems*, Winter, pp. 20-22.

Hanchey, C. M. (1995-96). *An Assessment Model for Surveying Graduates*. Journal of Computer Information Systems , Winter, pp. 67-75.

Mitchell, A. A. and Olson, J. C. (1981). Are Product Attitude Beliefs the Only Mediator of Advertising Effects on Brand Attitude? *Journal of Marketing Research*, August, pp. 318-332.

Van Auken, S. (1991). Outcomes Assessment: Implications for AACSB Accredited Business Schools and Marketing Departments. *Western Marketing Educators' Association Conference Proceeding*, April, pp. 34 - 37.

Chapter 13

A Personalized System of Instruction for Teaching Java

Henry H. Emurian
University of Maryland Baltimore County, USA

Ashley G. Durham[1]
Centers for Medicare & Medicaid Services, USA

INTRODUCTION

This chapter addresses the challenge of how to structure a learning environment to teach object-oriented computer programming to students who may need an introductory course in that discipline but who may lack the experiences to use symbol manipulations with confidence. In contrast to computer science students, information systems students sometimes exhibit these latter attributes, but they would nonetheless benefit professionally from acquiring rudimentary programming language knowledge and skill. To accomplish that objective, the Personalized System of Instruction (PSI), originally developed by Keller (1968), is described here to foster equivalent competence among students in an initial Java‰ coding assignment in an introductory programming course. The intent of integrating a Java tutoring system into the PSI framework as the first laboratory exercise is to ensure that all students in the class have at least this background experience in common prior to the introduction of advanced features of interface implementation that are taught during the remainder of the semester. Self-report and performance data are presented to support the use of this pedagogical approach in the classroom.

Previously Published in *Managing Information Technology in a Global Economy* edited by Mehdi Khosrow-Pour, Copyright © 2001, Idea Group Publishing.

The PSI methodology is based on the following five factors:

- *unit perfection*, in which progress from one step in learning to another step requires perfect performance in the prior step;
- *self-paced progression*, in which the student may move through a training experience at a self-determined rate;
- *focus on the written word*, in contrast to traditional lectures, to transmit information to the student;
- *repeated testing* of concepts; and
- *collaborations and discussions* with peers and experts.

These five factors together constitute the PSI proposed by Keller (1968) and implemented by Ferster and Perrott (1968). Many studies support the effectiveness of the PSI (e.g., Kritch & Bostow, 1998), which contains features that are intended to meet the needs of the individual learner in ways that have long been known to overcome individual differences and to promote high achievement levels in all students (Bloom, 1984).

This chapter reports the outcome of the use of the PSI in a graduate-level course that contains instruction in implementing graphical user interfaces with the Java Abstract Windowing Toolkit (AWT). The data reported here will show the use of the PSI to teach a class of students to write a Java Applet. The study extends our previous work, which validated a web-based tutoring system for training in fundamental aspects of Java by documenting improvements in programming confidence and competence immediately after students used the tutoring system (Emurian, Hu, Wang, & Durham, 2000). The present study broadens the number of assessment occasions to include a third assessment that occurred after the fifth PSI factor listed above had been completed by all students in a classroom discussion and collaboration setting. Finally, to assess the durability of learning, the study includes a fourth and final assessment that was administered during the last class of the semester, which occurred over three months after the third assessment occasion.

Our pedagogical approach emphasizes a programmed instruction methodology for implementing the first four factors in the PSI by means of the web-based tutoring system for Java training. Programmed instruction technology for teaching offers specific guidelines to follow in the construction of procedures that manage the moment-by-moment progress of a student during study events that are structured within the framework of a behavioral theory of learning (Skinner, 1958). The theoretical assumption is that the steps involved in learning a complex task, such as constructing a computer program, can be specified with sufficient precision that reinforcement contingencies can be applied to the component units that lead to task mastery. These ideas and concepts are grounded within the experimental analysis of behavior literature (e.g., Holland, 1960). This principle-based learning technology predates computer-based instructional systems, which now encompass a broad and multidisciplinary field of investigations and applications (Brock, 1997).

In the present tutoring system, the operational definitions of the information units to be learned by a student are based upon research in verbal learning that identifies at least three types of verbal information paradigms:

- *item information*, which records the occurrence of events and is commonly tested by recognition tests;
- *associative information*, which records relationships between separate events and is commonly tested by paired-associates tests; and
- *serial order information*, which records the temporal sequence of a string of events and is commonly tested by serial recall tests (Li & Lewandowsky, 1995).

The programmed progression among unit sizes studied here is based upon a functional account of verbal behavior, which suggests a systematic transition in learning from textual items to streams as a function of practice (Greer & McDonough, 1999). The adoption of the feature that learners be required to construct accurate responses by recalling units of increasing complexity is based upon earlier work by the authors in which learning and retention of UNIX command sequences were superior under conditions of recall in comparison to recognition of textual information items (Durham & Emurian, 1998).

TUTORING SYSTEM DESIGN

The technical and operational details of the tutoring system have been presented elsewhere (Emurian et al., 2000). The system consists of a series of Java Applets embedded within the WebCT' course management software that allows users to create guest accounts to access the system (http://webct.umbc.edu/public/JavaTutor/index.html). The design of the tutoring system is a synthesis of principles of programmed instruction (Skinner, 1958), verbal learning and memory (Anderson, 1995), the elaboration theory of instruction (Reigeluth & Darwazeh, 1982), practice and retention (Durham & Emurian, 1998), and instructional design (Tennyson & Schott, 1997).

The objective of the programmed instruction tutoring system is to teach a learner to construct a stream of 36 elements that together constitute a Java computer program that displays a text string in a Netscape browser window. The approach taken is first to specify the terminal performance, which is to write the program correctly, and then to craft a series of programmed instruction steps that progress to that goal. The outcome is tested mastery of the meaning of each of the 36 elements and the interrelationships among those elements in the production of the terminal performance. The 36 elements are displayed in Figures 3 and 4, which are discussed later in this chapter.

Overview

The learner progresses through the system in five stages. The full instruction set presented to the learner is available for observation within the online tutor.

Figure 1 shows the interfaces that the learner encounters during the first two stages of training. The left interface requires matching a displayed item. The right interface requires finding a displayed item in the list. These interfaces promote familiarity with the formal features of the symbols and with experience in detecting similarities and differences among the symbols.

Figure 2 shows the two interface types that are presented during the third stage of the tutor. The top interface teaches the individual items of code, which are displayed cumulatively in the white space as the learner enters the items correctly. This interface teaches up to three items of code, entered into keying fields at the bottom, and there are 14 of these interfaces in the tutor. This interface also requires passing a multiple-choice objective test on each item. Each successive item must be typed correctly in the keying field from memory before the learner may progress to a subsequent item. Next, the bottom serial stream interface is presented, requiring entering the items that were just learned. If the input is incorrect, the learner recycles again through the item interface, and that cycle repeats until the serial stream is entered correctly. Then the next item interface is presented.

After the completion of the item and serial stream interfaces, a row by row interface is presented for the fourth stage. Figure 3 shows two of the three row by row interfaces that are presented. The top view shows the first pass interface, and the bottom view shows the third pass interface. The second pass interface has small row labels on a white background. Each interface requires entering the lines

Figure 1: The interfaces presented during the first two stages.

Figure 2: The two interface types that are presented during the third stage.

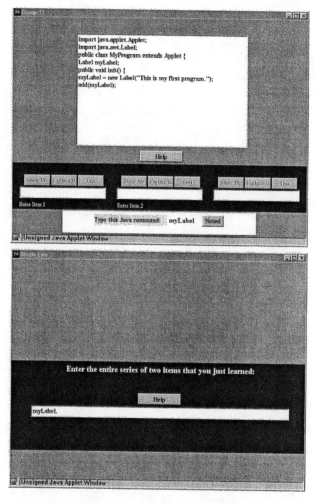

of code correctly, row by row. The input on a row is based on the format of the program that was displayed in the white space in the item interface. The input on a row must be accurate before the next keyin field is enabled. If the user can not enter the row correctly, the item interface for the code in that row is presented again, and that cycle repeats until the code on a row is entered correctly.

During the first pass, the user may select an optional "Hint" window, which displays a description of the objective of the code in that row. Additionally, a multiple-choice test must be passed on the objective of each row. The second pass interface has the "Hint" window available, but the third pass interface does not have this option. Accordingly, the learner must complete three passes of entering the code in a row by row format. A justification of this number of passes is presented elsewhere (Durham & Emurian, 1998).

Figure 3: Two of the three row by row interfaces that are presented during the fourth stage.

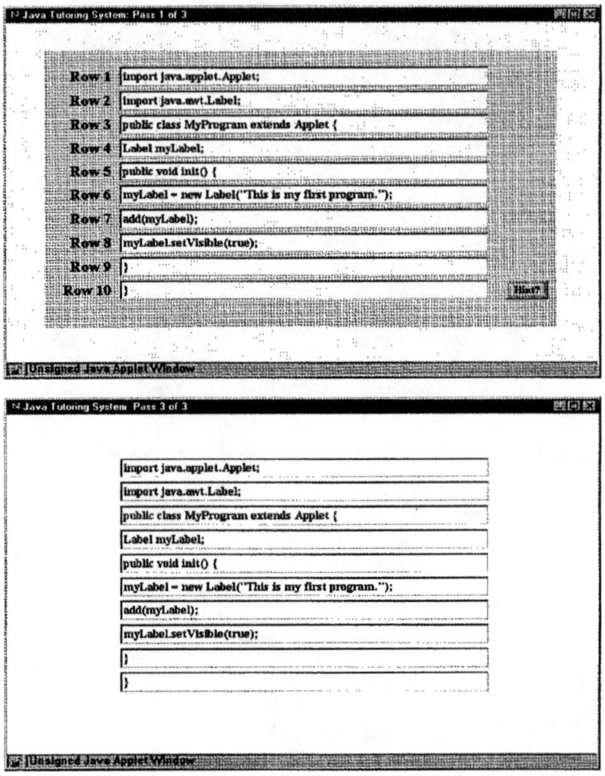

After the learner completes the row by row interfaces, a text editor emulation interface is presented for the fifth stage. Figure 4 shows this interface with correct code entered. This interface relaxes the format that was enforced in the preceding interfaces, and it evaluates the input as a stream. If the learner is not able to enter the code correctly, the "Review" button initiates a recycling through the third pass of the row by row interface. Accordingly, the learner may recycle back to the row and item interfaces as required to master the code. This text editor emulation interface exits when the code is entered correctly. Although the tutor does present further instructions about the running of the Applet on the world-wide web (www), these details are presented in a lecture and discussion format for the classroom work reported here.

PROCEDURE

The tutor was presented as the first exercise in a graduate course (Fall, 2000) entitled "Graphical User Interface Systems Using Java." There were 12 graduate students in the class (eight females, median age = 27.5; four males, median age = 30). Prior to using the tutor, each student completed a questionnaire in which was

Figure 4: The text editor emulation interface presented during the fifth stage.

presented two rating scales. The first rating scale assessed the student's prior experience with Java, and it consisted of the following instruction and five choices:

How would you describe your experience with Java as of this moment?

1 = No experience. (I am a novice in Java.)

2 = Some experience.

3 = Moderate experience.

4 = Much experience.

5 = Extensive experience. (I am an expert in Java.)

The second rating scale assessed the confidence that the student currently had in being able to use each of the 24 unique Java items to write a Java computer program. The rating scale consisted of the following instruction and five choices for each of the 24 items:

How confident are you that you can now use the following symbol to construct a Java program?

1 = Not at all confident. I do not know how to use the symbol.

2 = Only a little confident.

3 = Fairly confident.

4 = Very confident

5 = Totally confident. I know how to use the symbol.

The student was also asked to write a Java Applet to display a text string, as a Label object, in a browser window. Additionally, the questionnaire solicited demographic information. All data were collected and saved using the online assessment and recording features of WebCT.

At the conclusion of the two hours that were allotted to the tutoring system or whenever a student finished the tutor prior to that time, a post-tutor questionnaire was completed. The confidence assessment scale and the writing of the Applet were repeated, and three additional rating scales were administered. The first scale instruction and choices were as follows:

What was your overall reaction to the tutor?
1 = Totally negative. I did not like the tutor.
2 = Only a little negative.
3 = Neutral.
4 = Only a little positive.
5 = Totally positive. I liked the tutor.

The second scale instruction and choices were as follows:
In terms of learning Java, how would you rate your experience in using the tutor?
1 = Totally negative. The tutor did not help me to learn Java.
2 = Only a little negative.
3 = Neutral.
4 = Only a little positive.
5 = Totally positive. The tutor did help me to learn Java.

The third scale instruction and choices were as follows:
How would you rate the usability of the tutor?
1 = Totally negative. The tutor was difficult to use.
2 = Only a little negative.
3 = Neutral.
4 = Only a little positive.
5 = Totally positive. The tutor was easy to use.

The students were then dismissed from the class, and the tutor continued to be available for those students who were motivated to access the tutor outside of class.

During the immediately succeeding class period, which occurred one week later, the instructor discussed the Applet code with the students using a lecture format ("chalk and talk"). The approach was to have the students enter the code into a text editor at the time the items were presented and discussed on the board. The www directory tree and HTML file were also presented and discussed. The students then compiled the Java code and ran the Applet in a Netscape Communicator browser by accessing the HTML file as a URL on the web. During these latter events, the students were encouraged to help each other and to seek help from the instructor and course assistant as needed. After all students ran the Applet on the web, they again completed the confidence ratings and the writing of the Applet code in the assessment questionnaire. This identical assessment was repeated during the fourteenth class, the final class of the semester.

RESULTS

At the conclusion of the class time allotted for completing the tutor, six students had finished all parts of the tutor, and six students were still working on the row by row or text emulation interfaces. A comparison of the magnitude of the changes between pre-tutor ratings and the next two rating occasions did not support differences between these two groups in changes for post-tutor ratings, $F(1,10) = 0.75$, $p > .10$, and post-applet ratings, $F(1,10) = 2.48$, $p > .10$. Accordingly, the two groups were pooled for the following analyses.

Figure 5 presents box-plots displaying median confidence ratings for all subjects for the 24 distinct items that were used to compose the program. A box plot is presented across the four assessment occasions: (1) pre-tutor, (2) post-tutor, (3) post-applet, and (4) the final class. The figure graphically shows the progressive increase in self-reports of confidence across the four assessment occasions.

Figure 5: Box plots showing median confidence ratings for all subjects for the 24 distinct items that were used to compose the program.PRE = Pre-Tutor, POST = Post-Tutor, APPLET = Post-Applet, and FINAL = Final Class.

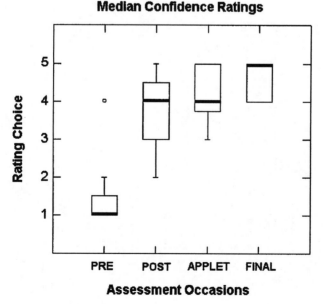

A MANOVA approach to comparing means based on the differences (D) between pairs of observations across the six combinations of assessment occasions for all subjects showed a significant effect of occasions, $F(5,66) = 18.12$, $p < .001$. Pairwise contrasts supported the conclusion that the most dependable changes in median confidence occurred over the first two assessment occasions. Since ordinal data are problematic for detecting and interpreting small effect size differences, replication is the preferred strategy for demonstrating the dependability of these observations.

Figure 6 presents the total number of correct Java programs that were written into the questionnaire across the last three assessment occasions. The data are presented as a cumulative total. Since no subject wrote a correct program during the pre-tutor assessment, the figure does not portray that outcome. The figure

Figue 6: Cumulative total correct programs written on the last three assessment occasions.

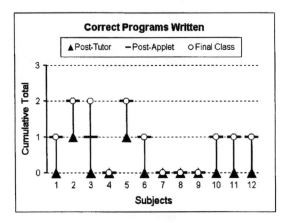

Figure 7: Self-report data on four scales.

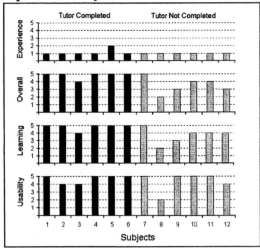

shows that immediately after completing the tutor, which required one accurate construction of the entire program, only two subjects (S2 & S5) were able to write the program correctly. After the subjects received classroom instruction and ran the Applet, eight of the 12 subjects were able to write the program correctly. Notably, however, on the final assessment occasion, which occurred 12 weeks later, only one subject (S3) was able to write the program correctly. These data show the improvement in performance over the first three repetitions of writing the program and the forgetting of the program after the 12-week delay interval.

Figure 7 presents rating choices on the following four self-report scales:
• prior experience with Java,
• overall impression toward the tutor,
• usefulness of the tutor in learning Java, and
• usability of the interfaces.

The data are grouped into those students who completed the tutor and those students who did not complete the tutor during the first classroom period. For Experience, only Subject 5 reported slight experience with Java prior to using the tutor. For Overall, five of the "completers" and one "non-completer" reported the maximum scale value. Although the values seem graphically lower for the non-completers, a Wilcoxon ranks test did not support a significant difference between the groups on this or any other scale (all $p > .20$). Similar effects were observed for Learning. For Usability, eight of the 12 subjects reported the highest scale value. It is also notable that Subject 8, who was in the "non-completers" group, gave consistently low ratings on these scales and also did not show accurate Applet construction on any of the three assessment occasions. Despite these reports, that subject did show an increase in reported confidence in the use of the Java items across the four assessment occasions. In summary, these self-report data support the conclusion that almost all subjects had positive reactions to the tutoring system and its methodology for programming a series of interactive instructional events.

DISCUSSION

This study investigated a PSI for acquiring fundamental knowledge of a Java Applet. The instructional design of a Java tutoring system followed programmed instruction principles, which were supplemented with students' personal interactions with the course instructors and collaborations with peers. In contrast to passive online tutorials that only display information, no matter how skillfully organized and delivered within a hypermedia environment, the present tutoring system required learners actively to construct correct responses during the training. The level of complexity of the learned and constructed response was systematically increased until the final response was the production of the entire Java program. The programmed instruction component was augmented by a discussion with an "expert" that culminated in the learner's running of the Applet on the world-wide web. These factors together characterize a Personalized System of Instruction.

Although the data generally show confidence and performance improvements at least across the first three assessment occasions, it is notable, however, that only one student was able to write the Applet code correctly at the end of the course. This outcome presents a challenge for interpretation, especially since the course content throughout was the cumulative construction of an interactive information system using Java.

One way to understand this outcome, perhaps, is to consider the fact that the Java Applet class was taught and discussed only during the first two sessions of the course. The other components of the Java AWT that were taught over the remaining class periods did not involve repeating the initial Applet construction. It is also the case that the instructor emphasized to the students the importance of seeking and using online information from Sun Microsystems, Inc. about the construction and manipulation of the interface components that were presented in the course. In that sense, the students were not encouraged to memorize Java code. They were encouraged to seek out and use information as professionals. Furthermore, students were not required to write Java code on examinations, although they were required to interpret code fragments based on information presented in the course study guides. Nevertheless, these findings indicate the importance of repetition in achieving a fundamental competence that sets the occasion for future confidence and learning, and they show that students within a group may require different amounts of practice to achieve the identical level of skill. They also show that competence displayed on one occasion may not be easily retained.

Despite these observations, the Personalized System of Instruction (Keller, 1968), with the Java tutoring system as the central component, has been adopted by the authors to good advantage in the classroom because it generates a history of symbol use and program construction competence in each individual student. It combines both teaching and testing within a single conceptual framework: programmed instruction. It allows the needs of the individual student to be met because it frees the teacher from relying exclusively on traditional approaches, such as lecturing and writing on the board, to deliver technical information to a group of students. Most importantly, perhaps, the present tutoring system combines knowledge delivery with learning, assessment, and documentation of competence. Although the number of subjects in the present study was low, the concentration on the behavior of the individual learner, rather than on group averages, together with past and planned future replications with different class groups, enables the cumulative development of a knowledge base that will document the reliability of the current findings under conditions that promote the generality of the programmed instruction methodology.

Much has been written about the nature of computer programming and the attainment of expertise as a high-level problem-solving activity (e.g., Anderson, Corbett, Koedinger, & Pelletier, 1995). Our classroom experience, however, continues to indicate the importance of not overlooking basic learning parameters of guided rehearsal and correct practice. These latter conditions help make computer programming accessible to inexperienced and unconfident students who may otherwise withdraw from the initial effort required to achieve the background competence necessary to acquire advanced programming skills. Although it is certain that complex problem-solving skills and conceptual understanding are considerations in the development of expertise as a computer programmer, there is, perhaps, underestimated value to fostering an inductive development of these important outcomes by the simple repetition of fundamental response patterns.

REFERENCES

Anderson, J.R. (1995). *Learning and Memory: An Integrated Approach.* New York: Wiley.

Anderson, J.R., Corbett, A.T., Koedinger, K.R., & Pelletier, R. (1995). Cognitive tutors: Lessons learned. *Journal of Learning Science, 4,* 167-207.

Bloom, B.S. (1984). The 2 sigma problem: The search for methods of group instruction as effective as one-to-one tutoring. *Educational Researcher, 13,* 4-16.

Brock, J.F. (1997). Computer-based instruction. In G. Salvendy (Ed.), *Handbook of Human Factors and Ergonomics* (pp. 578-593). New York: Wiley.

Durham, A.G., & Emurian, H.H. (1998). Learning and retention with a menu and a command line interface. *Computers in Human Behavior, 14,* 597–620.

Emurian, H.H., Hu, X., Wang, J. & Durham, A.G. (2000). Learning Java: A programmed instruction approach using Applets. *Computers in Human Behavior, 16,* 395-422.

Ferster, C.B., & Perrott, M.C. (1968). *Behavior Principles.* New York: Appleton-Century-Crofts.

Greer, R.D., & McDonough, S.H. (1999). Is the learn unit a fundamental measure of pedagogy? *The Behavior Analyst, 22,* 5-16.

Holland, J.G. (1960). Teaching machines: An application of principles from the laboratory. *Journal of the Experimental Analysis of Behavior, 3,* 275-287.

Keller, F.S. (1968). Goodbye teacher... *Journal of Applied Behavior Analysis, 1,* 79-89.

Kritch, K.M., & Bostow, D.E. (1998). Degree of constructed-response interaction in computer-based programmed instruction. *Journal of Applied Behavior Analysis, 31,* 387–398.

Li, S., & Lewandowsky, S. (1995). Forward and backward recall: Different retrieval processes. *Journal of Experimental Psychology: Learning, Memory, and Cognition, 21*, 837-847.

Reigeluth, C.M., & Darwexeh, A.N. (1982). The elaboration theory's procedures for designing instruction: A conceptual approach. *Journal of Instructional Development, 5*, 22-32.

Skinner, B.F. (1958). Teaching machines, *Science, 128*, 969-977.

Tennyson, R.D., & Schott, F. (1997). Instructional design theory, research, and models. In R.D. Tennyson, F. Schott, N.M. Seel, & S. Dijkstra (Eds.), *Instructional Design: International Perspectives* (pp. 1-16), Mahwah, NJ: Lawrence Erlbaum Associates.

Chapter 14

Places and Processes in Learning Environments

I.T. Hawryszkiewycz
University of Technology, Australia

The chapter describes ways to create a variety of learning environments. It suggests that good practices require both the definition of places of learning as well as clear definition of processes to be followed within such learning places. Different processes are often needed for different places. The paper then describes a metamodel for defining different environments and a system that implements the metamodel. The environments described include classroom teaching, group support, distance moderation and monitoring of groups. The chapter then describes a system, called LiveNet, which can be used to configure a variety of learning environments in terms of the metamodel, and describes experiences in its use. The experiences in particular indicate the need to clearly define processes to be followed and that the process changes depending on the learning environment and the support tools to facilitate the process with ensuing benefits to both teachers and students.

INTRODUCTION

Learning communities are now beginning to take many forms. There are the conventional classroom situations, but increasingly we are beginning to see new forms such as work based learning, distance learning, and virtual universities. Increasingly web based technologies are being used to support these learning environments. Such support is needed within the classroom situation to manage increasingly larger groups of students. It is also needed in other situations where

Previously Published in *Managing Information Technology in a Global Economy* edited by Mehdi Khosrow-Pour, Copyright © 2001, Idea Group Publishing.

support is needed across distance. The kind of support needed depends on the situation, the kind of subject taught and the way that it is taught. Each of these alternatives requires support of different kinds of roles and relationships within the teaching environment.

Computer tools that support learning environments must thus be configurable to support the different learning environments. What is needed is a way to design learning environments and configure support tools to support the environments. The paper proposes a framework for defining learning environments in terms of places, called workspaces in this paper. The goal is to provide ways to easily define learning models by customizing systems to support special relationships needed in a selected learning process. The paper also describes the need to clearly define processes to be followed in such environments. Such processes depend on the structure and goal of the environment and are related to those proposed for knowledge creation (Nonaka, 1994). A system called LiveNet, which can be used to customize such learning models, is described.

ORGANIZING LEARNING PLACES

The paper uses the workspace as the basis for representing learning models and shows how to implement the models using the LiveNet system. The workspace brings together people, materials and facilitate communication between them within a defined context. A number of people can then carry out these actions, possible on different objects, within the workspace.

Different places may be configured for different learning situations. Examples described in this paper include:
- A place for distributing and clarifying materials,
- A place for developing ideas,
- A place for guiding students through a case study,
- A place for students to set up their own applications.

Describing places of learning

We use the paradigm of workspaces to describe places of learning. The workspace paradigm is similar to other place paradigms such as rooms, although it is more generic in the sense that it provides an abstract model to describe any physical or logical structure. Thus for example workspaces can be organizational units or project repositories. A generic place structure is shown in Figure 1. It illustrates the basic concepts of the metamodel. A more detailed description of these concepts can be found in Hawryszkiewycz (2000). The central concept is the role, which has defined responsibilities in the workspace. These can be to access materials or carry our assigned actions. People are assigned to the roles. Roles or at least people assigned to the roles can also interact in a variety of ways.

Figure 1: Describing Places

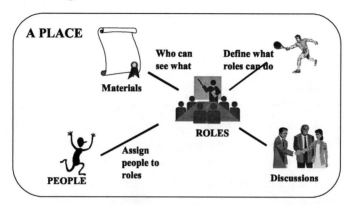

There are other concepts concerned with workgroup creation and a variety of awareness parameters.

Associated with this structure are the more dynamic semantics that define significant events and workflows and associated notification schemes.

The next question is to look in more detail at what makes up these places and how different places can be connected into learning environments.

Learning environments

The paper proposes that learning environments can be defined using the framework shown in Figure 2. The two main requirements are to:

- Define the structure together with the relationships and processes within it. It must also provide tools to create the structure and maintain the relationships and facilitate the processes. Such tools should assist both teachers and students, and
- Provide the tools to create the content and domain specific tools. Content creation is common to any subject whereas the domain problem tools are particular to subject domains.

Underlying the structure is the way to support interactions in the relationships. These include both the cardinality of relationships and whether they are synchronous and asynchronous.

Figure 2: The dimensions of support systems

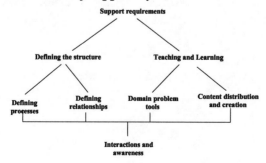

The important thing to remember in any system is to ensure that the effort needed to provide a course should not be greater than that needed in a course. This particularly applies to providing the teacher with tools, which reduce the preparation and management of material rather than being seen as an added workload component.

The system LiveNet, which is described here, includes ways to support both of these two kinds of requirements. This is in contrast to most other tools in this area. Most such tools concentrate on material distribution but do not provide the flexibility for easily setting up and managing a variety of learning environments.

The goal is to bring participants, who in most cases are students and teachers, into a commonly shared workspace (Hawryszkiewycz, 1999) and provide the flexibility to set up a variety of collaborative environments. The workspace is then populated with subject domain tools to support the learning process.

DESCRIBING LEARNING ENVIRONMENTS

This section describes a number of learning environments described in our study.

Model 1 – Supporting large class teaching

The simplest example is teaching environment to support large classes, whose structure is shown in Figure 3 in terms of place concepts. Here there is a workspace for each recognized activity. These are shown as clouded shapes in Figure 3 together with the roles that participate in the activities and the flows between the activities. The information used in the activity is shown as rectangular boxes. A place for material distribution is shown in Figure 4.

The main parts of a LiveNet, placed in Figure 4, includes background material about the subject, a set of actions that are possible in the workspace, documents that could be uploaded by users, and a set of discussions.

Figure 3: Describing an environment

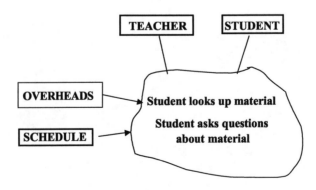

Figure 4: A Place for Accessing Materials

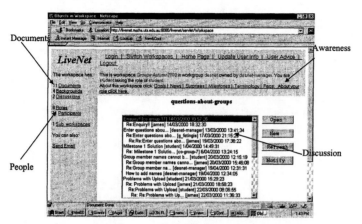

Processes

The process here is relatively straightforward and closely corresponds to socialisation in Nonaka's cycle. The process requires timely release of material to students and discussions about this material. This includes provision of agents that keep track of time and initiate release of materials such as problem solutions following completion of other outcomes. Notification schemes are associated with discussions and notify discussion participants whenever a new statement is entered into a discussion.

Model 2 - A Place for Interpretation

Another kind of learning environment is shown in Figure 5. Here there is a detailed evaluation with students developing theories and conclusions based on this data. This involves intense discussion with the tutor and continuous introduction of new background material.

Processes

The process here primarily concerns interpretation of material (Nonaka, 1995) and is primarily teacher driven to ensure participation during discussions. Guide-

Figure 5: A function oriented model

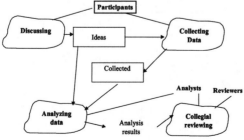

Figure 6: Distance moderation

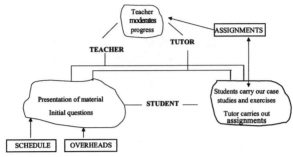

lines need to be provided by tutors and responses monitored and consolidated.

Model 3 – Distance moderation

Another model of teaching is shown in Figure 6. In this material is initially presented to students in an intensive course and followed through experience sessions moderated by a distant tutor with electronic assistance from the teacher. Thus the relationships established during the follow up phase are for direct interaction between tutor and student with monitoring and advice provided by the teacher.

Processes

The process here is similar to that found in Model 1. The major difference resulted from reduced faced to face interaction in the distant model. This has required closer monitoring of progress and provision of continuous feedback. It is thus a mix of socialization, interpretation and evaluation with emphasis on the first and last of these. Such a process calls for ways to maintain awareness of activities through students maintaining progressive updates on their work with responses by teachers. The process is thus predominantly teacher driven with teachers reminding students to continuously submit work and suggesting steps to be followed in such submissions.

Figure 7: Setting up student groups

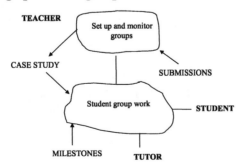

Model 4 – Supporting student groups

This is a more complex process where group formation and case study is facilitated by the system. The students form groups electronically using agents included in the LiveNet system to assist group formation. Once the groups are formed a .project repository is generated for each group which is subsequently used to create a working prototype based on LiveNet for their case study.

Processes

Considerable support can be provided here in the establishment of group workspaces. One is to support group formation itself. Thus students are provided with actions where they can register their availability for groups. The system will then notify others of their availability. The negotiation then takes place outside the system between the students. Should students agree to form a group they inform the system, which then creates a group space for them. Our next step is to extend workspaces to provide continuous feedback through gradual submission of case-work through LiveNet and provide feedback electronically through the integration of milestone submissions through workspaces. Students were given a number of milestones to aim for, starting with analysis, through design specification to setting up a prototype LiveNet system. Generally, these were successful in the sense that students understood the basic LiveNet modeling method and workspace description and set up prototypes with little effort. The social effect of this is to require students to pace their work according to the process rather, as is often the case, leaving it to the last minute. This has an obvious learning benefit although it is perceived as a nuisance by some students in that it requires them to follow a process.

COMBINING PLACES INTO AN INTEGRATED TEACHING ENVIRONMENT

Most learning environments require a combination of places. A teaching environment should allow users to combine a number of different kinds of workspaces. One common structure that we found useful is shown in Figure 8. It combines tutorial. Lecture material and groups. There are also a number of knowledge gates about particular subject areas.

LiveNet provides the tools to easily construct such networks. A detailed description of the tools used to set up the structures is out of the scope of this paper. In summary it allows a workgroup to be setup and workspaces created within the workgroup. Wizards are provided to guide users through the processes. Workspace structures like that shown in Figure 9 can be set up in a matter of minutes using wizards and templates provided by the system.

Figure 8: Workspace network

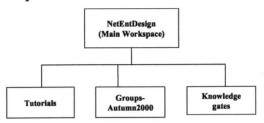

Figure 9: Setting up a multi-place environment

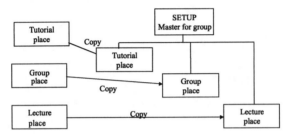

CREATING CONTENT

One issue in any teaching environment is that of creating content, and whether content creation should be separated from content use. One goal here may be to customize the interface to the way that people want to use the content. We thus assume here that content in the form of lecture material is available on FTP sites or some other system, although additional content can be provided through a learning tool. Thus LiveNet has a feature that enables new files to be added to the content database. Interface tools should also provide the context. This includes items such as news items, support for frequently asked questions among others. Such capture will emphasize interactions within the environment and ways of capturing tacit knowledge in these interactions through tools such as discussion systems. The paper then describes a prototype system, LiveNet that can be used to support such processes and its use in teaching.

Domain Specific Tools

A further goal is to provide domain specific tools within the server. These for example could include CASE tools in system development subjects. Currently, for example, we are developing tools for text and discussion analysis. These can be provided through the server on which LiveNet is based.

SUMMARY

The paper outlined the emergence of a variety of learning environments and the need for tools that can set up collaborative workspaces to match the processes in these environments. It described such a tool based on a workspace paradigm and described some applications. Our work with workspaces so far has covered the models described earlier in this paper and involve an average of 1000 students per semester. The majority of students used Model 1 although there has been an average of about 250 that used the other models. We have predominantly used the other models for feedback with students on assignments and clarification within a classroom situation. Students participated especially in seeking clarification of case studies and solutions.

One difference that we have found is the necessity to "push" the process in a number of environments – in particular Models 2 and 3 described above. This requires closer monitoring and driving by teachers.

ACKNOWLEDGEMENTS

A number of people contributed to the work described in this paper especially Dr. L. Hu and Dongbai Xue for assistance in the development of the LiveNet system and Dr. T. Rura-Polley, and Dr. E. Baker for their contribution to planning its use for knowledge creation.

REFERENCES

Hawryszkiewycz (2000). Evolving Knowledge Intensive Community Networks. *Proceedings of Ausweb2000*, Cairns, June.

LiveNet – http://linus.socs.uts.edu.au/~igorh/workspace/explore/livenet.htm.

Nonaka, I. (1994). A Dynamic Theory of Organizational Knowledge Creation. *Organization Science*, 5(1), 14-37.

Chapter 15

IS Program Issues:
From Origin to Accreditation

Douglas Leif
Bemidji State University, USA

*This chapter suggests the challenges of academic information systems pro-
grams are a product of origin and evolution. Based upon the literature and
survey results, the chapter suggests issues concerning origin, perceptions,
solutions, and accreditation.*

INTRODUCTION

The purpose of this chapter is to review information systems (IS) trends leading
to the present, and to raise issues concerning IS program accreditation. The
chapter discusses IS program origin, acceptance by other disciplines, and recognition from industry in reviewing answers to the following questions: Why and
how did higher education IS programs evolve; will widespread IS program accreditation lead to acceptance by other disciplines and recognition from industry;
how does a higher education IS program become accredited; and are clients
demanding accreditation? A discussion of information system program accreditation and client perception of accreditation follows.

BUSINESS BEGINNINGS

Business education is a relatively old and common discipline in higher education, borne out of demand for educated businessmen (Dudley, 1990; Dudley et
al., 1995). The need to enhance commerce produced a demand for business
education. Supplying business education eventually came to the hallowed halls of
higher education, leading to degrees in business education (Cudd, King & O'Hara,

Previously Published in *Managing Information Technology in a Global Economy* edited by Mehdi
Khosrow-Pour, Copyright © 2001, Idea Group Publishing.

1995). Business education initially included the traditional business cycle functions: management, finance, marketing, and accounting.

COMPUTER SCIENCE ARRIVES

Long after many years of business and commerce activity and the introduction of formal business education, computers made their appearance. The advent of this general purpose tool occurred in the 1950s. Computer technology advanced dramatically during the next two decades, stimulating a demand for computer education just as business activity generated a demand for formal business education. In response, higher educational institutions offer degrees in a discipline called computer science.

INFORMATION SYSTEMS EVOLVE

In the 1960s and 1970s, business education and computer science remained very distinct and independent disciplines in many, if not most, academic environments. Business functions, however, welcomed computer applications at operational levels. Implementing business computer applications employed graduates from computer science programs. Although success stories abound, major obstacles persist. Business professionals and computer science programmers were not communicating effectively (Smith & McKeen, 1992). Based solely on their major area of study, business graduates do not understand computers adequately, while computer science graduates generally do not have knowledge of business cycle intricacies. One business insider sums it up by confiding "We scrapped a new quarter of a million dollar accounting package after eighteen months because our accounting people and computer people didn't understand each other." This obstacle loomed only larger as businesses demanded applications for strategic advantages (Clemons, 1986; Kettinger et al., 1994; Weill & Olson, 1989). Businesses are no longer looking at computers to automate operations, but to improve efficiency and decision-making, and to increase product and service innovation (Kalakota & Whinston, 1993).

Business first demanded business graduates, then computer graduates, and once again demands a new type of graduate. The academia response was a degree in IS evolved from the academic blend of business and computer science disciplines. The structure and administration of IS vary among colleges and universities, but the curriculum content generally focuses on both computers and business. The computer core curriculum includes systems development, application development, database management systems, and telecommunications. The business core curriculum includes business cycle functions at levels of the organization encompassing business operations, operations, tactics, and strategies.

Information Systems Recognition and Acceptance

While IS programs are still very young, organizations covet IS graduates who understand business activity and management and are computer oriented. Forecasts indicate this trend will continue (Cale et al., 1991; Hawes, 1994; Minnesota Economic Trends, 1995). However, acceptance from academic disciplines and recognition from industry is proving to be a long process. Newspaper ads for positions responsible for business applications, development, support, and information center support often call for a technical degree, usually in computer science, instead of the business oriented IS degree (Todd, McKeen & Gallupe, 1995). Even academia cannot agree on a label, often seemingly randomly selecting among CIS, MIS, IS, BIS, and others (Gambill, Clark & Maier, 1999).

Several tools are available to further promote acceptance from academic disciplines and recognition from industry. Professional associations, with members representing industry and academia, can develop, prescribe, and enhance IS model curricula. An example is the traditional refinement of IS model curricula by the Association of Information Technology Professionals (AITP), formerly the Data Processing Management Association (DPMA), and the Association of Computing Machinery (ACM). Most recently, these two professional associations have joined the Association for Information Systems (AIS) to produce the 1997 IS undergraduate model curriculum guidelines.

Certification is a way to the top of a profession, and certification of computing professionals worldwide validates computing knowledge and experience internationally (ICCP, 1999). Certification provides a vehicle to demonstrate competency. The Institute for Certification of Computer Professionals (ICCP) administers examinations for the Certified Computer Professional (CCP), similar to the Certified Public Accountant (CPA) examination, administered by the American Institute of Certified Public Accountants (AICPA), for accounting professionals.

ACCREDITATION

Accreditation demands quality of IS programs. Used in conjunction with the former tools, accreditation may be a major contributor to increasing specific and accurate awareness of IS as a major discipline in the worlds of business, computer science, and information technology.

Generally, educational accreditation is a process established to ensure public protection of, and instill public confidence in, collegiate schools and programs (ACBSP, 1999). Institutional accreditation is the process by which an institution undergoes an independent appraisal. In the United States, post-secondary institutional accreditation is voluntary, sought by the institution, and conferred by nongovernmental bodies. In contrast to institutional accreditation, business program or school accreditation focuses its evaluation on the business units within the already accredited institution.

Two organizations are recognized nationally to accredit college and university business schools and programs: The American Assembly of Collegiate Schools of Business (AACSB) and the Association of Collegiate Business Schools and Programs (ACBSP). While several differences exist between AACSB and ACBSP, both have standards for curriculum, faculty credentials, scholarly and professional activities, educational innovation, outcomes assessment, and articulation and transfer relationships (Henninger, 1994).

AACSB accredits business schools. AACSB accredited business schools tend to be large research institutions with master and doctorate programs (Jantzen & Pendleton, 1994). AACSB (1916 inception) currently accredits thirty baccalaureate-only degree granting business schools, excluding accounting (out of about 398 accredited overall by AACSB) (2000). AACSB enjoys considerable name recognition amongst readers of business school and program accreditation related topics (Zoffer, 1987).

ACBSP accredits business schools and business programs. ACBSP accredited business schools and accredited programs attend to primarily undergraduate education which emphasize teaching in a student-learning environment. ACBSP (1988 inception) currently accredits approximately 150 baccalaureate-only and associate-only degree granting business schools and programs, including accounting (out of about 264 accredited overall by ACBSP) (1999).

A third option for business program or school accreditation is being developed by the International Assembly for Collegiate Business Education (IACBE).

Because IS programs are grounded in business, an IS program can obtain accreditation from AACSB or ACBSP. IS programs within accredited business schools or programs, satisfying all standards including a required business core can be accredited. Currently, this is the only course for national accreditation of an IS program.

Advantages and disadvantages of accreditation vary with each IS program and even then, may be speculative or empirical. Nonetheless, the following points serve as possible advantages of striving for IS program accreditation.

ACCREDITATION ADVANTAGES
University Perspective
- The reputation of the institution is enhanced by having a major degree granting area recognized by a national discipline-specific accrediting agency.
- In addition to academic enhancement, the recruitment and retention of students of all majors by the institution may improve (ACBSP, 1999).

- Accreditation may benefit the business area by providing an objective and informed reference for curriculum assessment and future development, evaluation of faculty credentials and professional development.
- Students will benefit because they are assured the business and IS program and faculty meet the requirements of a nationally recognized programmatic accrediting agency.
- University is assured that there is integrity in the business and IS programs (i.e., institution is doing what it purports to do) (ACBSP, 1999).
- University can advertise that it has quality business and IS programs because it has met the educational accreditation standards of a nationally recognized accrediting body (ACBSP, 1999).
- University enhances its attractiveness for purposes of recruiting and retaining business and IS students (ACBSP, 1999).
- University enhances its attractiveness for purposes of recruiting and retaining faculty.
- University provides assurance of quality to potential donors (ACBSP, 1999).
- Other universities may be exploring or seeking accreditation.
- No substantial additional costs by including IS program to business program accreditation process.

Faculty Perspective

- Faculty are interested in being associated with an institution that has a quality academic program in business as validated by a specialized accrediting body (ACBSP, 1999).
- Accreditation requires faculty to attain and maintain exceptional professional development standards in areas of scholarly activity (AACSB, 2000; ACBSP, 1999).
- Faculty are assisted in obtaining adequate support for quality (ACBSP, 1999).

Student Perspective

- Students are able to transfer their undergraduate course credit more easily from an accredited business and IS program (ACBSP, 1999).
- Students can apply for graduate school and receive full credit for their courses at the baccalaureate level (ACBSP, 1999).

Business/Industry Perspective

- Employers are assured that applicants for employment who have attended and/or completed training at accredited institutions have been exposed to a comprehensive and relevant curriculum (ACBSP, 1999; Elfrink & Johnson, 1994; Kim et al., 1996).

- Employers can expect better trained applicants for positions within their organizations (ACBSP, 1999; Elfrink & Johnson, 1994; Kim et al., 1996).
- International governments and companies career positions require candidates to graduate from accredited business and IS programs.

Societal Perspective

- Society is reasonably assured of high quality leadership from graduates of accredited programs (ACBSP, 1999).
- Society benefits from the increased productivity and international competitiveness resulting from quality business and IS education (ACBSP, 1999).
- Some project that unaccredited business and business related programs will be viewed as "third world" programs in years to come.
- Widespread business and IS program accreditation may provide a vehicle for clarification, knowledge and acceptance of the IS discipline and IS programs.

ACCREDITATION DISADVANTAGES

The following are potential disadvantages of striving for IS program accreditation.

- Accreditation (standardization) may limit the number of students entering the program, and therefore, the number of graduates entering the field.
- Programs can use accreditation as leverage to influence curriculum changes.
- Programs can use accreditation as leverage to influence funding from colleges or universities.
- Accreditation standards may be too prescriptive for programs (Jantzen & Pendleton, 1994).
- Accreditation standards and accreditation processes may not be in congruence with university, college, school, or program mission.
- Accreditation can be a step leading to potential loss or withdrawal of accreditation, leading to negative consequences.
- Meeting accreditation standards and undergoing accreditation processes may be very expensive, and potentially prohibitive from a cost standpoint.

ACCREDITATION OBSTACLES

There are several obstacles to accreditation of business and IS schools and programs. These obstacles, although not an exhaustive listing, vary dependent upon the structure and administration of the specific business and IS program.

- Limited pool of resources in which higher educational institutions exist.
- Required reassignment time (for faculty from teaching) necessary to prepare for the accreditation process, write the accreditation self-study, and to design and implement any necessary prescribed programs to treat deficiencies.

- Cooperation and coordination of the various departments and their faculty that will be part of the accreditation process (i.e., accounting, business administration, computer science, economics, IS, finance, management, marketing).
- Accreditation process is a long range, on-going entity.

SURVEY: STUDENTS PERCEIVE ACCREDITATION

Another important issue of accreditation is its perception among potential and current students, as well as alumni. A survey was conducted to determine the awareness of accreditation among a sample of 186 seniors from five high schools and 91 students from one university to determine if accreditation is a consideration in selecting a university program. Eighty percent (149) of the surveyed high school seniors plan to attend college (Table 1). The survey also elicits perceptions of accreditation, the media source of their perceptions, and asks respondents to define accreditation. The sample represents both genders from several majors and disciplines. (The complete survey results concerning media sources of accreditation information and accurate knowledge of accreditation are not within the scope of this paper and are not included.)

The pertinent portion of the survey results for this paper represents the awareness of accreditation among those sampled; and the degree accreditation affected their university and program selection. As Table 2, and Figures 1, 2, and 3 illustrate, university student respondents are aware of accreditation in larger numbers than are high school seniors respondents. Thirty-seven percent of the university students are aware of accreditation, while fifteen percent of the high school seniors are aware of accreditation. Twenty-two percent of all respondents are aware of accreditation. This raises an interesting question: Is the twenty-two percent awareness rate on the rise or decline over the past decade or two?

As Table 3, and Figures 4, 5, and 6 illustrate, high school seniors (47%) consider accreditation a factor in selecting a university program more than university students (33%). This may be explained by the fact university students have already selected an institution, while high school seniors are closer in proximity to the university or university program selection process. Overall, 43% consider accreditation a factor in selecting a university program.

One valid conclusion drawn from this portion of the survey results is that students are exposed to the concept of program accreditation, and they perceive something about it that makes accreditation a positive consideration in selecting a university program.

Table 1: High School Respondents with Higher Education Plans

No Indication of Plans to Attend College	37	20%
Plan to Attend College	149	80%
Total	**186**	**100%**

Table 2: Awareness of Accreditation

University Respondent		
No Indication of Awareness	57	63%
Aware	34	37%
Total	**91**	**100%**
High School Respondent		
No Indication of Awareness	158	85%
Aware	28	15%
Total	**186**	**100%**
Student Respondent		
No Indication of Awareness	215	78%
Aware	62	22%
Total	**277**	**100%**
University Respondent		
No Indication Accreditation is a Factor	61	67%
Factor	30	33%
Total	**91**	**100%**
High School Respondent		
No Indication Accreditation is a Factor	98	53%
Factor	88	47%
Total	**186**	**100%**
Student Respondent		
No Indication Accreditation is a Factor	159	57%
Factor	118	43%
Total	**277**	**100%**

Figure 1: Awareness of Accreditation

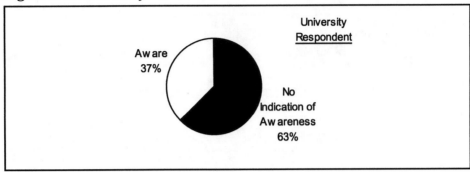

Figure 2: Awareness of Accreditation

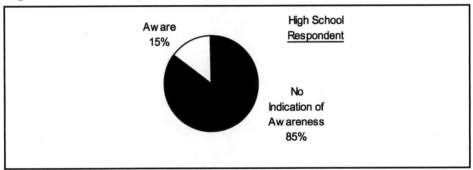

Figure 3: Awareness of Accreditation

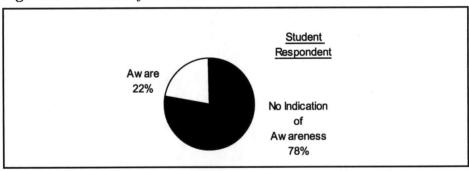

Figure 4:Importance of Accreditation in University Program Selection

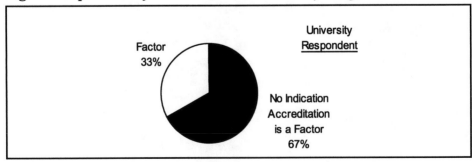

Figure 5: Importance of Accreditation in University Program Selection

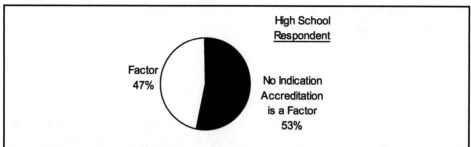

Figure 6: Importance of Accreditation in University Program Selection

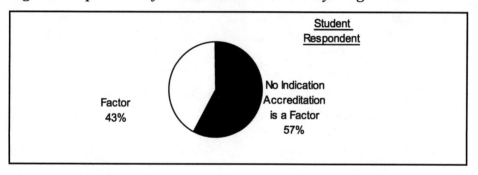

CONCLUSION

This chapter discussed issues from IS academic program origin to accreditation. The discovery by industry of the overwhelming benefits of business computer applications has generated many higher education derivative IS programs from business and computer science. IS, to many non-information technology professionals, remains unidentified, unfamiliar, or completely unknown. National certification exams and professional associations will continue to promote IS as a discipline. Accreditation of IS programs, as this paper proposes, should be gaining momentum. National accreditation of IS programs can promote acceptance and recognition by other disciplines and industry. Initial steps in the process are to investigate issues including examining accrediting agencies; analyzing cost and time resources involved in accreditation; and assessing student-client perceptions of accreditation.

IS programs can become accredited by one of two accrediting bodies, AACSB or ACBSP. By structuring IS majors around a common business core, IS can then proceed through the prescribed accreditation process with the business unit, without a substantial increase in cost.

Many current and potential students are aware of accreditation and perceive it positively. Though not the major factor in the decision to proceed to accreditation, it should not be altogether ignored.

Widespread accreditation of qualified IS programs will better prepare them to move out from under the shadow of its dominating, yet respected parents: Business and computer science.

REFERENCES

American Assembly of Collegiate Schools of Business (AACSB) (2000). St. Louis, MO. http://www.aacsb.edu/aacsb.html. December.

Association of Collegiate Business Schools and Programs (ACBSP) (1999). Overland Park, KS. http://okra.deltast.edu/acbsp, http://okra.deltast.edu/acbsp/institut.html, February 19.

Cale Jr., E. G., Mawhinney, C. H., & Callaghan, D. R. (1991). The Implications of Declining Enrollments in Undergraduate CIS Programs in the United States. *Journal of Management Information Systems*, 8(1), Summer, 167-181.

Clemons, E. K.(1986) Information Systems for Sustainable Competitive Advantage. *Information & Management*, 11(3), 131-136.

Cudd, M., King, J. O., & O'Hara, B. (1995). Assessment of the Nature and Status of the MBA Restructuring Trend. *Journal of Education for Business*, 71, October, 44-53.

Dudley, S. C. (1990). Is the Business Degree All It's Cracked Up to Be. *Journal of Career Planning & Employment*, 51, Fall, 32-37.

Dudley, S. C., Dudley, L. W., Clark, F. L., & Payne, S. (1995). New Directions for the Business Curriculum. *Journal of Education for Business*, 70, June, 305-316.

Elfrink, J. A. & Johnson, G. G. (1994). What Accounting Students Should Know About Business School Accreditation. *New Accountant*, March, 6-7 & 23-24.

Gambill, S., Clark, J., & Maier, L. (1999). CIS vs MIS...:The Name Game. *Journal of Computer Information Systems*, 39:4, Summer, 22-25.

Hawes, D. K. (1994). Information Literacy and the Business Schools. *Journal of Education for Business*, 70, October, 54-69.

Henninger, E. A. (1994). Outcomes Assessment: the Role of Business School and Program Accrediting Agencies. *Journal of Education for Business*, 69, June, 270-296.

Institute for Certification of Computing Professionals (ICCP) (1999). Des Plaines, IL. http://www.iccp.org, February 19.

Jantzen, R. H., & Pendleton, T. A. (1994). Preferences of the American Assembly of Collegiate Schools of Business. *Journal of Education for Business*, 70, October, 6-18.

Kalakota, R. S., & Whinston, A. B. (1993). The Future of Information Systems: Leadership Through Enterprise Integration. *Journal of Information Systems Education*, 5(1), Spring, 2-8.

Kettinger, W. J., Grover, V., Guha, S., & Segars, A. H. (1994). Strategic Information Systems Revisited: A Study in Sustainability and Performance. *MIS Quarterly*, 18(1), Spring 1994, 31-55.

Kim, K., Rhim, J. C., Henderson, W. C., Bizal, N. F., & Pitman, G. A. (1996). AACSB Accreditation: A Positive Signal in Accounting Job Markets. *Mid-Atlantic Journal of Business*, 32(2), June, 123-134.

Minnesota Economic Trends, Minnesota Department of Economic Security, Research and Statistics Office, St. Paul, MN (1995). *Minnesota Employment Projections*, 1995.

Smith, H. A. & McKeen, J. D. (1992). Computerization and Management: A Study of Conflict and Change. *Information & Management*, 22(4), 53-64.

Todd, P. A., McKeen, J. D., & Gallupe, R. B. (1995). The Evolution of IS Job Skills: A Content Analysis of IS Job Advertisements From 1970 to 1990. *MIS Quarterly*, 19(1), March, 1-27.

Weill, P., & Olson, M. (1989). Managing Investment Information Technology: Mini Case Examples and Implications. *MIS Quarterly*, 13(1), March, 3-18.

Zoffer, H. J. (1987). Accreditation Bends Before the Winds of Change. *The Educational Record*, 68, Winter, 43-44.

Chapter 16

Educating the Business Information Technologist: Developing a Strategic IT Perspective

John Mendonca
Purdue University, USA

The current business environment requires that all Information Technology (IT) professionals, not just managers, develop a strategic perspective toward their work. This chapter discusses the importance of that perspective for today's business information technologist and proposes a framework for teaching strategic IT to non-managers.

INTRODUCTION

The ways in which computers have been applied to business have evolved over the past forty years. It is convenient, albeit over-simplified, to describe that evolution in three over-lapping stages. This three-era model is commonly used to highlight changes in computer applications (Ward, 1996). The first era was dominated by a culture of automation—basically, computerizing labor-intensive manual processes. The next era emphasized the development and management of information systems, focusing on using data collection systems to create information useful to business managers. The third era—the one in which we now work—embraces IT as a valuable strategic resource and critical asset of the organization. Organizations expect IT to create new ways to compete, new products, new

Previously Published in *Managing Information Technology in a Global Economy* edited by Mehdi Khosrow-Pour, Copyright © 2001, Idea Group Publishing.

processes, new marketing channels, and even new organizational forms that promote "better-faster-cheaper."

Courses in management of information systems and technology, particularly leadership courses at the graduate level, have adapted to this new paradigm. These courses, designed for managers, regularly include management of information as a strategic resource and are amply supported by academic and professional literature. However, general undergraduate education in IT—that which produces the basic non-manager worker—continues to focus on producing programmers, systems developers, and systems analysts with first and second-era approaches to their work.

The demands on IT to deliver better-faster-cheaper require that all information technology workers adopt an entrepreneurial perspective consistent with third-era expectations. Organizations need more than traditionally educated programmers and analysts. They need business information technologists who understand such concepts as the organizational impact of IT, enterprise information architecture, enterprise application integration, rapid application development, and process re-engineering. A recent survey of 400 CEOs identified the most significant ways that IT delivers competitive advantage ("Competitve Edge," 2000). Many of these (for example, improved sharing and use of knowledge) require a strong strategic perspective for all IT workers.

This chapter explains the need for fostering a strategic information perspective for non-managers, proposes a framework for developing that perspective, and illustrates a practical application of the framework.

A STRATEGIC PERSPECTIVE

The context for discussing and pursuing "strategy" in IT has been developed primarily within the conceptual framework of Strategic Information Systems (SIS) and Strategic Information Systems Planning (SISP). Basically, a SIS is one that supports an organization's competitive strategy—that is, its strategy for gaining advantage over its competitors (Ward, 1996). An effective SIS is one that enables an organization to use information to exploit opportunities and thereby stay ahead of its competition in the marketplace. Chief Information Officers (CIOs), Chief Executive Officers (CEOs), Chief Technical Officers (CTOs) and other upper-level managers must have a strategic perspective for effective information resource planning, design, and implementation. However, to fully exploit the enabling value of IT as a deliverer of better-faster-cheaper, non-manager IT implementers must also embrace a strategic perspective.

Set within the framework of IT as a strategic resource, consider these realities that dominate the contemporary IT environment, and which are serious challenges to the pace and manner in which all IT workers work:

- The rapid pace at which new technologies (software and hardware) are introduced;
- The demand for expeditious development and implementation of new technologies, leading to new rapid development and implementation techniques;
- Development of non-procedural languages (visual and object-oriented programming);
- Telecommunications integrated into, and inseparable from, the computing environment;
- Modularization of hardware and software, emphasizing object assembly and processing (client-server computing); and
- Need for integration of seemingly incompatible diverse technologies.

The force behind these realities is the strategic use of IT. In response, an effective information technologist must adopt a strategic perspective that manifests itself in these work attributes:

- An appreciation of IT within the context of business value;
- A view of information as a critical resource to be managed and developed as an asset;
- A continuing search for opportunities to exploit information technology for competitive advantage;
- Uncovering opportunities for process redesign;
- Concern for aligning IT with organizational goals;
- A continuing re-evaluation of work assignments for added-value;
- Skill in adapting quickly to appropriate new technologies; and
- An object/modular orientation for technical flexibility and speed in deployment.

The challenge of developing a strategic perspective for the non-manager business information technologist is to find a simple framework that can be used to develop the necessary work attributes outside the context of SIS and SISP.

A PROPOSED FRAMEWORK

A beginning point for developing a strategic perspective might well be Porter's work on strategic management, particularly his and Millar's article on managing information for competitive advantage (Porter, 1985). Beyond this, the base of the framework is the "better-faster-cheaper" paradigm. It is an excellent characterization and summation of the concept "strategic" and provides a strong base. Because of its brevity and clarity, it is easily remembered and readily applied at the technical implementation level. Information technologists with a strategic perspective can not only use better-faster-cheaper as a standard for examining the value added by information technology activities, but also to uncover IT strategic opportunities. Building on the paradigm, the framework proposed here consists of the Value Chain business model (Porter, 1984), the Strategic Thrusts business model (Frenzel, 1999), and case analysis for application practice.

A note about Michael Porter's Competitive Forces model (Porter, 1980) which describes five competitive forces facing companies and is a staple for teaching strategic IT. Its value is limited for fostering a strategic perspective for non-managers. The model's inter-organizational perspective, its long-term focus and its complexity make it difficult to apply the simple better-faster-cheaper paradigm at a worker implementation level. Indeed, the model has been criticized for not reflecting the current fast-paced business environment because it does not include critical elements such as the importance of speed (first-to-market), and the digitization of products and product delivery (Downes, 1998).

A more appropriate model for non-managers, albeit one that was not designed as a framework for strategic initiatives, may be the Value Chain model. Also developed by Porter, it works well with the better-faster-cheaper construct partly because it is internally focused. The Value Chain concept has become a classic model for describing the primary collection of processes performed by businesses. It identifies five primary functions that form a linear flow through the business as inputs are converted to outputs and value is added at each step. The five functions are:

- inbound logistics;
- operations;
- outbound logistics;
- sales and marketing; and
- customer service.

While the Value Chain model focuses on processes, the Strategic Thrusts model focuses on kinds of value-adding activities that deliver better-faster-cheaper. First presented by Charles Wiseman and modified by Carroll Frenzel, the model relates strategic activities to six basic organizational thrusts:

- product and process differentiation,
- cost reduction,
- innovation,
- growth in market,
- alliances with other organizations, and
- time (first-to-market).

The integration of the two models provide a rich context for applying the better-faster-cheaper paradigm and uncovering strategic opportunities at a micro level. Working within the framework, information technologists who think strategically about their work might formulate questions such as the following: How can this work contribute to reducing costs (cheaper) in operations? For what functions does this work contribute better or faster or cheaper? How can I reduce development time in order to gain a time advantage (faster to market)?

CASE STUDIES

Developing a strategic perspective takes practice. Because different functions and thrusts may be combined in numerous ways, applying the framework to a variety of IT cases is important. Cases in which IT projects clearly contribute better-faster-cheaper should be contrasted with those in which IT activity does not play a strategic role—for example IT back-office functions that might consume resources but do not have strategic value. Cases can be examined both for successful completion of strategic IT efforts and for opportunities for strategic initiatives. Because the objective is to develop a strategic perspective for non-managers, applying the framework to smaller companies, where opportunities for individual contribution may be heightened, are especially valuable.

Real cases are relatively easy to find. Good sources for cases include texts, commercial and professional publications, vendor reports, and numerous websites serving the IT professional. Using the suggested framework, most IT cases can be analyzed for strategic elements, even when that is not the focus of the case or the intent of the author. Industry news magazines such as *Computerworld* and *Infoworld* are good sources for cases in which new technologies are being adopted by an organization or in thinking about how new technologies might be adopted for competitive advantage.

AN EXAMPLE APPLICATION

This section summarizes one application of the framework, a case that involves a small company. Rose Acre Farms is a family-run poultry egg producer based in Seymour, Indiana. The company's implementation of a Virtual Private Network (VPN) was reported by *PC Week Magazine* (Mullich, 1998).

As reported, Rose Acre Farms is a small business that turned to VPN technology pioneered by companies with powerhouse IT systems. The 50-year-old company has such a small staff that it didn't hire its first IT director until 1998. Roving managers are on the road, traveling among twenty-three farms to check flock health, making sure the chickens are properly fed, watered, and housed. Managers need to communicate with one another regularly, but attempts to communicate by telephone and written notes were time-consuming and inefficient. Although the company considered alternatives, it chose VPN as a solution because of its flexibility, quick installation, and cost. The installation costs for an Internet-based system, with email, was about $25,000.

Looking for better-faster-cheaper within the framework of the Value Chain and Strategic Thrusts models yields several observations about strategic benefits to Rose Acre Farms, including the following:
- Better-faster-cheaper is achieved in operations through faster communication among managers.

- Better-faster-cheaper is achieved in operations through better quality communications.
- Better-faster-cheaper is achieved in customer service through faster response time when problems occur.
- Better-faster-cheaper is achieved by uncovering alternative solutions that are effective and less expensive.
- Better-faster-cheaper is achieved through innovation—the VPN solution was not a common one at the time of implementation.
- Better-faster-cheaper is achieved through enabling Rose Acre Farms to overcome communications problems that could have been an impediment to its growth.

CONCLUSION

Having a strategic IT perspective is an important characteristic of today's business information technologist. The third-era view of IT as a strategic resource within a fast-paced, fast-changing competitive environment places the burden of strategic thinking on more than just higher-level IT managers and leaders. Education and practice for developing a strategic perspective is critical to meet the expectations of corporate leaders.

REFERENCES

The Competitive Edge (2000). *Computerworld Magazine*, August 21, p. 35.

Downes, L., and Chunka, M.(1998). *Unleashing the Killer App: Digital Strategies for Market Dominance*. Harvard Business School Press, Boston, MA, pp. 59-64.

Frenzel, C. W. (1999). *Management of Information Technology*. Course Technology, Cambridge, MA, pp. 39-40.

Mullich, J. (1998). *New Remote Access Recipes: Indiana chicken farm builds a VPN to tie together its 'Good Egg People,'* PC Magazine, Nov. 16.

Porter, M. E. (1980). *Competitive Strategy*. Free Press, New York.

Porter, M. E., and Millar, V. E. (1985). *How Information Gives You Competitive Advantage*. Harvard Business Review, July/August.

Speed-of-thought.com (2000). *Boeing soars into a Digital Future*. http://www.speed-of-thought.com/getting/explore_boering.html.

Ward, J. and Griffiths, P. (1996). *Strategic Planning for Information Systems*. John Wiley and Sons, London, pp. 10-24.

Chapter 17

Collaborative Ph.D. Examination

Mike Metcalfe and Samantha Grant
University of South Australia, Australia

In many universities, there is either no requirement for an oral examination or for examiners to guide Ph.D. candidates prior to submission of their thesis. This policy is usually the result of the "tyranny of distance" and/or the positivism philosophy of "impartial observer." This chapter argues for the Interpretivist approach of enriching the learning experience of examiner, candidate, supervisor and university by requiring the advantages of complex sustained interaction. Extensive evidence has shown that group learning is far more productive than individualistic learning. While individual universities need to make the resources argument for a more collaborative Ph.D. process, this chapter presents the management learning literature. It provides this literature in support of the argument that examiners need to be inter-actively involved with supervisors and examiners, especially in IS which changes rapidly and is experiencing a move from positive to interpretive methodologies.

INTRODUCTION

Many Information Systems (IS) schools are under pressure to change their Ph.D. supervision and examination practices. This has been discussed elsewhere with respect to the design of appropriate semi-structured first year programs (Wood Harper et al., 1999; Wood Harper et al., 1993; Metcalfe and Kiley, 2000; Lowry, 1997). This chapter looks at the examination process. As the writers are most familiar with the Australian system this will be used as the focus of this discussion.

Previously Published in *Managing Information Technology in a Global Economy* edited by Mehdi Khosrow-Pour, Copyright © 2001, Idea Group Publishing.

Many Australian Universities use the "tyranny of distance" or the positivism "impartial observer" arguments to encourage no interaction between candidate and examiners. An interpretive perspective concentrate's less on bias being a negative thing, rather it sees actor interaction bring about a deeper appreciation of a situation. Therefore, this paper argues that interaction between supervisors, examiners and candidates is important for effective learning of all parties, including the respective Universities. Of course, "fair" grading is essential, the issue is how to ensure the grading process become a learning system. Supporters of interpretivist knowledge gathering believe that the examination process will be considerably enriched if the examiners can appreciate the "richer" research picture by being involved in dialogue and collective thinking. This is especially true in a discipline like IS which changes rapidly and is experiencing a move from positive to interpretive methodologies. While there is a resources argument to be made this paper only address the "learning" literature.

Reasons for Change

One of main drivers for these arrangements to be re-considered is the enormous change in the demographics of students over the last two decades. For example, the number of students doing Ph.D.'s has increased dramatically. Schools, who in the past may have only had one or two Ph.D.'s, now, may have 10 or 20. The average age of a student has risen, with mature aged, experienced, managers returning to study. More students are enrolling in a Ph.D. that is very different from their initial studies, generally because the material they learnt as undergraduates is out of date. This is particularly true in IS where even the research methodologies suitable to their old studies may no longer be appropriate. There are more international students with a range of different skills derived from the undergraduate course structure of their first degree. More students are coming from industry, or doing their Ph.D. in conjunction with their industrial experience, where they are accustomed to producing brief reports with very different criteria to that required from academia. Furthermore, the motivations for doing a Ph.D. can be seen to be changing. For more and more IS workers the attraction of a Ph.D. is that it may help them move into international consulting. Fewer want it solely as a ticket for a tenured lecturer's job, or for some kind of life changing social experience. This changing environment combined with the Australian Federal Government's support for mass tertiary education means that the old, quaint if indulgent, academic style of voluntarily supervising "one or two" Ph.D.'s needs re-thinking.

Other drivers for change come from the globalisation of business and from the "humanisation" of business studies. International recruitment companies are demanding more standardised qualifications. With the dominance of American multinationals, it is their methods that are being seen as the norm. In addition to this, the more frequent meeting of international colleagues means more consultants are provided the opportunity to compare different educational, and examination styles. This highlights the newness of the Australian Universities arrangements, which were largely designed around the concept of "boating scripts back to the home country to be marked." Moreover, the contrasting effects of a monarchy versus republican perspective on students' rights become apparent. These issues can be considered cultural or ethical, and are typical of some of the problems raised by globalisation. A related one is that of dominant epistemology.

Epistemological Differences

Many people would acknowledge that the history of the United States has led it down a technological path supported by a positivist epistemology. In contrast, the socially turbulent history of Europe has made it more interested in the Critical Perspective and the social impacts of technology. This has given social enquiry more dominance along with its associated interpretive epistemology. Given the development of technology as an international effort, Ph.D. students in Information Systems are increasingly under moral pressure to be true to their personal preferred epistemology relative to the enquiry at hand. The days of being confined to a supervisor's, or a discipline's preferred epistemology are ending in IS. Indeed, considerable time and effort needs to be taken by students in identifying what knowledge gathering methods are convincing to them and seeking to align those with the demands of their research question. For an increasing number, maybe reflecting the learning from the discipline itself, the epistemological basis of the 'variables' measurement approach is questioned. The limits of enquiry that result from the statistical analysis of slight variations in variables while purposely-ignoring experience and context have been reached and exceeded. The complexity of organisations and the human issues that are involved in their functioning necessitate enquiry approaches that build new and revealing perspectives. Galliers (1991) lists fourteen research approaches, including laboratory experiments, field experiments, surveys, case studies, and action research, presently in use in Information Systems inquiries. Action (case) Research for example, as defined in IS involves researchers being involved in significant organisational changes, and having to deal with a range of very different stakeholders. Finding impartial, international examiners, who are aligned with the students preferred epistemology, is becoming increasingly hard.

LEARNING TO LEARN

Love and Street (1998) suggested that supervision be reframed as a "collaborative problem solving process... drawing on theories of counselling and conflict resolution." It is suggested here that we need to go further and include the examiner to become part of a strategic organisational learning system for Universities. This paper suggests that these issues, the need for greater openness and examiners' responsibility in education and the shortage of skilled supervisors, mean that it is time to re examine the supervisor and examiner's role. Moreover, a new system is required that uses what has been learnt from Argyris and Schon's (1996) reflective **group** learning ideas to ensure that the supervision and examination process provides learning not only to the student but also to the wider academic community. This means more than just individual supervisors and, examiners, but their employers, their Universities, and their peers. Group consensus is required to ensure the examiners are learning something useful not just deluding themselves they are learning from personal reflection.

The message in Argyris and Schon's (1996) work on "Organisational Learning" is that organisations have to design an organisational system that allows staff to learn to learn. This also applies to postgraduate supervisors and examiners. But learning not only needs to be made about the research topic itself (e.g., Information Technology) but also in the process of enquiry adopted by the student. This is not an "administrative efficiency" issue but one very relevant to the research topic. The way we enquire determines what we find. Supervisors and examiners need to learn how to direct enquiry. Managers, or examiners, working in isolation, unaccountable for their actions, getting no feedback from peers, are not functioning in a good learning environment. From Aristotle to Habermas through Hegel and Popper, the message has been that individuals need to have their personal impressions tested against a universal audience before it can be assumed to be useful knowledge.

Argyris and Schon (1996) are also supporters of the Action Research methodology. This term is used very differently across disciplines. In the Information Systems literature, it assumes the researcher is a full participant in a specific change project that includes a process of reflection. The argument (thesis, theory) and practice form a complementarity (see Baskerville and Wood-Harper, 1998); action (or practice) generates new/revised argument which in turn generates more practice. It is about learning from doing. The Ph.D. process itself can be seen as an Action Research project, with the supervisor and examiner as the researcher-consultants. The Ph.D. study is the action. Learning occurs because the researchers, and other stakeholders, reflect together both during and after the project. The absence of any reflection by all those involved would negate the learning. This supports the need for group learning as a continuous process.

Small Group Learning

Working in small groups provides an effective learning system preferable to working alone. This has been supported by numerous sources. Examples from a wide management literature include, for example, empirical research from tank crews performance to forecasting accuracy has found a good learning environment requires working in small groups, made up of one's peers in a equi-power relationship. This literature confirms, despite the rhetoric about committees, that small groups outperform individuals in both the generation and application of ideas. The Hollywood image of charismatic, lonely, inventors is not supported by history nor experimentation (Metcalfe, 1995). The argumentation literature in management also shows those decisions, problem solving and purpose setting only make sense through an explicit, human interactive, argumentative process, rather than by people working in isolation. Further support for group learning comes from the philosophy literature, simple examples coming from Butler (2000) and Aristotle (in *Rhetoric*) who argue that enquiry needs to be a social process, where knowledge has to be tested and constructed from interaction with a universal audience.

There is a range of possible interactive models for Ph.D. examination. At one extreme the supervisors and examiners could make up a small group, which oversees the recruitment, preparation, empirics and write up of a Ph.D.. Examiners should work closely with the supervisors and candidates throughout the candidature, so that all are equally responsible when candidate and committee make themselves available at a public viva (oral examination). This committee, which the literature on small groups suggests should not exceed 5 persons, may include supervisors able to help with technical, political and organisational issues. It may have people from other disciplines to ensure cross discipline learning. Given the increasing numbers of IS Ph.D. students, and the increasing use of small Doctoral Schools, this committee may be responsible for several candidates. The committee will need to meet at regular intervals and allocate tasks to members. Their main purpose is to learn about supervising and examining research, so some method of reflective learning is appropriate including a post-mortem of candidate's work. The public viva (oral) provides an important opportunity for one form of such reflection, very much in the Aristotelian tradition. This process has the added advantage of not only extending learning across disciplines but also makes the examiners, and supervisors more accountable for their advice. It is an important, if perhaps socially difficult, learning device.

At the other end of the spectrum of interactive models for Ph.D. examination is to only introduce the oral examination. This is common in most Universities around the world. Australia is an exception, but this is changing aided by developments in conferencing technology.

Replacing the Lone Scholar
The usual form of Ph.D. supervision and examination in Australia still involves Phillips and Pugh's (1987) lonely apprentice approach. This applies to the stu-

dents, supervisors and the examiners. Phillips and Pugh (1987) found that difficulties with supervisory skills were a real problem, one that constituted a considerable obstacle for many students. Supervisors will sometimes complain that students expect too much of them, yet the student often has few alternative sources of support. Moreover, it is unreasonable to expect one person to play the roles of academic expert, teacher, "hands-off" research manager, confidante and counsellor to a variety of personalities, some of which they might not always agree with or feel sympathetic towards. Sadly, some supervisors use the apprentice metaphor as an argument to justify their own unreasonable or sloppy behaviour towards students in their care. Students with two supervisors can sometimes fare better. However, if these two are not working closely together students can be placed in a tenable position where they cannot satisfy the conflicting demands of their supervisors.

A number of semi-structured programs for research students have appeared in some Australian universities in recent years. These do at least offer the opportunity for alternative sources of support for students, and an excuse for supervisors to talk to colleagues about the enquiry process. But many of these programs do not emphasise the social aspects of learning by group sharing of core competencies, found so essential for innovation (Lawson, 1999). This lack of group learning for students mirrors the lonely scholar, or individual assessment mind set which blocks experimentation with group learning. This is particularly unfortunate in the IS discipline in which group learning and teamwork are highly valued. While more and more supervisors are learning from students in seminar programs, it is unusual for examiners to be involved. Yet without this sort of social interaction it is hard for tacit knowledge about enquiry processes to be developed.

Objectivity

At the centre of the traditional Ph.D. examination system is an epistemology that assumes objective knowledge, including observer independence. A thesis becomes a "object," which can be impartially observed, and classified, by the impartial judge-examiner. In management enquiry and in IS enquiry in particular this perception is being questioned. For example, see Landry's (1995) definition of "the problem" which constructs the objective, subjective and constructionist view of "problems." In the constructionist view of a Ph.D., pretence of impartiality of the observer on what is observed is either naive or dangerous (see Broad and Wane, 1982). Examiners are not impartial, they are carefully selected to either be compliant, sympathetic or of one perspective. The clever candidate finds ways to informally engage possible examiners during candidature. So, rather than turn a blind eye to failures in the assumption of impartiality, it is preferable to be explicit about the examiner's obvious influence in the research process.

External examiners in Australia are often modelled on the Lords High Court approach. There is no oral examination, the examiners are not involved until "it's finished" making it difficult for them to participate constructively in the process. In many cases the rationale for their decision can be totally confidential. Not only does this make them unaccountable, but also it excludes them from the students', the supervisors' and their own learning process. It is understandable how Australian universities came to have this system given that they did not award Ph.D.'s until the 1950's. There are many professors in Australia whose career has benefited from having to go overseas to get a Ph.D. because none were available in Australia. Maybe as part of the 50 years celebration of Australian Universities awarding and examining their own Ph.D.'s, consideration could be given to using the systems adopted in more experienced countries. In the UK external examiners are only brought in at the end, but the oral examination at least provides some attempt for group learning and accountability. The US, which prides itself on its sense of equity and open contracts has been issuing Ph.D.'s for about 100 years longer than the UK and are the architects of the "every lecturer should have a Ph.D." culture. Much more use is made of the Ph.D. committees in the US, which includes the supervisors, the examiners (internal or external) and peers, from other disciplines. This guides the student from the start of candidature, and ends with a public (literally) defence of their thesis.

The purpose of gaining a Ph.D. includes more than merely producing "a book" or the confirming of the conclusions of one student's piece of research. Given the changing demographics mentioned earlier, especially the background of the candidates, the Ph.D. is starting to be seen more and more as "training" in research. In this role the candidate should receive supportive, directed, continuous feedback as an exemplar of how to learn. Again, given the constructionist view of research, and the subjective aspects of problems, Ph.D. candidates should be as concerned with becoming useful members of a research community and in that way influence what is considered a worthy future research problem.

An Open Learning System
Demands for a more democratic, group learning experience also come from the expectations of today's "students." Increasingly the students have several years of management experience of learning to design innovative and complex Information Systems in an organisational setting. These commercial settings can be comparable, if not better, learning experiences than some University departments. The practitioner coming to start a Ph.D. can have a lot more experience than the supervisors or examiners, both in large project management and publishing reports. Further, in a professional discipline, that is attempting to better inform practice, there is little sense in drawing people from their place of practice to

attend the University. The work place is where the phenomena to be observed reside. Asking managers to break their career in order to fit in with Universities' traditional science laboratory perceptions of education may result in a very bias sample. Rather, it may be more sensible to engage "consultant-candidates" in their work place and ask them if they wish to "reflect" on their work for their Ph.D. (Action Research). There will be exceptions; especially where the research is critical of organisational behaviour, but in most cases the research is not controversial to the organisations being studies.

So different is the modern IS Ph.D. from the historic hard science Ph.D. that even the traditional University language and selection criteria are irrelevant. The term's "student" and "supervisor" are inappropriate; they actually dissuade candidates from starting. Something like "candidate" and "academic mentor" may be better. The authors suspect the term "examiner" is less offensive as many practitioners fully understand the concept of having to come up to a client's requirements. The term examiner does describe the role well. However, the examiners have to be identified, be accountable for their decisions, and be required to defend (legally if necessary) their position. This is already being reflected in a change in the journal referee process for some journals. They publish submitted articles for public review on the Internet. The comments and names of referees, after the double blind review, are also published. This makes the authors and reviewers more accountable.

Despite their interest (or maybe as a result of it) in Critical Studies, in the UK vivas are common but usually behind closed doors. A more open contract system is at least advocated in the US. The literature on argumentation, from education (Crosswhite, 1996), from psychology, from research methodology, from philosophy (Walton, 1998), from decision-making (Myer and Seinbold, 1989) and from the problem solving domain (Neiderman and Desantis, 1995), suggests that public debate is most likely the best and fairest approach to learning. While a universal audience may not be achieved, it should be sought. Metcalfe (2000) presents the case for corporations using public debate or a 'mock court-room' when making major organisational changes. The same image can be used with the oral defence of research findings but maybe in this case the Royal Commission or European court system would be preferable. The candidate, having previously submitted the thesis for reading by the examiners (judges) starts by making a short summary of the thesis, which is then cross-examined by the judges. The academic supervisor assists the candidate but the student must independently present the viva. Last, the public can ask questions through the judges. To conclude, the judges confer and pronounce a verdict. This layout makes the examiners and the examination public. It also allows the candidate to present in two forms, so if there is some weakness in their written style they get a further chance with the oral.

CONCLUSION

It has been argued that examining a Ph.D. should be a learning experience for the candidate, supervisor and the examiner. Not just on the Ph.D. topic but also with respect to the process of enquiry, which is so important in determining what is learnt. Learning, in an organisational setting has been found to benefit from small group interaction, some would say it defines knowledge. It therefore seems logical to suggest that supervisors and examiners work more closely as a group. The United States often use a committee system that includes the examiners throughout the candidature. The arguments against this usually draw on an objectivity epistemology. This view of how knowledge is created which is most likely wrong, has caused numerous cases of fraud in the sciences, and is increasingly being dropped in social enquiry methodologies. The pretence of objectivity in examiners needs to be set aside. Examiners should be more involved through the whole Ph.D., so they can learn, not by un-validated self-reflection but rather by interaction with a universal audience. If this is not possible then at the very least oral examination should be used. It is about interactive learning. This is a much more reliable method of knowledge creation. What is good for student learning should also be good for academic learning. A public viva or oral examination, conducted under the rules of evidence used in Royal Commissions (in Australia) nicely contributes to this while also adding a touch of accountability. Overall the system should reflect a more open environment for both the students and the supervisors and examiners. Providing a collaborative learning process.

REFERENCES

Argyris, G. and Schon, D. (1996) *Learning Organisations II*, Addison Wesley, Mass.

Baskerville, R. and Wood-Harper, A.T. (1998). Diversity in Action Research Methods, *European Journal of Information Systems*, Vol.7, pp. 90-107.

Broad, W. and Wane, N. (1982). *Betrayers of the Truth*, Simon and Schuster, New York.

Butler T. (2000). Making Sense of Knowledge, *European Conference on Information Systems*, Vienna, 3-5 July.

Crosswhite J. (1996). *The Rhetoric of Reason*, University of Wisconsin Press.

Galliers, R. D. (1991). Choosing appropriate information systems research approaches: a revised taxonomy, In H-E Nissen, R. A. Hirschheim, & H. K. Klein (Eds.), *The information systems research arena of the 90s*. IFIP 8.2 Workshop, Copenhagen, Denmark, 14-16 December, 1990. Amsterdam, The Netherlands: North Holland.

Lawson, C. (1999). Towards a Competence Theory of the region, *Cambridge Journal of Economics,* Vol. 23, pp. 151-166.

Landry, M. (1995). A Note on the Concept of problem, *Organization Studies,* 16(2), pp. 315-343.

Love, A. and Street, A. (1998). Supervision and Collaborative Problem-solving, *3rd Quality in Postgraduate Education Conference,* Adelaide, April.

Lowry, G. R. (1997). Postgraduate Research Training for Information Systems: Improving Standards & Reducing Uncertainty, *Eighth Australasian Conference on Information Systems*, Australian Computer Society, Adelaide, pp. 191-202.

Meyers, R.A. and Seibold, D.R. (1989). Perspectives on Group Argument, *Communications Yearbook*, Vol. 14, pp. 268-302.

Metcalfe, M. (1995). Decision-Making in Small Groups, *International Journal of Computer and Engineering Management*, 3(1), pp. 40-54.

Metcalfe, M., forthcoming (2000). Multiviews II and Argument, *European Conference on Information Systems,* Vienna, July.

Metcalfe, M. and Kiley, M. (2000). Arguing for Ph.D. Coursework, *Australian Journal of Information Systems*, Vol. 7, pp. 52-59.

Niederman, F. and Desantis, G. (1995). The Impact of the Structured Argument Approach on Group Problem Formulation, *Decision Sciences*, 26(4), pp. 451-474.

Phillips, E. M. & Pugh, D. S. (1987). *How to get a Ph.D.* Milton Keynes, Open University Press, United Kingdom.

Walton, D. (1998). *The New Dialectic*, University Press, Toronto.

Wood-Harper, T. et al. (1993). Designing Research Education in Information Systems, In Khosrow-Pour, M., and Loch, K., (Eds.), *Global Information Technology Education: Issues and Trends.* Harrisburg, Pennsilvania, USA: Idea Group Publishing.

Wood-Harper, T., Metcalfe, M., Robbins-Jones, T. and Hughes, J. (1999). Designing a Unique Australian Research Education in Information Systems: Towards a Global View, *Australasian Conference on Information Systems - ACIS99*, Wellington, New Zealand, December.

ACKNOWLEDGMENTS

The authors would like to thank Dr. Glen Lowry for his valuable comments on this chapter.

Chapter 18

Information Systems and Computer Science Model Curricula: A Comparative Look

Anthony Scime'
State University of New York College at Brockport, USA

Computer science and information systems are interrelated disciplines that both cover the technical and functional aspects of computing. They are fields of study in high demand by students and employers. Yet, many colleges do not have the resources to offer multiple computing departments. So, professional organizations have developed model curriculums to help define the knowledge necessary for information technology majors. This chapter provides a discussion of model IS and CS curricula. It is hoped that IT departments will be able to develop an information technology curriculum, which suits their student's needs.

INTRODUCTION

Computer science, information systems, and management information systems are in high demand. Industry needs the graduates. The shortage of qualified information technology specialist is well known. Students want an information technology education to be able to fill the demand.

The demand for information technology (IT) workers will not decrease in the near future. It is fueled by the decrease in physical size of IT hardware, the decrease in price of information technology hardware and software, and the in-

Previously Published in *Managing Information Technology in a Global Economy* edited by Mehdi Khosrow-Pour, Copyright © 2001, Idea Group Publishing.

crease in performance, reliability, and flexibility. These affordability factors have caused IT to become critical to business operations and personal daily activities. This demand is not limited to the United States, the raising world wide demand is pushing the shortage to a global problem (Freeman & Aspray, 1999; Watson, Taylor, Higgins, Kadlec & Meeks, 1999).

All organizations today depend on information technology. Computers and information systems are essential to business and government. The information itself is a resource similar to finances, personnel, material, and equipment, which must be managed. To effectively management information requires technical knowledge of hardware, software, and information production, distribution, and integration. Therefore, the information technologist requires both technical and organizational knowledge (Davis, Gorgone, Couger, Fienstein & Longnecker, 1997; IRMA, 1999; Freeman et al., 1999).

WHAT IS INFORMATION TECHNOLOGY

Information technology involves the "design, development, implementation, support or management of computer-based information systems, particularly software applications and computer hardware (ITAA, 1997)." An IT worker is someone who performs at least one of those activities as 50% of their job. IT workers can be further classified into one of four categories: conceptualizers developers, modifiers, and supporters (Freeman et al., 1999).

Conceptualizers are workers involved with the conception of the basic nature of an IT system or part of an IT system. Developers are people who specify, design, construct, and test IT. The workers who modify information technology work with existing hardware or software. Finally, there are those who support the existing systems by delivering, installing, operating, maintaining, or repairing. Undergraduate institutions should emphasize preparing students to work as developers, modifiers, or supporters or for further education to become conceptualizers.

IT is not a homogeneous field, it has many different and diverse academic and professional origins. IT uses as reference disciplines mathematics, management and engineering (Denning, 1998; Freeman et al., 1999; Myers & Beise, 1999; Watson et al., 1999). Depending on the interests of academic faculty the IT major originated from one of three reference disciplines. In business, computers were first used in accounting departments to track accounts receivable and accounts payable. This quickly led to university business departments investigating computing as it applied to management control and accounting. Mathematicians found the algorithmic and logical nature of programs to be a resurrection of these fields of mathematics. Mathematics departments began investigations into the theoretical aspects of software. Electrical engineering is of course necessary to construct the hardware components of the computer. From the academic perspective, computing may have originated in the business department focusing on information systems, the mathematics department focusing on software, or in electrical engineering as computer engineering. IT is now an umbrella-term for the fields of computer engineering, computer science, software engineering, information systems, and management information systems.

INFORMATION TECHNOLOGY DEPARTMENTS

The rise of IT and the variation of business and technical emphasis has lead to many program names. Even with different schools calling programs by different names, most IT programs teach students the following areas: develop hardware or software, maintain information systems in organizations, and provide information services (Denning, 1999; Freeman et al., 1999).

To help schools and departments develop appropriately structured curriculums professional organizations, particularly the Association of Computing Machinery (ACM), in conjunction with the Computing Society of the Institute of Electrical and Electronic Engineers (IEEE-CS); the Information Resources Management Association (IRMA) in conjunction with the Data Administration Management Association (DAMA); and the Association for Information Systems (AIS), in conjunction with the ACM and the Association of Information Technology Professionals (AITP) have developed model curricula. Model curricula have also been developed by other organizations, in particular the Information Systems-Centric Curriculum (ISCC) committee. This chapter provides a comparison of model curricula. From these models, computing departments should be able to develop an IT curriculum, which suits their particular needs.

TOPICS COVERED IN INFORMATION TECHNOLOGY

Information Technology consists of various technical topics, which the curriculum models address. Topics range from a theoretical understanding of computing through the design of practical applications. These topics collectively represent the body of IT technical knowledge expected of bachelor's degree IT graduates.

- Use of Software Tools - Practice and theory in the use of software development tools to construct small decision-making systems.
- Overview of IS - A survey of information systems specifically their business application and effect on society.
- Operating Systems - Control mechanisms for the execution of computer programs in an environment of multiple resources.
- Architecture - Computer organization for the implementation of processors, memory, communications, and software interfaces.

- Programming, Languages, Algorithms and Data Structures - Design and construction of application programs using computer languages.
- Networking - Hardware and software data communication concepts and the design, development, and management of computer networks.
- Systems Analysis and Design - The analysis and specification of requirements and the design and development of the system.
- Database and Information Retrieval - The modeling and implementation of databases.
- Project Management - Planning and management of complex software development projects.
- Artificial Intelligence, Robotics, and Decision Support - Design, development, and management of systems that support decisions.
- Ethics - A survey of the legal and moral issues of computer and system usage.
- Internship or Design Project- An opportunity to apply classroom knowledge in a professional setting.

These topics were derived from a collective analysis of the curriculum models. Each of the model's courses was then assigned to the topic most closely matching the course. This provides for a comparison of courses across models as shown in Table 1.

The table does not discuss the depth of knowledge or imply equivalence between the courses. It only shows the coverage by course of the topics. For example, the Systems Analysis and Design topic has one course from ACM's CS, and the IRMA/DAMA models and two courses from the IS '97, and ISCC '99 models. All of these courses discuss elements of requirements analysis and systems design.

It is possible that topics in a model are covered in courses of the model but not specifically identified as such a course. For example, the ethics of computing in the IS '97 and IRMA/DAMA models may be discussed in Overview of IS courses, whereas, the ISCC '99 model has two specific half-courses.

INFORMATION RESOURCES MANAGEMENT MODEL

Information Systems (IS) is the combining of business and computer science. As a discipline it is composed of two parts: information management and systems development. The acquisition, deployment, and management of information technology resources and services are studied in the information management portion. The development and evolution of technology infrastructures is the focus of the systems development portion (Davis et al., 1997).

The Information Resources Management Association's (IRMA) IRMA/DAMA 2000 model has a business approach to IS. Taking a top down approach to IS education this model stresses learning general principles before specific implementation details. Specifically, programming is left to the third course after the concept of information as a resource is well understood.

Table: Comparison of Courses to Topics (electives in Italics)

Topic	IRMA/DAMA 2000[1]	AIS '97	ISCC '99	ACM-CS[6]
Software Tools		IS'97.P0 Knowledge Work Software Tool Kit[3,4] IS'97.2 Personal Productivity with IS Technology[3,4]		
Overview of IS	IRM1 - IRM Principles[2] IRM2 - Information Systems Technology *IRM 8 - Global Information Management* *IRM10 – Selected Topics in IRM*	IS'97.1 Fundamentals of IS[3,4] IS'97.3 Information Systems Theory and Practice[4]	ISCC-11 Information Systems in Enterprises ISCC-44 Dynamics of Change	
Architecture		IS'97.4 Information Technology Hardware and Software		CS 201 Introduction to Computer Systems CS 301 Computer Organization and Assembly Language CS 306 Architecture
Operating Systems				CS 302 Software Systems CS 305 Operating Systems
Programming, Languages, Algorithms and Data Structures	IRM3 - Algorithm Concepts and Information Management	IS'97.5 Programming, Data and Object Structures[4]	ISCC-21& Information Systems Architecture I ISCC-31 Information Systems Architecture II	CS 101 Intro to Computing I CS 102 Intro to Computing II CS 202 Analysis and Design of Algorithms CS 304 Programming Lang.
Networking	*IRM 7 - Communication Technology and Information Management*	IS'97.6 Networks and Telecommunications	ISCC-43 Telecommunications and Networking Issues/Methods ISCC-51 Distributed Systems	
Systems Analysis and Design	IRM6 - IRM Design and Implementation	IS'97.7 Analysis and Logical Design of an IS[4] IS'97.9 Physical Design and Implementation with a Programming Environment	ISCC-42 Human Computer Interaction and Methods ISCC-53 Comprehensive Enterprise Information Systems Engineering	CS 303 Software Engineering
Database and Information Retrieval	IRM5 - Data Resource Structures and Administration	IS'97.8 Physical Design and Implementation with DBMS	ISCC-41 Information Databases and Transaction Processing	
Project Management		IS'97.10 Project Management and Practice		
Artificial Intelligence, Robotics, Decision Support	IRM4 – Data Warehousing, Data Mining, and DSS *IRM 9 - Executive Information Systems Management*		ISCC-45 Applications of AI in Enterprise Systems	
Ethics			ISCC-22 Ethics I[5] ISCC-52 Ethics II[5]	
Internship or Design Project			ISCC-61 Comprehensive Collaborative Project	*CS Design Elective*

1. The IRMA/DAMA model requires the selection of an elective.
2. Course recommended for all business students.
3. Courses recommended for all students.
4. Courses part of the minor program.
5. This is a half-course.
6. Includes 6 concentration electives, not shown.

Figure 1: Information Resource Management Model

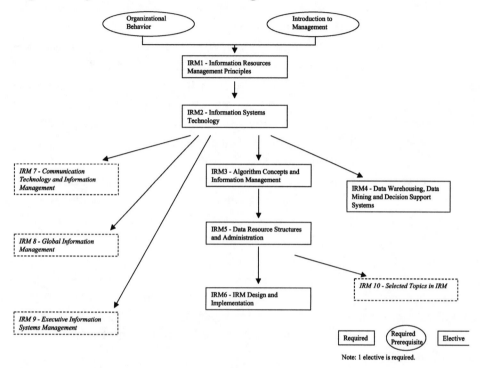

Note: 1 elective is required.

Central to the IRMA/DAMA curriculum is the recognition of information as the major organizational asset. This preparation for an IT profession revolves around the application of IT to business problems. Effective verbal and written communication, time management, leadership, and delegation of authority skills are stressed in this program.

The proposed curriculum consists of 10 courses of which the student must complete 7, 6 required and 1 elective selected from the remaining five (IRMA, 1999). The traditional application programming, systems programming, and computer hardware is de-emphasized. How information is used in decision-making and how information effects the various components of a business are the basis of the courses. The elective courses provide management refinement and specialization (IRMA, 1999). See Figure 1 and Table 1.

INFORMATION SYSTEMS '97 MODEL

The Association for Information Systems (AIS) Model Curriculum for Information Systems, IS' 97, provides for the technical aspects in information systems as well as a foundation in business processes. The AIS's model comes from a body of knowledge developed "from surveys of practitioners and academics" (Davis et al., 1997).

This model is strong in fundamental computing and information systems knowledge. The curriculum is divided into three components. The first level stresses the development of small office and personal systems, the effective use of organizational systems, and the identification of a quality system. The second part specializes in the technology; courses in the hardware and the software of information technology, software programming, and systems analysis and design. Emphasizing teamwork in systems design, development, and project management is the final portion (Davis et al., 1997). This three level structure allows students to leave the program and still have obtained an organized body of knowledge, and perhaps a minor, in information systems.

The curriculum is divided into ten required courses and one prerequisite (IS'97.P0). The prerequisite course provides students basic knowledge in office applications. There are no specified technical electives.

Because IS professionals need to be able to communicate within a business organization effectively, courses in communications, quantitative and qualitative analysis, and organizational functions are necessary. Courses outside of IT are also necessary to provide technical background and breadth in business functions. Therefore, non-technical required, but not specified, courses include courses in communications, mathematics, and business functions (Davis et al., 1997). See Figure 2 and Table 1.

Figure 2: Information Systems '97 Model

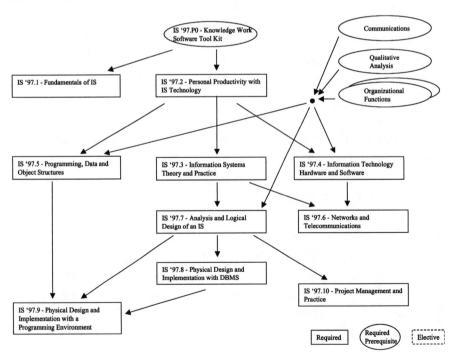

INFORMATION SYSTEMS-CENTRIC CURRICULUM '99

A collaborative Academe/Industry Task Force has developed a third model known as the Information Systems-Centric Curriculum '99 (ISCC '99). It is heavy in ethics and practical skills. The authors are seeking the endorsement of the AIS, the ACM, and the IEEE (Lidtke, Stokes, Haines & Mulder, 1999).

This curriculum looks at information as an enterprise asset, which must be managed. The management is accomplished through large-scale, complex information systems. It is the building of complex systems that takes precedence in this curriculum. This is an engineering development approach to information systems. However, it does not exclude interpersonal skills, which are necessary in the teamwork environment of systems development.

The key components of the ISCC'99 curriculum are the close relationship with industry and education through teamwork. By using innovative pedagogical techniques such as teaming, just-in-time learning, and guy by the side, the courses place students into an active learning role. The last course is a project that comes from an industrial sponsor of the program.

Figure 3: Information Systems-Centric Model

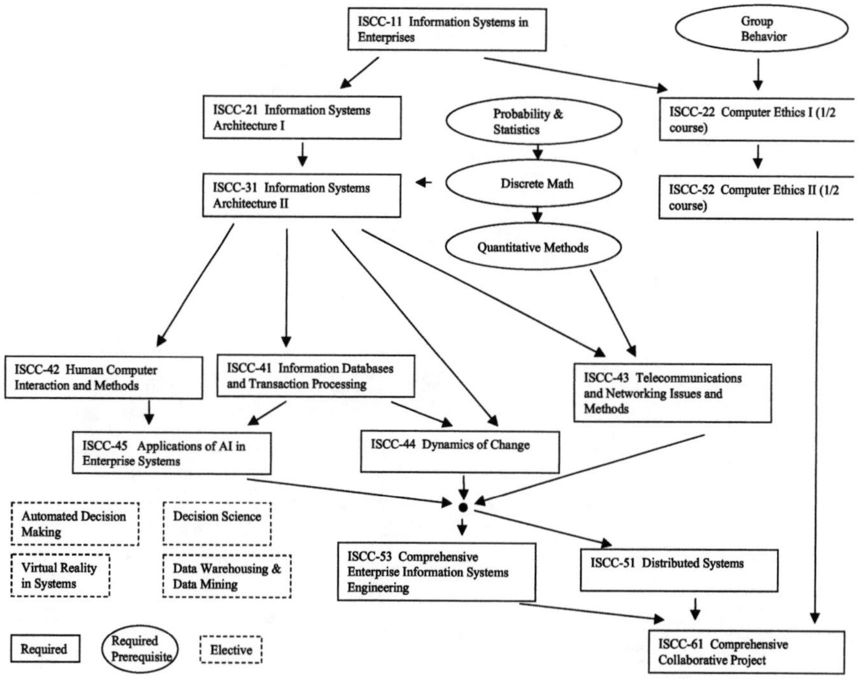

The curriculum consists of 11 full courses and 2 half courses as well as 4 required foundation courses. The model also contains 4 technical electives and identifies a number of non-technical courses to bring in business aspects such as economics, project management, and business functions. The model encourages students to include in their studies courses that require interpersonal, systemic thinking, and problem solving skills (Lidtke et al., 1999). See Figure 3 and Table 1.

COMPUTER SCIENCE

In 1991, the ACM and IEEE-CS published computing curricula models for computer science (Tucker, Barnes, Aieken, Barker, Bruce, Cain, Conry, Engel, Epstein, Lidtke, Mulder, Rogers, Spafford & Turner, 1991). The method used was to divide the material considered important in computing into concepts known as knowledge units.

The recombination of knowledge units allows creation of multiple courses and curriculums from the same body of knowledge. The ACM/IEEE-CS task force created 12 different curricula. All the curricula have a heavy programming emphasis. We will consider here only the Computer Science program meeting the accreditation requirements of ABET and CSAC (Tucker et al., 1991). Engineer-

Figure 4: Computer Science Model

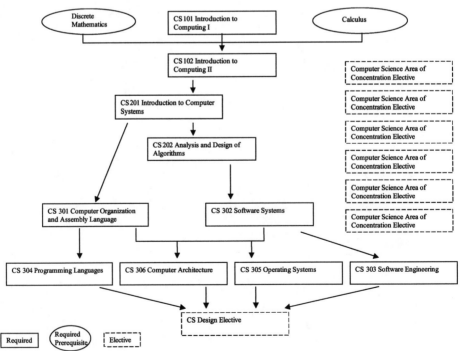

ing programs in the United States are accredited by the Accreditation Board of Engineering and Technology (ABET). The nationally recognized accreditation organization for computer science is the Computer Science Accreditation Commission (CSAC).

Mathematics plays a strong part in all the curricula, but most of the courses are not specified. None of the programs has a requirement for business courses. However, there is recognition for the need for humanities, the social sciences, and communication skills.

The curriculum consists of 16 courses: 10 required, 6 concentration electives and a design elective. The required concentration may be in software engineering, multiprocessing, knowledge-based systems, or a similar area. The program is capped with a design course (Tucker et al., 1991). See Figure 4 and Table 1.

SIMILARITIES AND DIFFERENCES

The CS model begins with programming courses in a higher order language. The inverted curricula proposed by the IRMA, AIS, and ISCC present at least one course that establishes a foundation in information technology before focusing on the more narrow aspects of IT. The introductory course serves two purposes. First, it provides an introduction to the field for potential majors. Second, it serves as an overview to the field for other majors. It provides the non-major with an understanding of IT and acts as a gateway for majors and minors (Freeman et al., 1999).

Most new students do not know the difference between the computing fields and typically start in computer science. With the introductory course as programming, there are high attrition rates; and it becomes a rite of passage course (Freeman et al., 1999; Shaekelford & LeBlanc, 1994). This can present a problem with switching majors from computer science to information systems. These students have already completed courses, specifically programming, which come latter in the IS curricula. These transfer problems need to be worked out between the programs at individual schools.

The four models represent a continuum of the reference disciplines from business to mathematics (Figure 5). IRMA/DAMA provides a business management approach to IT education. This model treats information as a business resource, which needs efficient and effective management. To manage the information it is necessary to manage the production and storage tools (hardware and software) and to understand the business needs.

The AIS model provides for both the business and technical aspects of IT. The structure recognizes that some IT knowledge is important to everyone. Course sequences are provided for all college students and IS minors as well as IS majors. The building nature of these sequences allows students to start slowly and continue or switch majors without loss of effort.

Figure 5: Business Mathematics Continuum

Business   Mathematics

IRMA   IS '97   ISCC '99   ACM CS

The ISCC '99 model is oriented toward large-scale system design and implementation. This model stresses the need for teamwork in problem identification and solution. The focus is on the construction of the tools necessary for information management.

The ACM computer science model has no business component. The courses focus on programming and the architecture of the computer. The approach is the most theoretical. Programming related courses comprise nearly a third of the computer science implementation. Architecture and operating systems comprise another third. The final third are electives in an area of concentration.

The IRMA/DAMA, ISCC, and ACM models contain elective courses. The ACM model in computer science requires that the electives form a technical area of concentration. The AIS model recommends additional courses in business to complete the curriculum. Each model also requires prerequisite work in mathematics.

The standard college education is based on an eight-semester sequence of courses. The courses provide for a general education and specialization in one particular field - the major. The courses in the major are generally interleaved with the general education requirements. This allows students an opportunity to explore different fields and select an appropriate major. Therefore, the number of semesters to complete the major courses may be less than eight.

	Required Courses	Required Prerequisites	Specified Electives	Minimum Semesters to Complete
IRMA/DAMA 2000	7[1]	1[2]	4	5
AIS - IS '97	10	4[3, 4]	---	6[4]
ISCC '99	12[5]	4	4	7
ACM - CS	17[1]	2	7	7

- Includes required electives.
- May be Organizational Behavior or Introduction to Management.
- Specific organizational functional courses are not specified; this table assumes one such course.
- Includes computing prerequisite.
- The two ethics courses (ISCC-21 and ISCC-52) are half courses and counted as one here.

Table 2 Number of Courses and Semesters

The courses in the major are normally arranged is a hierarchical, prerequisite structure. This provides for increased depth of knowledge as the student's education proceeds. For the curriculum to be do-able, it must fit into the 8-semester time frame.

The IRMA/DAMA model is designed to start in the third year. If the prerequisite business courses are completed in the first two years, the model requires at least five more semesters to complete the required courses. This is a problem because the student has only four semesters left. However, if the IRMA/DAMA program is started in the fourth semester (2nd year) this problem is resolved. Because the model also suggests the first course (IRM 1) be part of all business majors this is not a serious problem.

The IS '97 model is a six semester sequence of courses. This includes one semester for the prerequisite computer literacy course (IS'97.P0). It is expected many new students will come to college with these computer literacy skills and be able to complete the IS '97 curriculum in five semesters. Plus, this model identified 2 courses for all students and a 5 course minor beyond the prerequisite. With this philosophy there is no loss of effort on changing majors.

The ISCC '97 and ACM CS models, including prerequisite courses, comprise a seven-semester sequence. This leaves little slack for entering the program late without extending beyond four years.

CONCLUSION

All of these models have good points. Most schools will not be able to adapt a model in its entirety. Rather each school needs to assess its educational philosophy and student needs to choose and modify the model best for them. By closely following a model the school's prospective students, student's potential employers, and graduate schools know the type of education received by the graduates. The school administration is assured that the IT department is providing a recognized curriculum, which covers all the central topics of information technology. Although the models differ in emphasis, businesses will need information technologist from each of the models presented here.

Each of these models is under continuous review. IRMA/DAMA updated their model in 2000. AIS expects to update in 2000, as well. The ACM expects to publish a new set of models in early 2001 (ACM, 2000). IRMA/DAMA's most recent draft is available at http://gise.org/IRMA-DAMA-2000.pdf. AIS is currently collecting data and comments over the World Wide Web at http://www.IS2000.org/. The ISCC's Web site http://www.iscc.unomaha.edu includes an opportunity to comment on the model.

REFERENCES

Association of Computing Machinery (ACM) (2000). *Computing Curricula 2001* (CC2001), (2000) The Joint Task Force on Computing Curricula IEEE Computer Society and Association of Computing Machinery, March 2000 (Draft).

Davis, G. B., Gorgone, J. T., Couger, J. D., Fienstein, D. L., & Longnecker, H. E. (1997). *IS'97 Model Curriculum and Guidelines for Undergraduate Degree Programs in Information Systems*. Association for Information Systems.

Denning, P. J. (1998). Computer Science and Software Engineering: Filing for Divorce?, *Communications of the ACM*, 40 (8) p 128.

Denning, P. J. (1999). Our Seed Corn is Growing in the Commons, *Information Impacts Magazine*, March 1999; http://www.cisp.org/imp/march_99/denning/03_99denning.htm (retrieved Sep 19, 2000).

Freeman, P. and Aspray, W. (1999). *The Supply of Information Technology Workers in the United States*; Computing Research Association, Washington D.C.

Information Resources Management Association (IRMA) (1999). IRMA/DAMA Curriculum Model, IRMA, Hershey; http://gise.org/IRMA-DAMA-2000.pdf; (retrieved Nov 15, 1999).

Information Technology Association of America (ITAA) (1997). *Help Wanted: The Workforce Gap at the Dawn of a New Century*, Arlington, VA, p. 9.

Lidtke, D. K., Stokes, G. E., Haines, J., and Mulder, M. C. (1999). *ISCC'99 An Information Systems-Centric Curriculum '99 Program Guidelines for Educating the Next Generation of Information Systems Specialists, in Collaboration with Industry*.

Myers, M. E., & Beise, C. M. (1999). Recruiting IT Faculty, *Communications of AIS*, 2 (13).

Shaekelford, R. L. and LeBlanc, R. J. (1994). Integrating "Depth First" and "Breadth First" Models of Computing Curricula, *Selected Paper of the Twenty-Fifth Annual SIGCSE Symposium on Computer Science*, New Orleans; pp 6 - 10.

Tucker, A. B., Barnes, B. H., Aieken, R. M., Barker, K., Bruce, K. B., Cain, J. T., Conry, S. E., Engel, G. L., Epstein, R. G., Lidtke, D. K., Mulder, M. C., Rogers, J. B., Spafford, E. H., and Turner, A. J. (1991). *Computing Curricula 1991: Report of the ACM/IEEE-CS Joint Curriculum Task Force*, Association of Computing Machinery.

Watson, H. J., Taylor, K. P., Higgins, G., Kadlec, C., & Meeks, M. (1999). Leaders Assess the Current State of the IS Academic Discipline, *Communications of AIS*, 2 (2).

Chapter 19

E-Commerce Curriculum Development and Implementation

Linda V. Knight and Susy S. Chan
DePaul University, USA

The very nature of e-commerce requires a rapid, flexible approach to curriculum development. This chapter describes a successful model for the design and development of an e-commerce curriculum, and chronicles the experiences of DePaul University's School of Computer Science, Telecommunications, and Information Systems in developing an e-commerce master's degree. Eight key principles for universities seeking to embark on a new e-commerce curriculum are identified. The chapter updates earlier work presented at the 2000 Information Resources Management Association Conference (Knight & Chan).

BACKGROUND

In an Internet age, a university must respond quickly to external changes. It is no longer appropriate, at least not in the e-commerce arena, to agonize at length over curriculum changes. The very nature of e-business demands flexible and rapid curriculum development to keep pace with rapid changes, not just in technologies, but in business models and the external competitive environment as well. This chapter chronicles the experiences of DePaul University's School of Computer Science, Telecommunications, and Information Systems in meeting that challenge.

Previously Published in *Challenges of Information Technology Management in the 21st Century* edited by Mehdi Khosrow-Pour, Copyright © 2000, Idea Group Publishing.

The DePaul experience indicates that it is possible for a university, even a large one with over twenty-one thousand students, to move quickly and effectively in curriculum development. The entire e-commerce master's curriculum was developed and approved, students admitted and the program launched within just seven months. In February of 1999, two DePaul faculty members first considered the idea of developing an e-commerce related master's degree. By March 1999, a design team was formed, the underlying curriculum design principles were determined, the background research was conducted, and the courses were defined. Shortly thereafter, in April 1999, the appropriate committees within the school met and approved the plan. In May 1999, the school's faculty approved the degree. In June 1999, the entire university faculty and the university president approved the program. In September 1999, the first fifty students enrolled in the program. Enrollment grew steadily to reach about 400 majors within the program's second year.

DePaul University in Chicago was not the only university to pioneer e-commerce programs. For example, Claremont Graduate University in California, Carnegie Mellon University in Pittsburgh, Creighton University in Omaha, Marlboro College in Vermont, and National University in San Diego all were among the first to offer such master's degrees (Memishi, 1999). In addition to degree programs, many schools offer certificates or concentrations in the area. Some institutions, including Stanford University and Harvard University, have opted not to separate e-commerce from their traditional programs, but instead to include e-commerce coverage in their existing curricula (Memishi, 1999). Among universities offering degrees in e-commerce, the vast majority of programs are offered through business schools, rather than through schools of computer science, information science, engineering, or technology (Knight, 2001).

The growing number of e-commerce degrees is based solidly in the growth of e-commerce itself. According to Forrester Research Inc. (2001), global Internet business will reach nearly $6.8 trillion in 2004, up from $657 billion in 2000. The rapid growth of e-commerce has resulted in an increased demand for e-commerce IT professionals. In Computerworld's Annual Technology Skills Survey, 30% of the 307 participating IT managers indicated that they would hire or retrain staff for Internet applications development in the year 2001, with 28% saying that they would hire or retrain for e-commerce application development (Goff, 2000). According to the same study, Web-based applications, including supplier-facing, customer-facing, industry exchange, and marketplace systems are among the top IT agenda items for 2001. Despite the decline of the dot-coms, high demand IT jobs continue to include Internet and intranet developers (Radcliff, *IT Jobs*, 2001), while high demand skills continue to include those central to much Web information system development: HTML, Visual Basic, Java, and Active Server Pages (Radcliff, *Hot Skills*, 2001).

A MODEL FOR E-COMMERCE CURRICULUM DESIGN

In this model, the curriculum is based upon two sets of guiding principles: student learning goals and curriculum design principles. These are the most crucial elements of the model, and they are discussed in detail in the next two sections. In addition, the model shows substantial input into the curriculum coming from IS faculty, students and business practitioners, as well as three major IS model curricula.

The Information Resources Management Association / Data Administration Managers Association 2000 Curriculum Model (Cohen, 2000), the IS '97 Curriculum, and the Information Systems-Centric Curriculum '99 (ISCC '99) are model curricula for undergraduate IS programs. Nonetheless, they identify many significant considerations for a graduate level e-commerce curriculum, including the importance of industry input, ties to future employment, timely curriculum updates, technical skills, oral and written communication skills, team skills, and appreciation for information's role as a strategic asset, as well as the business purposes and organizational context of IT systems (Knight & Chan, 2001). Beyond the model curricula, practitioners should provide substantial input into the e-commerce curriculum. They play a particularly crucial role in insuring that the curricu-

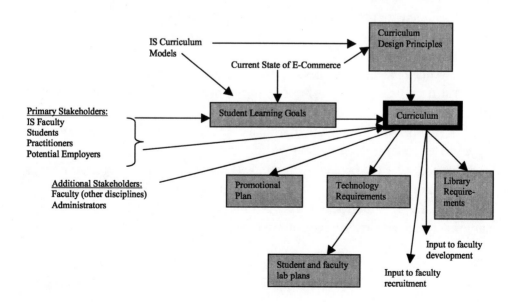

lum accurately represents the current state of e-commerce. Universities embarking on a new e-commerce curriculum should develop close working relationships with key players in the e-commerce arena before beginning to think about a curriculum. As guest lecturers, clients for student projects, sponsors for student internships, and adjunct faculty, they can come to know the school and its students. Students too are key stakeholders in any new curriculum. For DePaul's MS in E-Commerce Technology, students' active support of existing e-commerce classes, closing every section every quarter, provided internal support for the very suggestion of an expanded e-commerce program. In addition, master's students working in the field provided valuable insight into the needs of local employers.

CURRICULUM DESIGN PRINCIPLES

Perhaps the most significant element of the model is the underlying curriculum design principles. DePaul's MS in E-Commerce Technology followed these five underlying principles:

1.   Expose students to a broad and ever changing mix of technologies, programming languages, and tools. Reasoning: The Internet has few dominant technologies, and those that do appear to be dominant today may change tomorrow.

2.   Build in program flexibility for adapting rapidly to future changes in either technologies or industry norms. Reasoning: E-commerce as a discipline is in a constant state of change. One of the major curriculum challenges is to anticipate what master's students will need to know when they graduate two years hence. This requires the active use of feedback loops throughout the e-commerce curriculum development model.

3.   Emphasize practicums and application development for real clients in an authentic e-commerce environment. Reasoning: E-commerce, by its very nature must be an applied curriculum.

4.   Anticipate industry needs and forge a long-term partnership with e-commerce leaders. Reasoning: Business contacts are crucial for keeping the program in sync with a rapidly changing environment.

5.   Emphasize the integration of business strategies, development methodology, and technologies throughout the curriculum. Do not isolate technology in separate courses from business principles. Reasoning: E-commerce stimulates the integration of technology solutions while building a bridge between strategy formulation and solution development. Students should learn e-commerce in the same integrated fashion in which they will practice it.

STUDENT LEARNING GOALS

Student learning goals are both technical and managerial in nature because successful implementation of e-commerce solutions requires an understanding of business models and principles, as well as practical knowledge of the technologies used to support them. For DePaul's MS in E-Commerce Technology, student learning goals include the following:

1. Knowledge and understanding of practical applications and evolving e-commerce business models within the context of organizational strategy.

2. Knowledge and understanding of Web site design principles and engineering processes.

3. Hands on experience with technologies and tools.

4. Experience using rapid Web engineering processes to integrate business models, strategies, design and technology solutions.

5. Experience developing solutions both individually and in a collaborative team setting.

THE CURRICULUM

Because the basic curriculum design principles require a responsive, flexible curriculum, few specific technologies are referred to in DePaul's course descriptions. Instead, the courses are designed to teach principles, but with the understanding that current technologies will always be used, and that students, by the time they graduate, will have a broad basis in many different technologies. The appendix to this paper provides abbreviated course descriptions for e-commerce courses that are part of DePaul University's MS in E-Commerce Technology.

Once a curriculum is developed and approved, there are still three critical support areas that must be in place for the curriculum to succeed. These three supports may be thought of as the three legs of the curriculum stool. No e-commerce curriculum can stand without promotional resources, faculty resources, and technical resources (Knight, Chan, Epp & Kellen, 1999).

PROMOTIONAL RESOURCES

A new curriculum, no matter how snazzy the technology, cannot survive without any promotion. For DePaul, this involved internal promotion of the new degree to faculty, students, staff and administrators, as well as external promotion in the way of press releases, advertising and mailings to past and present students. Underlying all of these promotional efforts must be a clear understanding of who the potential students are. This understanding should be clearly developed and stated early on, as the curriculum development process is just beginning. For DePaul, that target audience was defined internally as follows:

This program is directed toward those who plan to work in the rapidly expanding field of e-commerce application development. As a technical program, it will appeal primarily to those who are already working in the Information Technology field, and want to move into a new high-growth area within IT. We expect the majority of students to be new students, attracted by the currency and uniqueness of the program and DePaul's reputation for technological excellence.

FACULTY RESOURCES

Since the technology behind e-commerce is so new, it is unlikely that many faculty members will have prior experience working with it. The e-commerce business models, either new or modified from those serving traditional companies, pose similar challenges. Therefore no e-commerce curriculum development effort is complete without a tie to the university's faculty recruitment and faculty development efforts. With an enrollment growth rate of approximately 25-30% annually, DePaul University's School of Computer Science, Telecommunications and Information Systems has been able to meet the human resource needs of its new e-commerce curriculum through a combination of current faculty and normal faculty expansion. For example, three new IS full-time faculty joined the school in the first year of the e-commerce program. They were complemented by two new industry practitioners hired to teach part-time in the e-commerce area. As is the case with any new program, this program required hiring of additional full-time and part-time faculty members, commensurate with enrollment growth. Because of the high salary cost for recruiting new e-commerce faculty, development of current faculty becomes a critical strategy (AACSB, 2000). In addition, the rapidly changing technology basis for e-commerce demands that those teaching e-commerce embark on perpetual and aggressive professional development activities. In the words of one e-commerce faculty member, "We train and prepare our students to work in a fast-paced, radical environment" (Baeb, 1999). Further, e-commerce faculty work in an arena where few textbooks exist, and those that do exist begin becoming obsolete the day they are printed. The necessarily heavy reliance of e-commerce courses on non-text material makes additional demands on e-commerce faculty, who experience constant pressure to keep up-to-date. They must expend a considerable amount of time and energy building a thorough knowledge of the ever-changing Internet and developing industry relationships. Partnerships with industry allow faculty to contribute toward the development of their partners' business strategies and projects while at the same time maintaining currency in a rapidly changing field.

TECHNICAL RESOURCES

A new e-commerce curriculum automatically generates technical resource requirements. These include library, computer, and network resources and support specialists. E-commerce applications typically require support for servers that the university computing services department does not normally provide (Dhamija, Heller & Hoffman, 1999). Therefore, adequate support for client-side and server-side technology is a significant issue for those launching an e-commerce program. In terms of physical resources, students in DePaul's e-commerce program have ready access to the school's existing state-of-the-art computing environment, including multi-media classrooms, student classroom laboratories, and research laboratories suitable for collaborative industry research. Like other students, e-commerce students are also able to access the Internet from home and from student laboratories at different campuses. To support the program, the dean built an e-commerce laboratory housing approximately fifty student computers fully equipped with application software, development tools and multimedia presentation audio/visual devices. Additional facilities have been built to house specialized e-commerce servers, and a full-time staff of three has been assigned to maintain and support the servers. DePaul's e-commerce program's location in a school that includes many technical specialists provides it with a broad basis of technical support.

CONCLUSIONS

For universities seeking to embark on a new e-commerce curriculum, eight key principles emerge:

1.   Business practitioners are a key resource in insuring that an e-commerce curriculum is in sync with reality; as such, they should be brought into the project early, and partnerships with them kept active throughout the life of the curriculum.

2.   Any e-commerce curriculum must emphasize technology as well as business strategies and models. No firm succeeds in e-commerce by doing just one of these well.

3.   The rapidly changing nature of the Internet demands a flexible curriculum that is not based in any one vendor or technology.

4.   Students seeking e-commerce positions need both theory and practical hands-on experience. Working with real clients or on realistic projects stimulates learning.

5.   A dual emphasis on individual assignments and group projects allows students to strengthen their capacity to engage in both self-directed inquiry and collaborative teamwork (Chan & Wolfe, 1999, 2000).

6.   As with any curriculum development effort, an e-commerce curriculum must have its roots in a clearly stated definition of who the target students are.

7.   Development of an e-commerce curriculum cannot be isolated from technology requirements, promotional plans, library requirements or faculty recruitment and development efforts. For a new e-commerce curriculum to succeed, all these areas must respond promptly and appropriately to the curriculum design.

8.   An e-commerce curriculum should emphasize the dynamic interaction among organizational strategy, the e-commerce development process, and ever-changing technologies. This requirement addresses the ongoing transformation that is taking place in the market and within organizations.

REFERENCES

AACSB. (2000, Winter). Hurr-e up: b-schools striving to get e-business courses and resources up to speed. AACSB Newsline. Accessed December 1, 2001 from http://www.aacsb.edu/Publications/Newsline/view.asp?year=2000&file=wnhurreup_1.html.

Baeb, E. (1999, August 23). Internet's ivy league. Crain's Chicago Business. Accessed December 1, 2001, from http://www.crainschicagobusiness.com.

Chan, S. & Wolfe, R. (1999, August). Collaborative team learning approach for web development. *Proceedings of the 1999 Americas Conference on Information Systems*, 181-183.

Chan, S. & Wolfe, R.J. (2000). User-centered design and web site engineering: An innovative teaching approach. *Journal of Informatics Education and Research*, 2(2), 77-87.

Cohen, E. (Ed.). (2000). Curriculum model of the Information Resource Management Association and the Data Administration Managers Association. Accessed July 30 2001 from http://gise.org/IRMA-DAMA-2000.pdf.

Dhamija, R., Heller, R. & Hoffman, L. (1999, September). Teaching e-commerce to a multidisciplinary class. *Communications of the ACM*, 42(9), 50-55.

Forrester Research, Inc. (2001). Accessed March 15, 2001, from http://www.forrester.com.

Goff, L.J. (2000, December 4). The skills that thrill. Computerworld. Accessed December 1, 2001, from http://www.computerworld.com/storyba/0,4125,NAV47_STO54596,00.html.

ISCC '99. (1999). Information Systems-Centric Curriculum '99. Accessed March 15 2001 from http://www.iscc.unomaha.edu.

IS '97 Curriculum (1997). Accessed March 15 2001 from http://www.is-97.org.

Knight, L. V. (2001). E-Commerce curricula patterns and projections. In B. Saghafi (Ed.), *Proceedings of the Thirty-Seventh Annual Midwest Business Administration Association Conference, Information Systems and Quantitative Methods*, 102-106.

Knight, L. V. & Chan, S. S. (2000). A conceptual model for e-commerce curriculum design and development. In M. Khosrow-Pour (Ed.), *Challenges of Information Technology Management in the Twenty-First Century, Proceedings of 2000 Information Resources Management Association Conference*, 555-557.

Knight, L. V. & Chan, S. S. (2001). E-commerce curriculum strategies and implementation tactics: an in-depth examination of DePaul University's experience. In E. Cohen (Ed.), *Challenges of Information Technology Education in the Twenty-First Century*. Hershey, PA: Idea Group Publishing, 190-208.

Knight, L., Chan, S., Epp, H. & Kellen, V. (1999). Internet commerce in the information systems curriculum. In Haseman, W. D. and Nazareth, D. L. (Eds.), *Proceedings of the Fifth Americas Conference on Information Systems*. 201-203.

Memishi, R. (1999, December). Ready or not, schools roll out e-commerce graduate degrees. *E-Commerce World*, 28-34.

Radcliff, D. (2001, November 12). Hot skills for a cold market. *Computerworld*. Accessed December 1, 2001, from http://www.computerworld.com/storyba/ 0,4125,NAV47_STO65450,00.html

Radcliff, D. (2001, November 12). IT jobs in high demand. *Computerworld*. Accessed December 1, 2001, from http://www.computerworld.com/storyba/ 0,4125,NAV47_STO65451,00.html.

APPENDIX

DePaul University's School of Computer Science, Telecommunications and Information Systems MS in E-Commerce Technology abbreviated course descriptions follow.

Prerequisite Courses (a partial list of the most relevant courses)
Fundamentals of Web Development.

A survey of Internet technology, tools and theory. Introduction to the concepts of Web architecture, Web software development languages and tools, and common e-commerce applications. Students will develop a basic understanding of HTML, create a Web site using an authoring tool and supplement it with Java applets.

Web Application Development with Scripting.

Application development for e-commerce. Includes development of small-scale e-commerce transaction applications. Students will design and build a retail Web site that accesses a database for online order processing.

Required Courses (a partial list of the most relevant courses)

Design and Strategies for Electronic Commerce.

An integrated study of strategies, design, and technology issues for consumer oriented electronic commerce. Mercantile models, mass customization, interactive marketing, search engines, and digital payment systems. Web engineering process, requirement analysis, design, usability testing, prototyping, implementation, promotion, and site evaluation. Team projects will develop commercial web sites using authoring tools and scripting.

Database Technologies.

An introduction to database technology and systems including: database architecture, data models, query languages, integrity, security, functional dependency and normalization.

Foundations of Distributed Systems.

An examination of current software architecture (e.g., client/server), protocols (e.g., LDAP, OpenDoc, DCOM/ActiveX, CORBA), and tools (e.g., Java RMI) for distributed systems. Platform, performance and concurrency issues. Overview of development tools.

Usability Issues for Electronic Commerce.

Design, prototyping and evaluation of e-commerce web sites. Content of usability in the project development life cycle. User/task analysis with emphasis on the first time and the infrequent user. Content organization. User testing with low fidelity prototypes. Issues of perceived privacy and security. Students' projects involve design and/or evaluation of actual electronic commerce sites.

Intranets and Business Intelligence.

An in-depth study of enterprise portal applications and their integration with enterprise databases and legacy systems. Internet based business strategies for managing distribution channel and call centers. Architecture and solutions for leveraging legacy systems and business intelligence through interface with data warehousing, knowledge management, and decision support. Tools and technologies for client, server, and content management. Web information systems development methods and process. Students will conduct case studies and group projects

Internet Supply Chain Management.

A study of business-to-business electronic commerce strategies, technologies, and infrastructure requirements. Web-based supply chain management and XML. Planning of Extranets, ROI analysis, and development life cycle. Building collaborative Extranets, automated version control, software configuration management, considerations for global Extranets. Security, performance issues, database and legacy systems integration, and Internet Virtual Private Networks.

Secure Electronic Commerce.

Concepts, strategies, tools, and implementation of secure e-commerce transaction processing. Cryptography, digital certificate, digital signatures, cryptographic key management, and authentication. Transaction security, SSL, and SET protocols. Models and technologies for electronic cash and digital payment, including e-cash, smart card, electronic wallet, virtual point-of-sale, internet electronic fund transfer, and bank credit card systems. Implementations of secure transaction systems and technologies.

E-Marketplace Technology.

This course concentrates on modeling online trading applications supporting complex interactions and transactions. Theoretical models of online business negotiations such as: auctions, brokerages and exchanges/marketplaces will be discussed. Server/client side applications utilizing the models and distributed data access will be developed. Assignments will include business case analysis as well as application development projects using Java.

Electronic Commerce Management.

This capstone course focuses on the development of e-commerce strategies and organization of resources. Planning of digital strategies, technology assessment and forecasting, global market analysis, and implementation plans, marketing, product life cycle, and funding strategies. Organization models for e-commerce application development, staffing, project management, and sourcing options. Students will develop business and organization plans for e-commerce development operations for in-house support, consulting practices, or entrepreneurship. This course should be taken at the conclusion of the ECT program.

Chapter 20

The Challenge of Teaching Research Skills
to Information Systems
and Technology Students

Beverley G. Hope
Victoria University of Wellington, New Zealand
and City University of Hong Kong

Mariam Fergusson
PricewaterhouseCoopers, Australia

As the information systems discipline grows, so do the number of programs offering graduate research degrees. These include one-year post-graduate (honors) programs, masters by research, and doctoral degrees. Graduate students entering their first research degree are faced with a quantum leap in expectations and required skills. The burden is significant: they need to find a referent discipline, select a research method and paradigm, defend the research relevance, and fulfill the requirements of adding to a body of knowledge. The purpose of this chapter is to inform discussion on the issue of teaching and learning graduate research skills. We identify the core research skills needed and present three pragmatic models for teaching them. This provides a basis for a shared knowledge and discourse based on lessons learned.

Previously Published in *Challenges of Information Technology Education in the 21st Century* edited by Eli Cohen, Copyright © 2002, Idea Group Publishing.

INTRODUCTION

Student experiences of conducting information systems and technology (IST) research in Australia generally begin in graduate programs. At the undergraduate level, IST education focuses on fundamental concepts, applications, and skills for practice. This vocational education acts as a terminating point for many students, but an increasing number are continuing or returning to graduate education in order to broaden their options in the labor market. Many of these graduate programs include a research component and, to meet the needs of employment-focused students, this research needs to be both rigorous and relevant.

The question is, how do we train people to become good researchers? What are the required knowledge, skills, and abilities of a good researcher? And how do we foster these in our students? If these are cognitive skills, *can* they be taught and learned? We believe the answer to the last question is a firm "yes." We learned to research; our students also can learn. But how best do we achieve this?

The objective of this chapter is to examine issues of how to foster research skills in novice IST research students. We propose a minimal set of skills and understandings (thought processes and concepts) as part of the researcher's repertoire, and outline some teaching strategies that can foster their development. The important assumptions underlying the chapter are:

- research is situated, that is, what constitutes knowledge and good research are defined by the audience or discipline; and,
- research skills are not innate, they are learned (and, consequently, can be taught).

THE IMPERATIVE FOR TEACHING RESEARCH

Research requires a spectrum of cognitive abilities, from the simple ability to establish facts to the more complex ability to judge and evaluate. In higher education we might reasonably expect students to be led through this spectrum to the point where they are able to criticize, to analyze, and to reach a deep understanding of knowledge. Typically, however, students are graduating from their first degrees in IST with limited research training and under-developed critical thinking skills. One reason for this may be that undergraduate IST education is seen as a professional qualification rather than the first step in an academic career. The need for practitioner skills and the ever-increasing knowledge base in IST leaves little time for research skilling. At the undergraduate level, we teach *what* is known, not *how* it is known. Furthermore, an increasing number of students are entering graduate programs with strong professional experience in lieu of academic prerequisites. So, IST students are entering graduate research degree pro-

Figure 1: IST research: A juggling act

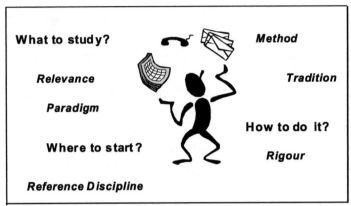

grams without understanding the research process and without possessing research skills.

Graduate research degree programs vary in content and structure, but the output invariably includes a written document, whether a research project, published paper, thesis, or dissertation. The document is the culmination of many months or years of study and serves not only to communicate findings but also to evidence the student's ability to conduct credible research. To be credible in the IST field, the research must be both relevant and rigorous.

Relevance and rigor are paradigmatic issues because our world views guide both the selection of phenomena to study and the acceptability of methodologies (Wand & Weber, 1986; Weber, 1997). As such, paradigms set the scene for the selection of a *good* topic (relevance) and provide a benchmark or standards for evaluation (an aspect of rigor). In contrast to established disciplines, IST is at best multi-paradigmatic and at worst non-paradigmatic. It remains to a large degree a complex "fusion of behavioral, technical, and managerial issues" (Keen, 1980, p.10), that are difficult to untangle. The discipline borrows theories, models, and methods from the physical and social sciences, as well as from professional business disciplines. As early as 1980, Keen noted the plethora of reference disciplines in practice, including computer science, experimental social psychology, cognitive psychology, and political science (Keen, 1980, p.10). There are no fewer today. The 1993 *Keyword Classification Scheme for IST Research Literature*, for example, contains 16 reference disciplines (Barki, Rivard, & Talbot, 1993). It is not surprising, then, that Galliers' (1991, p.328) review of the literature identifies 14 research approaches used in IST. With no single accepted paradigm, multiple reference disciplines, and a variety of research approaches, IST researchers must make some important decisions up front. They must select an "appropriate" discipline from which they can set standards, draw theories, select methodologies, and find criteria for evaluating research (Keen, 1991). The novice IST researcher is on a very steep learning curve.

Research students in more mature disciplines do not normally share the ambiguities facing novice IST researchers. For example, science and engineering students have a well-defined research paradigm that is both normative and scientific. At masters and PhD levels, these students are likely to become part of a research team with an established area of study. The *apprentice within a team* approach provides for a rapid start, an effective mentoring system, and the benefits of collegiality. Typically, IST students entering research programs do not have these advantages. The lack of a team support structure is particularly marked under the British or Oxbridge PhD tradition followed in most of Australasia. The structure imposed by course-led programs such as those in North America mitigates this to some extent. We use the term 'course' here and throughout this chapter to denote a unit of study, sometimes referred to as a paper, unit, or subject.

The early stage in the research life of a student has been identified as being critical (Fergusson, 1997). In an empirical study students reported a big leap in expectations and skill requirements upon entry to an honors (first graduate research) program, but found the step up to PhD study less problematic (Mullins & Kiley, 1998). The difference between these steps is knowledge and experience of research. A rapid start is particularly important for honors students who have a short time to complete their program of study, but is also important for masters and PhD students seeking a timely completion date. To ease students into research, we argue that they need to begin their graduate research degree programs with research training.

TEACHING AND LEARNING RESEARCH SKILLS

Research skills, like any other skill, can be learned. Just as students once learned to analyze an information system and draw a DFD, so they can learn to analyze literature and write academic articles. Even creativity can be learned (Gerity, 1997). But how are research skills best acquired? While there is a plethora of books to assist students in completing theses (see, for example, Creswell, 1994; Leedy, 1997), these usually address the research process rather than the component skills. It has even been argued that textbooks can be a barrier to creative thinking as they "instill judicial thinking" (Evans, 1991, p.47). The term judicial thinking implies a correct way of critiquing, judging, or solving problems. Thus books, while providing a useful framework for the process of producing the research output, do not replace the valuable contribution of the research instructor, mentor, or class.

Teaching research skills represents a shift from focusing on the research topic to focusing on learning outcomes. Student learning outcomes "encompass a wide range of student attributes and abilities, both cognitive and affective" (Baddeley, 1979, p.4). In describing doctoral research training, the Australian Vice-Chancellors' Committee noted that it:

> Provides training and education with the objective of producing graduates with the capacity to conduct research independently at a high level of originality and quality. The student ought to be capable by the end of their candidature of conceiving, designing, and carrying to completion a research program without supervision (Australian Vice-Chancellors' Committee [1990] cited in Brown [1998]).

A subsequent review modified and softened this definition of traditional research training:

> Research training, through good supervision, should provide the student with an ethical framework and generic workplace competencies as well as research-related skills.... Some universities have embraced this broader concept of research training through the establishment of graduate schools which appear to be more focused on the multiple dimensions of research training and the different career paths that research training provides (Review Committee [1997, p.3] cited in Brown [1998]).

The differing approaches to research education can be arrayed on a continuum ranging from the lone scholar approach to the student cohort approach. At the lone scholar extreme, novice researchers work largely on their own to prove themselves capable of self-skilling in the research process and of providing a unique contribution to knowledge. At the other extreme a cohort of students are led through the research process in a series of classes or workshops with ongoing peer and mentor support.

The lone scholar approach is the traditional form of research training in Australasia as it is in the United Kingdom. Here, students work with supervisors in a one-to-one relationship. In theory, this provides students with a way of internalizing the work habits and expertise of a seasoned researcher by association; in reality, the student will rarely observe their supervisor in action. As Wood-Harper, Miles, and Booth (1993, p.455) observe, "The culture of individualism within UK academia is such that post-graduate students are expected to make their own way in the research world."

There are many possible learning outcomes at this end of the training continuum. Learning can be serendipitous, and dependent upon both the problems that the student encounters and the skill and attitude of the supervisor. If the supervisor is a subject but not a research specialist, acquisition of research skills can be minimal. The success of the relationship can be affected by the chemistry of the personality mix and the workload or availability of the supervisor. At one end there are students who are left to "muddle along" and teach themselves research skills. They learn from books or from emulating a method from published research. Learning is most often just-in-time, exposing the student to the risk of learning too late that an essential step was omitted earlier in the process, perhaps invalidating results. While they may become adept in the chosen method, they are unlikely to be knowledgeable in a variety of methods or to even know of their existence. These researchers acquire a narrow view of the research process and are likely to become method rather than problem driven. The implication of method-driven research is that knowledge is circumscribed by the method by which it is acquired. The lone scholar approach emphasizes depth at the expense of breadth and individualism at the expense of collegiality and debate (Baddeley, 1979; Davies, 1990).

The self-taught student is the poor cousin in the research arena, because, as Baddeley (1979, p. 130) observes, "Most subsequent occupations are likely to involve interacting with other people, writing in such a way as to interest and influence them, and meeting reasonably short deadlines. The PhD student is given neither training nor experience in any of these."

The problems of the lone scholar may be overcome by the collegiality, support, and structure at the cohort end of the training continuum.

The cohort approach is more common in the United States, but is fast being taken up by other regions, including Australasia. Students learn about a variety of research methods through a combination of attending seminars, analyzing published research, completing practical assignments, and writing papers. Course content may be dependent upon the prevalent paradigm of the particular IST department or the bias of the instructor. Some address only positivist paradigms and are heavily quantitative, but increasingly the interpretivist paradigm and qualitative methods are being taught. The coursework mode fails to realize its potential when the curriculum favors a particular paradigm or methodology, or fails to include experiential learning.

Constructivist theory of knowledge suggests that actual knowledge is not transmitted from one person (the teacher) to another (the student); rather it is constructed in the mind of the student (Cronin, 1997; Jonassen et al., 1995). This is achieved by situating learning in real-world contexts and grounding concepts in experiential learning. In research education, this involves practicing research skills on real or realistic research problems with all their complexity, to provide context to the process, thereby enhancing learning. Students are then more likely to be able to articulate and clarify concepts, and to develop critical thinking abilities (Metz & Tobin, 1997).

While all modes may lead to success, we propose that more benefits are obtained at the cohort end of the continuum. Coursework provides a focused and structured learning environment, ensuring better coverage of a broad range of research paradigms and methods. In addition it is more economical both of staff and student time. By providing the right kinds of experiences, we can enhance our student's ability to search the literature, think critically, and write concisely in an academic style. They can learn how to challenge assumptions, critique methodologies, and improve article organization. A particular strength of the research classroom is that students are able to learn from each other's experiences as well as their own. This enriches their view of the approaches to research, and allows them to work together on essential skills, but independently on their own research projects. They also learn through debate to articulate and defend their argument, an important skill. In the long term, the structured teaching of research methods and skills must benefit the IST discipline as graduating students go on to conduct research and disseminate their findings.

To construct a research training program, we need to be able to identify the skills and techniques used by experienced researchers. These provide a framework around which research programs can be organized.

CRITICAL RESEARCH SKILLS

For the purpose of identifying critical skills it is convenient to conceptualize research as a linear series of steps grouped according to the common milestone outputs. In reality, the research process is likely to involve several iterations and include feedback loops (Barrow & Thomson, 1997). From the literature (see for example, Kumar, 1996) and from our experience, we posit the following process and outputs:

Phase I - Topic Analysis
1. Choose a topic area
2. Survey the literature (and practice)
3. Identify a relevant research problem/opportunity
4. Identify the audience for the intended research output
5. Identify the research approach suited to the problem and the audience

Phase II - Research Proposal
1. Thoroughly search the literature and synthesize the findings
2. Define the research questions, with hypotheses where required by the paradigm
3. Develop a research design and method, including a time plan for the research
4. Identify key assumptions and limitations

Phase III - Research Report
5.   Collect and analyze "data"
6.   Interpret results in light of existing knowledge and theory
7.   Communicate the findings (thesis, paper, article)

These skills can be grounded in the student's own research. Outputs at the end of each phase are the practical applications of the lessons learned in the student's actual research: topic analysis, research proposal, and research report (thesis, conference paper, or journal article). The outputs provide the formal framework within which the students' understanding can be expressed and subsequently discussed as a cooperative group learning experience.

This process suggests a "minimum" set of critical skills that the novice researcher must acquire to complete good research. These are shown in Table 1 under the headings "Cognitive skills" and "Research techniques." Although the distinction between cognitive skills and research techniques is not clear cut, the separation is intended to provide a classification against which to target particular areas for development and to compare the offerings of existing courses.

Reading Table 1 across and then down provides a loose matching with the research process steps set out earlier. The six essential skills can be used to benchmark existing or proposed courses for novice researchers. The skills can be taught to a group while allowing sufficient diversity for individual development. In addition, the list of skills can be used as a reference for criterion-based assessment.

Because relevant research frequently involves study of IST within organizations, we can add to the required skill set, consultancy skills. According to Metzger (1993), these include: diagnostic ability, problem-solving skills, specialized knowledge, communication skills, marketing and selling abilities, and business acumen.

Table 1: Essential Research Skills

Cognitive skills	Research techniques
Selecting a topic and defining a research problem	Conducting a comprehensive search of the literature
Evaluating and synthesizing existing research	Designing the research and "data" collection
Selecting and justifying a research paradigm	Writing an academic paper

RESEARCH PROGRAMS

Programs of study for research students tend to vary considerably. They vary both in terms of the relative proportions of coursework to research and the amount of prescribed research methods coursework. For example, at Victoria University, honors study begins with an intensive one-week program (Lowry, 1997); at the Australian Defence Force Academy, students take one research methods course; and at Victoria University of Wellington, honors students take four research-focused courses. The objective of each program is to focus students on defining a research question, developing a research plan, and conducting credible research. These three programs are summarized next.

Case 1: Honors at Victoria University (VU), Victoria, Australia

Lowry (1999) reports a semi-structured approach to research education at VU. The approach was developed and successfully implemented earlier while Lowry was at the University of Tasmania (see Lowry, 1997). Of the 22 students participating in the research training program at VU in 1998, 17 were PhD candidates, three were DBA candidates, and two were master's students. Of the 17 PhD candidates, 13 were serving members of the academic staff. The nature of the student body, particularly the high proportion of academic staff enrolled, favored an intensive, workshop approach to research training.

Program aims included development of an appreciation of the broad nature of the IS discipline, an awareness of the range of research methods, an ability to articulate research questions, and competence in "framing, conducting, arguing, and reporting research in a convincing yet conventional way" (Lowry, 1999). Additional objectives included the rapid completion of PhDs, particularly by serving academic staff, and increased publication output from the PhD research.

Training begins with an intensive, week-long orientation in which participants begin their thesis with identification of a preliminary research question and development of a working title. The initial workshop is followed with three workshops, at monthly intervals. These workshops, which are "social as well as academic events", are held in an executive seminar setting and are characterized by strong student input and interaction. In describing the earlier, Tasmanian, program, Lowry (1997) describes the workshop structure as:

1. In the first follow-up workshop, students report their progress and focus on the literature review and research questions. They are expected to have substantially completed their focused reading and to have written a draft literature review.

2. In the second workshop students report progress, focusing on refinement of the research question, hypotheses, scope, and assumptions. They are expected to have completed the thesis introduction (Chapter 1) and literature review (Chapter 2).

3. In the third workshop, students focus on research design and plans. They are expected to have fully revised previously presented chapters, and to have a good first draft of the methodology (Chapter 3).

In describing the subsequent VU program, Lowry reports that at the end of the first semester, students are expected to have developed a formal research proposal and substantially completed the first three to five chapters of their thesis. Outcomes of the training have included increased staff publications, higher PhD completions, and development of three research groups within the department-organizational, technology, and technology-induced change management,

Case 2: Honors at the Australian Defence Force Academy (ADFA), University College, UNSW Canberra, Australia

Students enrolled in the honors program at ADFA are full-time students and personnel in the Australian Defence Force. Most have limited or no prior research training.

The aims of research training are to facilitate completion rates, decrease student frustration, and improve the quality of research outputs. Students are required to take four courses and a thesis over one calendar year, with Research Methods prescribed in the first semester. A course is the equivalent to 36 contact hours. Each student is allocated a research supervisor.

The assessments for the Research Methods course are: topic analysis, literature review, research presentation to the school, and a research proposal. Assessment is criterion referenced and marked independently by the course lecturer/manager and the student's supervisor. The role of the supervisor is to provide topic-specific expertise and advice, including help with finding the relevant literature, and choosing a suitable research paradigm.

Students are encouraged to find a topic themselves. Students who ask their supervisors for a research question tend to be more organized with their work and able to focus early on the body of knowledge surrounding their topic. Their enthusiasm for the topic is typically high initially, and reduces gradually over the year. Students who elect to find their own topic are slower to "settle," though they tend to maintain momentum until the end of the year. There is no perceived difference between the final performance of students who choose their own topic and those who obtain one from a supervisor.

The identified cognitive skills are covered in the course material and practiced in assignments. Workshops and mini-tasks are used to assist the students with selecting a topic and defining a problem, as well as evaluating and synthesizing existing research. Research paradigms used in IST are discussed in lectures, and justification of the research paradigm is a required part of the research proposal. Training in research techniques tends to be limited to writing skills, and this mostly by feedback on submitted work. Students have an on-line resource center, which "guides" them through the research process as presented in the course. The greatest weakness of the students by the end of the semester-long research methods course is in providing alternate research designs.

Following the introduction of the research methods course, formative evaluations were requested of research supervisors. These consistently reported significant improvement in student performance, better understanding of the topic areas, and perceptions of greater levels of motivation among students. Feedback obtained from around 25 students over a three-year period was positive with respect to their own research. Students were all able to identify direct benefits of having completed the course. About 20% of students reported that "learning about all the 'other stuff' (research paradigms that they did not use) was useless." It would seem that grappling with the breadth of the IST discipline, on top of learning how to do research, might be a little too much to ask of an honors student in a single semester, though the vexatious question of how to expose them to the range of paradigms and methods remains.

Case 3: Honors at Victoria University of Wellington (VUW), Wellington, New Zealand

(Despite name similarity there is no connection with Case 1). The honors year in the School of Information Management at Victoria University of Wellington also serves as the first year of a two-year master's-by-research degree. An important objective of the IST honors program is to provide the foundation skills needed for students to progress to the master's thesis and eventually, we hope, to a doctoral degree.

The majority of students are full-time, recent graduates of the school's undergraduate program, but a few graduates from other universities in New Zealand and overseas join the program. In any given cohort, one or two students are likely to be part time, while also working downtown or in the home. Whatever the circumstance, students generally have little prior academic research experience.

The program of study consists of eight courses, of which four are prescribed. Elective courses are content specific and include options in areas such as e-commerce, the virtual organization, and IT in the new organisation. Two electives may be chosen from cognate disciplines, and common choices include marketing, management, and library and information science.

All four prescribed courses are devoted to research issues and practice. They are: Foundations of Information Systems Research, Research Methods in Information Systems, Current Issues in Information Systems Research, and Research Project in Information Systems.

Foundations of Information Systems Research is a first-semester course, which introduces the IST discipline and includes ontological foundations of IST, an overview of the main streams of IST research, and the skills and techniques required to write a literature review. A skills workshop on searching the university online catalog and online databases is provided. Assessments include bi-weekly article critiques, bi-weekly search and writing exercises, and an academic literature review. Topics for the literature reviews are selected from a list of topics to be offered by staff as research projects in the following semester. In this way, students get an early start on their second semester research project.

Research Methods in Information Systems is also a first-semester course, which provides a critical examination of methodologies used in IST research. Both qualitative (case research, grounded theory, ethnography, action research) and quantitative methods (survey, experimental study) are included. Skill workshops include introductions to NU*DIST and SPSS. Assessment includes weekly assignments describing research methods and reviewing related articles, a research journal describing the student's learning process, an end-term test, and a research proposal. The research proposal is the major course output and brings together the skills and knowledge of the course. It also provides some depth in an otherwise broad coverage of research methods. Students are encouraged to write their research proposal for their proposed project in the following semester, and to this end they incorporate into the proposal the literature review completed and edited in the *Foundations* course.

Current Issues in Information Systems Research in the second semester builds on the *Foundations* course. It involves a critical examination of recent literature in the domain of strategic, managerial, and organizational aspects of IST research. Relevance of research is a strong theme in this course. The issue of relevance is also addressed through the incorporation of a practitioners' forum. Assessment includes bi-weekly article reviews, two mini-projects or literature reviews, and an end-term test.

The Research Project in Information Systems provides an opportunity for students to synthesize the learning in all other courses and prepares them for entry into Part II of the master's program, the thesis. Students work with a selected supervisor on a project offered by that staff member. In our first year of offering the program, we allowed students to select and define their own research question, but we found that students were taking too long, often half the semester, to define their topic. Since honors is a one-year, eight-course program, this was clearly unacceptable and the quality of some projects reflected this. Since moving to the 'select from a list' approach, students have completed the assignment in a more timely manner, projects have substantially improved, and students are less stressed. Under the revised scheme, students can refine the research question but they are helped by the provision of a general research topic. A conference-style presentation to staff and students is required at the end of the course.

The VUW honors program is thus an intensive introduction to research incorporating both cognitive skills and research techniques. Students work long hours and burnout is a potential problem. The program does not meet every entrant's needs. Those who enroll expecting to receive consultancy training are disappointed, but those who enroll for the intended research degrees are well served. We have been impressed by the quantum leap in understanding and practice evidenced by our students following on to theses from the honors program. Many have subsequently published their research projects.

These three research training programs are not intended to be prescriptive. Rather, they are examples of approaches designed to meet the differing needs of differing cohorts at different institutions. We hope that they will foster debate and serve as starting points for others to develop (and report) their own research training initiatives. The reviewed programs had similar aims and all assumed a cognitive apprenticeship model within the constructivist educational paradigm. All programs were considered successful by participating teachers, research supervisors, and research students.

CONCLUSION

As a discipline without an accepted single paradigm, IST presents novice researchers with many challenges. The applied nature of the discipline imposes the dual requirements of rigor and relevance, which can be difficult to meet even for seasoned researchers. Consequently, IST students entering graduate research degree programs benefit from structured research training experiences. Decomposing the research process into a set of critical skills can assist in developing research training programs and criterion-referenced assessments.

To demonstrate the applicability of the skill-set, we described three quite different programs, each of which were considered to meet the needs of their constituents. VU offers an intensive, week-long introduction, followed by three, day-long workshops; ADFA, offers a single, semester-long course which combines theory with practice; and VUW offers a series of courses. Courses include both cognitive skills and research techniques, though techniques are more frequently practiced in the longer training program at VUW.

Further research is needed to explore the different modes by which students acquire research skills and to assess the relative effectiveness and efficiency of each. Such research could help us to identify which modes are best suited to which learning aims and objectives. From our experience and from our review of the literature, we recommend that any research training be given a strong contextual grounding. The skills taught must be relevant to both future academics and future practitioners.

REFERENCES

Australian Vice-Chancellors' Committee (1990). *Code of Practice for Maintaining and Monitoring Academic Quality and Standards in Higher Degrees*. Canberra: AVCC.

Baddeley, A. (1979). Is the British PhD system obsolete? *Bulletin of the British Psychological Society, (32)*, 129-131.

Barki, H., Rivard, S., & Talbot, J. (1993). A keyword classification scheme for IS research literature: An update. *MIS Quarterly, 17*(2), 209-226.

Barrow, P. D. M., & Thomson, H. E. (1997). Choosing research methods in information systems. In *Proceedings of the 2nd UKAIS Conference* (pp. 239-251). Southampton, United Kingdom.

Brown, D. (1998). The PhD as professional qualification: Is research education enough? In Kiley, M. and Mullins, G. (Eds.), *Quality in Postgraduate Research: Managing the New Agenda*. Adelaide: University of Adelaide. Available at: http://www.usyd.edu.au/su/supra/quality.pdf (last accessed March 12, 2001).

Creswell, J. (1994). *Research Design: Qualitative and Quantitative Approaches*. Newbury Park: Sage Publications.

Cronin, P. (1997). *Learning and Assessment of Instruction*. Web document. http://ww.cogsci.edu.ac.uk/~paulus/Work/Vranded/litconsa.htm (last accessed March 8, 2001).

Davies, G. (1990). New routes to the PhD. *The Psychologist, 3*(6), 253-255.

Evans, J. R. (1991). *Creative Thinking in the Decision and Management Sciences*. Cincinnati, OH: South-Western Publishing Co.

Fergusson, M. (1997). The Ferrett: A Web tool for postgraduate supervision. In Sutton, D. (Ed.), *Proceedings of the 8th Australasian Conference on Information Systems,* (pp. 529-539). Adelaide, Australia.

Galliers, R. D. (1991). Choosing appropriate information systems research approaches: A revised taxonomy. In Nissen, H. E., Klein, H. K., & Hirschheim, R. (Eds.), *Information Systems Research: Contemporary Approaches and Emergent Traditions* (pp. 327-345). North-Holland: Eslevier Science Publishers.

Gerity, B. P. (1997). *Teaching Creativity: A Cognitive Apprenticeship Approach to the Instruction of Previsualization in Art.* Web document. http://cc.usu.edu/~slqxp/TCResear.html (last accessed March 15, 2001).

Jonassen, D., Davidson, M., Collins, M., Campbell, J., & Haag, B. (1995). Constructivism and computer-mediated communication in distance education. *The American Journal of Distance Education,* 9(2), 7-26.

Keen, P. (1980). MIS research: Reference disciplines and a cumulative tradition. In Mclean, E. (Ed.), *Proceedings of the First International Conference on Information Systems* (pp. 9-18). Philadelphia, USA.

Keen, P. (1991). Relevance and rigor in information systems research. In Nissen, H. E., Klein, H., & Hirschheim, R. (Eds.), *Information Systems Research: Contemporary Approaches and Emergent Traditions* (pp. 27-49). Amsterdam: North Holland.

Kumar, R. (1996). *Research Methodology: A Step-by-Step Guide for Beginners.* Melbourne: Addison Wesley Longman.

Leedy, P. (1997). *Practical Research: Planning and Design,* 6th ed. New Jersey: Prentice Hall.

Lowry, G. R. (1997). Postgraduate research training for information systems: Improving standards and reducing uncertainty. In Sutton, D. (Ed.), *Proceedings of the 8th Australasian Conference on Information Systems* (pp. 191-202). Adelaide, Australia.

Lowry, G. R. (1999). Building a research culture at the Victoria University greenfields site. *Australian Council of Professors and Heads of Information Systems (ACPHIS) Curriculum and Research Workshop,* Macquarie University, NSW, September 30-October 1, 1999 (invited paper).

Metz, P., & Tobin, K. (1997). Cooperative learning: An alternative to teaching at a medieval university. *Australian Science Teachers' Journal,* 43(1), 3-28.

Metzger, R.O. (1993). *Developing a Consulting Practice.* Newbury Park: Sage.

Mullins, G., & Kiley, K. (1998). Quality in postgraduate research: The changing agenda. In Kiley, M., and Mullins, G. (Eds.), *Quality in Postgraduate Research: Managing the New Agenda* (pp. 1-13). Adelaide: University of Adelaide.

Review Committee. (1997). *Learning for Life–review of Higher Education Financing and Policy: A Policy Discussion Paper.* Canberra: AGPS.

Wand, Y., & Weber, R., (1986). On paradigms in the IS discipline: The problem of the problem. In *Proceedings of the 1986 Decision Sciences Institute Conference* (pp. 566-568). Honolulu, Hawaii.

Weber, R. (1997). *Ontological Foundations of Information Systems*. Melbourne: Coopers & Lybrand.

Wood-Harper, A.T., Miles, R.K., & Booth, P.A. (1993). Designing research education in Information Systems. In Khosrowpour, M., & Loch, K. D. (Eds.), *Global Information Technology Education: Issues and Trends* (pp. 453-487). London: Idea Group Publishing.

Chapter 21

Towards Establishing the Best Ways to Teach and Learn about IT

Chris Cope, Lorraine Staehr and Pat Horan
La Trobe University, Bendigo, Australia

In this chapter we report on an ongoing project to improve the ways we teach about IT in an undergraduate degree. Using a relational perspective on learning, we have developed a framework of factors to encourage students to adopt a deep approach to learning about IT. We describe the design, implementation, evaluation and refinement of learning contexts and learning activities based on the framework. Results are encouraging and show a significant positive effect when compared with a previous study by other researchers involving a different teaching and learning context.

INTRODUCTION

A challenge for IT education in the 21st century is to find ways to produce graduates who meet IT employers' expectations. Recent research indicates that employers are not satisfied with the understanding and skills of new IT graduates, claiming that curricula are unrealistic and unsuited to business needs (Hawforth & Van Wetering, 1994; Misic & Russo, 1996; Roth & Ducloss, 1995; Trauth, Farwell & Lee, 1993).

So what is wrong with current IT undergraduate curricula? Is there a problem with the content, as suggested by IT employers? Our review of the IT higher education research literature identified a strong focus on curricular content. Widely

Previously Published in *Challenges of Information Technology Education in the 21st Century* edited by Eli Cohen, Copyright © 2002, Idea Group Publishing.

available model curricula for IT courses have existed for many years and have been regularly updated and published in the literature (for example Cohen, 2000; Couger et al., 1995; Davis et al., 1997; Longenecker et al., 1995; Mulder & van Weert, 2000). The design of these model curricula incorporates direct input from industry and the research literature on the skills and knowledge requirements of IT professionals (Athey & Wickham, 1995; Doke & Williams, 1999; Lee et al., 1995; Richards & Pelley, 1994; Richards et al., 1998). It is unlikely that the problem lies with the content of IT curricula.

Could the problem lie in 'how' we teach our curricula and, consequently, 'how' our students learn about IT? Are we teaching about IT in the best ways possible? If our strategies for teaching about IT are inappropriate, then it is unlikely that students will be gaining the understanding and skills required by employers. In reviewing the literature on IT teaching, we found reports on implementations of a number of new strategies for teaching about IT. However, these strategies were not, in general, underpinned by any contemporary, research-based view on teaching and learning and have not been evaluated in any structured way. Therefore, the problem of employers' concerns with the skills and understanding of our graduates could lie in 'how' we teach about IT.

In this chapter we report our contribution to overcoming employers' dissatisfaction with IT graduates. We have begun the long process of establishing the best ways to teach and learn about IT. A number of steps have been taken:

1. We have sought a contemporary, research-based view on student learning which would adequately underpin teaching and learning about IT in the 21st century and should produce graduates with the qualities required by IT employers. We have chosen a relational perspective on student learning (Biggs, 1999; Marton & Booth, 1997; Prosser & Trigwell, 1999; Ramsden, 1987, 1988). From this perspective the best ways to learn about a discipline are to use the deep learning approaches known to lead to high quality learning outcomes. The best ways to teach are to identify and implement in the learning contexts and learning activities the discipline-specific factors likely to encourage students to use deep learning approaches. We describe in detail and justify a relational perspective later in the chapter.

2. We have reviewed the IT education research literature for insights into the best ways to teach and learn about IT. Our review sought to identify the IT-specific learning context factors and learning activities likely to encourage deep learning approaches. In general we found little attention to the area within the IT education literature.

3. The next step was an iterative one. Based on a relational perspective on learning and, to a limited extent, the IT higher education research literature, we have identified and implemented learning context factors and learning activities

we believe likely to encourage deep learning approaches in IT students. Importantly, we have evaluated in a structured way the learning approaches students adopted in response to our learning contexts. This has led to an ongoing process of modification and evaluation of our learning contexts and learning activities.

In this chapter we report our progress to date in attempting to establish the best ways to teach and learn about IT. While we do not have definitive answers as yet, we believe our progress is worth reporting. While some of the learning context factors and learning activities we have identified are not new, the way in which we designed, justified, implemented and evaluated our teaching and our students' learning from within a relational perspective on student learning is. We hope that the chapter will provide fresh insights into teaching about IT and encourage other IT academics to assist with establishing the best ways to teach and learn about IT. Only through the use of research-based, considered, evaluated teaching can we hope to produce graduates of a quality acceptable to IT employers.

BACKGROUND

We believe that a problem confronting IT education at the beginning of the 21st century concerns 'how' the content of our curricula is being taught. To begin to address this problem, we have reviewed the IT education literature looking for insights into the best ways to teach and learn about IT. Before reporting this review, we need to establish what we mean by 'best ways to teach and learn about IT.' According to Biggs (1999) efforts to improve teaching and learning require reflection on current practices based on an explicit theory of learning and teaching. Our explicit theory is a relational perspective on student learning and teaching, which we now describe. Later in the section we use a relational perspective to review some of the important teaching strategies and learning activities proposed in the IT education research literature.

A Relational Perspective on Student Learning

A relational perspective is a contemporary, research-based view of student learning in higher education, first proposed by Ramsden (1987, 1988), but used in this chapter to also unify the ideas of other educational researchers, principally Biggs (1999), Marton and Booth (1997) and Prosser and Trigwell (1999). The relational perspective research focused on identifying and understanding students' perceptions of their own learning experiences as the impetus for improved teaching and learning. In doing this, the research contrasted with earlier and concurrent studies which focused on external observers' and teachers' perceptions of students' learning experiences, students' behaviours and students' cognitive structures. The relational perspective research identified the nature of and systematic relationships between students' perceptions of their own learning situations, approaches to learning and quality of learning outcomes. We have summarised what we believe to be the essential aspects of a relational perspective on student learning in Figure 1.

Figure 1 shows that the quality of a student's learning outcomes is related to a learning approach which, in turn, is related to the student's perception of their learning situation. A student's perception of their learning situation is influenced by their previous learning experiences and a complexity of contextual factors. We will now describe in more detail the various aspects of the relational perspective illustrated in Figure 1, moving from right to left.

Quality of Learning Outcomes

Many qualitative studies have found that a particular concept, topic or course area can be conceptualised in a limited number of different ways (for example Crawford et al., 1994; Johansson, Marton & Svensson, 1985; Lybeck et al., 1988; Prosser & Millar, 1989). Of considerable importance, this research has presented the different conceptions in a hierarchy. Higher quality learning outcomes were those conceptions higher in the hierarchy that represented a more complex and complete understanding. Higher quality learning outcomes were found to build

Figure 1: A Relational Perspective on Student Learning (arrows represent empirical relationships)

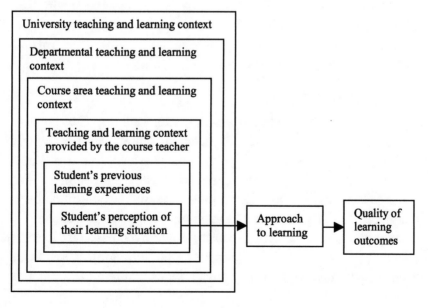

on and be inclusive of lower quality learning outcomes. This finding contrasts with some constructivist and cognitive perspectives on learning in which the learning process involves higher level understandings completely replacing lower levels of understanding. These cognitive and constructivist views find it difficult to explain empirical findings that the same student can use different levels of understanding of the same phenomenon in different contexts (Marton, 1998).

Approach to Learning

One of the most important findings of research into student learning from a number of different research perspectives, and central to a relational perspective, is that students' learning approaches can be categorized broadly as either surface or deep. There have been many attempts to generalize the description of surface and deep learning approaches, for example those of Biggs (1999), Marton and Säljö (1976, 1997) and Ramsden (1988, 1992). A comprehensive description is given by Prosser and Trigwell (1999, p.3):

Surface Approach

… students see tasks as external impositions and they have the intention to cope with these requirements. They are instrumentally or pragmatically motivated and seek to meet the demands of the task with minimum effort. They adopt strategies which include focus on unrelated parts of the task; separate treatment of related parts (such as on principles and examples) a focus on what are seen as essentials (factual data and their symbolic representations), the reproduction of the essentials as accurately as possible, and rote memorising information for assessment purposes rather than for understanding. Overall they would appear to be involved in study without reflection on purpose or strategy, with the focus of that study being on the words, the text or the formulae.

Deep Approach

… students aim to understand ideas and seeks meaning. They have an intrinsic interest in the task and an expectation of enjoyment in carrying it out. They adopt strategies that help satisfy their curiosity, such as making the task coherent with their own experience; relating and distinguishing evidence and argument; looking for patterns and underlying principles; integrating the task with existing awareness; seeing the parts of a task as making up the whole; theorizing about it; forming hypotheses; and relating what they understand from other parts of the same subject, and from different subjects. Overall they have a focus on the meaning in the argument, the message, or the relationships, but they are aware that the meanings are carried by the words, the text or the formulae.

Of great significance to this chapter, a deep approach seeks meaning in a learning task by trying to relate the task to other tasks and/or existing understanding and/or personal experience. A deep approach focuses on developing a cohesive whole by seeking relationships between the various tasks. These relationships are considered to be vital components of an understanding (Entwistle, 1998).

It is important to note that deep and surface learning approaches allow for different preferred learning styles. It is not so much the nature of the way students go about their learning that distinguishes deep and surface learning approaches, but the difference in the intention with which the learning styles are applied. Deep approaches have an intention to understand, surface approaches do not.

Relation Between Approach to Learning and Quality of Learning Outcome

Logically it would seem that high quality learning outcomes involving a deep understanding are unlikely to occur unless a deep learning approach is taken. Only deep learning approaches seek understanding by looking for links between aspects of content. Many empirical studies have confirmed this contention (for example, Cope, 2000; Crawford et al., 1994; Hazel, Prosser & Trigwell, 1996; Marton & Säljö, 1976; Prosser & Millar, 1989).

Students' Perceptions of Their Learning Situation

As deep learning approaches are the vital stepping stone to high quality learning outcomes, it would seem reasonable to investigate how to get students to use deep learning approaches. It has been proposed that learning approach is a characteristic of a student. In fact, students have been found to vary the learning approach they use (Biggs, 1993). Direct instruction in deep learning approaches has been tried, but has been found to lead to poor quality learning outcomes (Marton & Booth, 1997). It seems that instruction in learning techniques leads to a focus on the strategies of learning rather than the intention. A focus on an intention to understand is at the core of a deep learning approach. So how can we encourage students to adopt deep learning approaches? The research has identified certain factors in learning contexts and learning activities which influence the learning approaches students adopt. To understand these factors we firstly need to consider the concept of a student's perception of his/her learning situation.

Many studies of students' perceptions of learning contexts have shown that different students will perceive the same context in different ways (for example, Entwistle & Ramsden, 1983; Prosser & Millar, 1989; Ramsden, 1979). This is not surprising given the complexity of a learning context and the variation among students. When a student sits in a lecture, tutorial, workshop, etc., they are immersed in a context which is far more complex than their immediate surrounds (see Figure 1). Indeed, Biggs (1999, p.25) proposes five critical components of a learning context. These are:

1. The curriculum being taught
2. The teaching methods used
3. The assessment methods used
4. The environment created in the interaction between the teacher and the students
5. The institutional (university) climate

In addition to these components, Entwistle and Ramsden (1983) propose that the departmental context is important, and Ramsden (1997) also includes the course area context.

The myriad, complex components of a learning context appear to be filtered by students' prior learning experiences so that only a limited number are perceived by a student at any one time (Prosser & Trigwell, 1999). As students in a particular learning context are likely to vary greatly with regard to previous learning experiences, they will perceive the learning context differently. The interaction between a student's prior learning experiences and a learning context has been called a learning situation by Prosser and Trigwell (1999). Components of a learning context which have been found empirically to be vital parts of a student's perceptions of their learning situation include the quality of the teaching, the clarity of the curriculum goals, the appropriateness of the workload, the nature of the assessment and the amount of choice in learning (Entwistle & Ramsden, 1983). As explained in the next section, it is a student's perception of their individual learning situation which influences the learning approach they will use.

Relation Between Perceptions of Learning Situation and Approaches to Learning

The approach to learning students adopt has been found to be related to perception of learning situation, that is the aspects of the learning context perceived by students as a result of their previous learning experiences (Prosser & Trigwell, 1999; Trigwell & Prosser, 1991; Ramsden et al., 1997). In studies involving many thousands of students across many different subjects, deep learning approaches have been associated with perceptions of good teaching, clear goals and independence in learning. Surface learning approaches have been associated with perceptions of too high a workload and inappropriate assessment, that is, assessment which is perceived to require rote learning.

Returning to our earlier intention to establish what we mean by 'best teach and learn about IT,' part of the answer is now apparent. To best learn about a discipline area like IT means applying a deep learning approach. To best teach about a discipline area like IT means to provide a learning context and learning activities which students are likely to perceive as requiring deep approaches to learning. While the general nature of these learning contexts and learning activities are known, it is significant that the specific details have been shown by research to be discipline dependent (Prosser & Trigwell, 1999). That is, the learning context factors and learning activities found to encourage a deep approach to learning about physics are similar in general but different in detail from the factors likely to encourage a deep approach to learning about humanities or IT, for instance. To establish the best ways to teach about IT, then, we need to identify the IT-specific learning context factors and learning activities which, if perceived by students, will encourage deep learning approaches. To begin this task we turned to the IT education research literature.

A Review of the IT Education Research Literature

We reviewed the IT education research literature hoping to learn about the specific learning context factors and learning activities likely to encourage IT students to adopt deep learning approaches. We found the literature to be limited and unstructured. There was little mention of learning context factors. The focus was on new teaching strategies and, to a lesser degree, learning activities. The impact on students' approaches to learning was rarely mentioned. It was possible, however, to make some limited inferences about the learning contexts intended by the teaching strategies and learning activities.

New teaching strategies were proposed, in general, in response to criticism of the lecture/tutorial strategy considered to be predominant in an IT education context (Avison, 1991). From a general learning perspective, the lecture/tutorial model has been shown by Jackson and Prosser (1989) to be effective in transferring knowledge from a lecturer to students but ineffective in promoting conceptual understanding. From an IT education perspective, the limitations of teaching about IT to undergraduate students using a lecture/tutorial approach are well documented (for example, Cope & Horan, 1994; Fritz, 1987; Little & Margetson, 1989; Mantelaers & Creusen, 1990; Mitri, 1993; Mowete, 1993; Nunamaker, Cougar & Davis, 1982; Osborne, 1992; Schuldt, 1991; Yaverbaum, 1987). The concepts, skills and techniques needed by an IT professional working in a business environment cannot be learned simply through transfer of knowledge in a lecture/tutorial situation, as students do not develop any idea of how to apply the concepts and skills. Academically successful students have been found to pass exams by memorizing the knowledge and mechanically practicing the skills with little or no understanding or mastery of concepts.

In recognition of the problems with a lecture/tutorial teaching strategy, a number of alternative teaching strategies have been proposed in the IT education literature. In general, these strategies were intended to encourage active, cooperative, experiential learning. Some significant examples are now given.

Active participation by students in IT subjects has been promoted as a contrast to the passive approaches encouraged by the conventional lecture/tutorial model. A preference by students for active rather than passive participation was demonstrated by Lu (1994). Students perceived active participation as a more effective way to learn and made more effort when taught in this way. Active participation was encouraged by Wagner (1997) through using the World Wide Web (WWW) as a discovery-based learning tool. Students were encouraged to learn for themselves rather than being told the answers by the lecturer. Learning then becomes an active process of "modifying one's mental framework or knowledge chunks to allow them to comprehend a broader range of life experiences rather than the memorization of discrete facts" (p.76). This learning process is compatible with a deep approach to learning.

An activity that can be used to extend the advantages of active participation in IT subjects through the incorporation of cooperative learning is role plays (Cope & Horan, 1996; Mowete, 1993, Sullivan, 1993). Cope and Horan, for instance, used role plays in introductory IS classes as an adjunct to a lecture/tutorial teaching approach. The role plays involved a re-creation of a real-life scenario, with the students role playing an IS developer and an actor role playing the client. The students, working in small groups, were required to interview the client three times, once in a large group lecture situation and twice in small-group tutorial situations. The interviews were a means of determining the client's requirements for an IS. Cope and Horan evaluated the impact of the role play activity by investigating students' perceptions of the learning situation in which the role play activity took place. The evaluation sought to determine if students perceived the need to apply a deep learning approach to the role play activity. The role plays were found to be more effective than a lecture/tutorial approach in encouraging students to use deep learning approaches.

An activity intended to extend the advantages of active, cooperative learning by making learning more experiential is the use of small-group, long-term, real-world or simulated projects (for example, Crow & Rariden, 1992; Little & Margetson, 1989; Mukherjee & Cox, 1998). Projects generally require students working cooperatively in small teams to research an information storage and retrieval problem for a client in a business environment. The project includes the design, construction, documentation and implementation of a solution. In general projects are of an extended length, compared to more usual learning tasks such as assignments. IT projects are experiential in that they are "hands on" and provide students with an experience of a business context. An advantage of projects claimed by Crow and Rariden (1992 p.53) is that "Students will learn better if involved in an active and real mode."

Two other significant examples in the literature described learning activities that focused on principles compatible with deep learning approaches. These principles were the seeking of the meaning of the content being taught and the necessity for students to be aware of their developing understanding of the content and approaches to learning about IT.

The first example by Godfrey (1995) used Participative Course Design (PCD) to encourage holistic learning approaches in IT students with a focus on understanding concepts and principles. PCD is a collaborative instructor-student activity which establishes shared expectations for learning goals and learning processes early in a subject. While Godfrey does not describe holistic learning approaches in any detail, Svensson (1984) describes them as trying to form a cohesive whole. This is consistent with a deep approach to learning where students try to relate the different aspects of the content to one another.

The second example by Thomson (1994) describes the use of the principles of Total Quality Management (TQM) in IS subject design and implementation. Applying TQM to learning about IS involved considering students as clients and focusing on the learning process and its continued improvement. Students were required to view the classes as learning experiences, and design and implement their own way of learning about their choice from a number of topics. Regular meetings of the group of students exposed students to variation in understanding and the learning process, leading to continual improvement in both the learning process and understanding of the content. The use of TQM in this way is consistent with the ideas of Marton and Booth (1996, 1997) and Cope (2000) that the intention to understand, so critical to a deep learning approach, is best encouraged by having students reflect on the differences between their own and other students' levels of understanding and approaches to learning.

Considering the relevant contributions from the IT education research literature, what can be inferred about the IT-specific learning context factors and learning activities likely to encourage deep learning approaches? Little is known about the specific learning context factors appropriate for IT learning contexts, although learning activities should involve IT students trying to seek a cohesive whole with regard to the content. To achieve this aim, students need to reflect on both the content and approaches to learning about the content. Experiential learning activities are needed in which learning is active rather than passive and in small groups where students have to co-operate in the learning process.

Considering the limited input from the IT education research literature, from a relational perspective we must conclude that the best ways to teach and learn specifically about IT have not been established. We cannot rule out inadequate teaching as the cause of employers' dissatisfaction with our graduates. At the beginning of the 21st century, this is not a good situation for IT education.

To move towards establishing the best ways to teach and learn about IT, we have, over a period of time, used the research-based knowledge inherent in a relational perspective on learning to change the nature of our learning contexts and learning activities. On the basis of an iterative process of structured research, we have designed and implemented these learning contexts and activities, evaluated the resultant learning approaches used by students, and refined the learning contexts and activities. In the next section we describe the framework we used to give structure to our research.

A Framework for Action

The purpose of changing our learning contexts and learning activities was to encourage IT students to use deep learning approaches. Only through using deep learning approaches are IT undergraduates likely to develop the understanding and skills required by employers. As a benchmark for the best ways to learn about IT, and against which to design our changes and to evaluate their impact, we have used the comprehensive description of surface and deep learning approaches given by Prosser and Trigwell (1999, p.3), presented earlier in the chapter.

To encourage our students to use deep learning approaches as described by Prosser and Trigwell (1999), we have constructed a framework of factors around which to design our learning contexts and activities. The factors were derived principally from the general relational perspective literature (Biggs, 1999; Gibbs, 1992; Martin et al., in press; Marton & Booth, 1996, 1997; Ramsden, 1988, 1992) with some input from our review of the IT education research literature. The factors have been established either empirically or logically as encouraging deep learning approaches. The framework is divided into factors relating to the learning context and those relating to learning activities.

The factors included in the framework guided the design of our learning contexts and the learning activities. The practical implementation of the framework is described below.

IMPLEMENTATION

We have implemented the framework in the learning contexts and activities we use in courses in the information systems stream of the Bachelor's of Computing

Table 1: Framework of Factors Likely to Encourage Deep Learning Approaches

1.	*The learning context* – The following factors are important to achieving a learning context likely to encourage deep learning approaches:
a.	The course is well organized and has clear goals
b.	Teaching approaches support the explicit aims and objectives of the course
c.	The student has responsibility for his/her own learning, including some control over the content and approach to learning
d.	The workload is manageable
e.	The student is given help in learning within the context of the subject matter
f.	The teaching makes the structure of the individual topics, and the course as a whole, explicit
g.	Assessment tasks require the demonstration of conceptual understanding
h.	Teaching and assessment methods foster active and long-term engagement with learning tasks
i.	The teaching identifies and builds on what students already know
j.	A supportive classroom environment is provided where students feel comfortable to openly discuss their conceptions and learning approaches
k.	The emphasis is on depth of learning rather than breadth of coverage
l.	The teaching is stimulating and demonstrates the lecturer's personal commitment to the subject matter and stresses its meaning and relevance to the students
m.	Feedback is appropriate and timely
2.	*The nature of learning activities* – The following factors are important in the design of learning activities. Learning activities should:
a.	Be active and experiential
b.	Tackle real-world problems that are compatible with the experiences of the students
c.	Encourage students to relate the learning to situations outside the educational context
d.	Encourage students to reflect on the content *and* the learning process
e.	Use group interaction to expose students to variation in the ways other students understand the content and approach their learning

taught in the Department of IT at La Trobe University, Bendigo. We have evaluated the impact of our learning contexts and activities over a number of years and consequently refined them. A brief description of the latest implementation follows. In the description, the figures in brackets (for example 1b) refer to the specific learning context factors and learning factors which make up our framework for action, described in Table 1. Full detail of our learning contexts and learning activities can be found in Cope, Horan and Garner (1997), Horan (1996, 2000), Staehr (1999) and Staehr and Cope (1999).

Our current teaching of IT includes the following features.

Learning Objectives

We specify learning objectives for each course and for each topic in a course. Following Ramsden (1997), the objectives clearly specify learning outcomes or processes which should result from studying the course or topic. The objectives are published on the Web and are frequently referred to by the lecturer during classes (1b, 1f). The objectives present students with the course goals (1a) and enable them to evaluate their progress throughout the semester (2d).

Workshops

We have found that most of the factors in the framework are implemented more effectively in workshops than lectures. Consequently we have restructured the delivery of our courses. For example, in one subject, a two-hour workshop and a one-hour tutorial each week have replaced two one-hour lectures and two one-hour tutorials. We have reduced the total number of contact hours per week as we expect our students to spend at least an hour a week on the reading material they are given (1d). The reading material comes from a book of readings we prepare each year as an alternative to prescribing a textbook.

We use the Web to indicate which topics are to be covered in a particular workshop, to provide an introduction to each topic and to indicate the readings which are appropriate. Prior to attending a workshop students are expected to identify the topic that is relevant, to read the appropriate readings and to make their own notes on the topic. Not all topics relate to the information systems discipline, some are specifically included to help the students learn, for example, note taking, concept mapping and rich pictures (1e).

A typical workshop contains 25–30 students and is structured in the following way. During the first 20 minutes or so, the lecturer gives an overview of the topic and relates the topic to the course as a whole (1f). Any questions arising from the readings are dealt with by a general discussion. The remainder of the workshop involves students actively working on experiential problems in small groups (typically three or four students) (2a, 2e). These learning activities explore the topic for the workshop. The activities are centered around a case study designed to be compatible with the real-world experiences of the students (2b, 2c). Student groups are asked to report their solutions to the problems to the rest of the students in the class, thus exposing students to variation in levels of understanding (2e). This workshop format gives staff the means and time to consult with the small student groups to discover the stage of learning reached by individual students and to demonstrate limitations in existing student conceptions (1i, 1j).

In the middle and at the end of semester, workshops are allocated which do not introduce new topics but allow students to consolidate the topics already covered and to catch up with assignment work (1d, 1k, 2d). In these workshops, learning activities designed to integrate topics are used. For more detail on our use of workshops, see Staehr and Cope (1999).

Rich Pictures

We have used Rich Pictures (RPs) as the cornerstone of our learning contexts. RPs were originally proposed by Peter Checkland (1981), as part of his Soft Systems Methodology. Checkland used RPs to graphically describe and analyze IS contexts. Important features of rich pictures are that they are flexible and non-prescriptive, can be used and interpreted by anyone, and can be used to display concrete and abstract factors. Our students use RPs, individually (1c) and in groups (2e), both as a standard IS documentation tool (2c) and, importantly, as a way of developing, reflecting on and recording both their understandings of our topics and courses and the learning process (2d). RPs also provide a medium for discussion with and feedback from the teacher (1j, 1m). For a detailed description of our use of RPs, see Horan (2000).

Case Studies

We use case studies of typical business applications as a means to integrate the content of our Courses (1f). A case study is introduced at the beginning of the semester, and the weekly topics over the semester are all introduced and developed within the context of the case study. This provides continuity as different topics are progressively illustrated in the same context (1h). The experiential learning activities in the workshops (2a), mainly group-based (2e), are based on the case study, and some of the assessable assignment work involves extending aspects of the case study. Although of necessity simplified for the classroom, the case study links the topics of the course to the real world (2b, 2c). For more detail on our use of case studies, see Cope and Horan (1996) and Horan (1996).

Assessment

Each assignment we give to our students lists the learning objectives underlying the design of the assessment (1b). All assignment work is marked, annotated and returned to students promptly so that they can evaluate their progress and seek early assistance if needed (1m). The learning portfolio assignment best illustrates the application of our framework to assessment. Students are asked to choose any two topics covered in the course so far and to demonstrate their understanding of those topics using two different methods. We place strong emphasis on the importance of demonstrating a deep understanding of the material rather than presentation of isolated facts (1g). Some methods are suggested, for example, letter to a friend, a workshop plan or a rich picture, but students are free to come up with their own method (1c). Students are given the opportunity to have a draft of one of their topics commented on by staff well before the assignment is finally handed in for marking (1m).

In summary, the implementation of our framework (see Table 1) was intended to modify the learning contexts and learning activities we provide for our students. The framework was used in such a way that students' previous learning experiences and perceptions of their learning situation could be perceived by the teacher and made explicit to the students. It was incorporated into the learning context, including materials and tasks made available to the students, both within and outside formal classes. All of the techniques described reinforce one another by exhibiting characteristics likely to encourage a deep learning approach.

EVALUATION

Structured evaluations of new teaching strategies are essential to establishing the effectiveness of different ways to teach and learn about IT, yet are not commonly reported in the literature. We have endeavored to evaluate quantitatively and qualitatively the impact of the changes to our learning contexts and learning activities. A description of one of these evaluations and the outcomes is now given. For further examples of our evaluations, see Cope (1997, 2000), Cope, Horan and Garner (1997), Cope and Horan (1996, 1998) and Staehr and Cope (1999).

Quantitative Evaluation

We have centered the quantitative evaluations of our learning context and learning activity changes on the learning approaches used by students taking the second-year course, Information Systems Development. From a relational perspective on learning, the aim of any changes to learning contexts or activities should be to encourage more students to use deep learning approaches. The impact of any changes can be evaluated by comparing the numbers of students adopting surface and deep approaches before and after the changes.

In Information Systems Development we changed from a lecture/tutorial to a workshop/tutorial teaching strategy in 1998. The workshop/tutorial strategy attempted to implement the learning contexts and learning activities we described in the previous section. At the end of each implementation of Information Systems Development, from 1997 (before the change) through 2000, students completed a questionnaire (Appendices A and B). The questionnaire contained a number of Likert scale questions from the Study Process Questionnaire (Biggs, 1987) and short, open-ended items which investigated the students' approaches to learning. Using the descriptions of surface and deep learning approaches of Prosser and Trigwell (1999), two researchers independently categorized each questionnaire as representative of a surface, surface/deep or deep learning approach, following Prosser and Millar (1989). A surface/deep learning approach demonstrated some, but not all, elements of a deep approach. The researchers then compared categorizations and discussed differences until agreement was reached. The results are shown in Table 2.

To obtain an indication of the consistency of academic ability over the study period, the mean Tertiary Entrance Ranks (TER) of students in each year was compared using a single-factor analysis of variance. A TER is the university entrance score of a student in Victoria, Australia, obtained from academic performance in the last year of secondary school. The results of the single factor analysis of variance showed no significant differences in TER between years. Therefore, with respect to TER, and by implication academic ability, the profile of students was similar for each year.

Table 2: Students Categorized by Learning Approach

	Learning Approach					
	Surface		Surface/Deep		Deep	
Year	No. Students	% Students	No. Students	% Students	No. Students	% Students
1997	45	76.3	8	13.6	6	10.2
1998	39	66.1	14	23.7	6	10.2
1999	45	77.6	8	13.8	5	8.6
2000	35	62.5	17	30.4	4	7.1

The results in Table 2 were analyzed with a Chi-square test for independence using exact significance levels (SPSS exact tests). This test showed no interaction between year and learning approach and therefore indicates similar response profiles across all years. In other words our changes had no statistically significant effect on the number of students using major aspects of deep approaches in their learning.

Table 3 compares our results in the year 2000 (see Table 2) using the workshop/tutorial learning context with a study by Prosser, Walker and Millar (1994) that involved a lecture/tutorial learning context. We chose our results from the year 2000 because by this time, the two lecturers involved were thoroughly familiar with the new learning context. By studying the method used by Prosser, Walker and Millar, we determined that by combining our surface/deep and deep categories, we could make a valid comparison of the results of the two studies using 95% confidence intervals for the percentages in each cohort. The upper 95% confidence limit for students using aspects of a deep approach to their learning is 14.2% in the study by Prosser, Walker and Millar, and our lower limit is higher at 24.8%. Therefore, our teaching strategy resulted in a significantly higher proportion of students using significant aspects of a deep approach to learning in comparison.

Qualitative Evaluation

Qualitative feedback has been obtained from our students through in-depth interviews, questionnaires and focus groups. In general, students readily perceived

Table 3: A Comparison of Two Studies Using Different Learning Contexts (the errors are based on the 95th percentiles of the normal distribution and represent two standard deviations)

Study	Course	No. of students	Learning context	Significant aspects of a deep approach	Surface approach
Prosser, Walker & Millar (1994)	Physics	84	Lecture/ tutorial	8.3% ± 5.9%	91.7% ± 5.9%
Table 1 (2000 results)	Information Systems	56	Workshop/ tutorial	37.5% ± 12.7%	62.5% ± 12.7%

the difference between the deep learning approaches required in our subjects and the rote learning surface approaches required by many of their other subjects. Although many found the deep approach more difficult than a surface learning approach, they acknowledged its value.

We discuss the implications of our evaluations in the next section. We also consider how a global research approach is required to most efficiently establish the best ways to teach and learn about IT. This will be an important challenge for IT education in the 21st century.

DISCUSSION AND CONCLUSION

We began this chapter by suggesting that the concerns expressed by employers about the quality of IT graduates may be the result of problems with 'how' we teach and 'how' our students learn about IT. Our review of the IT education research literature and our evaluation results support this proposition. Even after the implementation and refinement of the changes we have made to our learning contexts and learning activities, fewer than half of our students were using significant aspects of the deep learning approaches likely to lead to the understandings and skills required by employers. The majority of our students are not learning about IT in the best ways. Given that recent research by Prosser, Trigwell and Taylor (1994) and Trigwell and Prosser (1996) has demonstrated an empirical relationship between teachers' approaches to teaching and students' approaches to learning, we must also conclude that we continue not to be teaching about IT in the best ways possible.

We have proposed that teaching and learning about IT based on a relational perspective on learning, and the framework of learning context and learning activity factors derived from the literature, should, logically, lead to an improvement in the proportion of students using deep learning approaches and resultant higher quality learning outcomes. What empirical evidence do we have regarding this claim? Our evaluation of the course Information Systems Development found no statistically significant change between 1997 and 2000 in the proportion of students using deep learning approaches in response to our interventions. Should we continue with a relational learning perspective and our framework of learning context and learning activity factors as the foundation for our attempts to establish the best ways to teach and learn about IT? We now present what we believe to be evidence that encourages us to continue our efforts.

Our failure to detect a statistically significant change in the proportion of students using deep learning approaches is not unexpected. One possible cause of this failure may be lack of statistical power due to the relatively small numbers of students in each year. In our IT context we would need a very large change in students' learning approaches to produce a statistically significant change. Given the generally recognized slowness of educational change, we are not discouraged by our results. Indeed we, as teachers, have been learning as we go in implementing our new learning contexts and learning activities. We did not expect immediate and striking results.

Further encouragement for continuing with the thrust of our present research comes from the significant difference we have been able to demonstrate in the comparison of the results of our study in the year 2000 with those of Prosser, Walker and Millar (1994). The results of this comparison are encouraging for two reasons. Firstly, the students in the Prosser, Walker and Millar study were first-year undergraduate students and our students were second-year students. Biggs (1987, p.8) states that "there is a general decline in the deep approach from first to final year for those completing first degrees in both universities and colleges." This decline in the deep approach was shown in Prosser, Walker and Millar's study. At the beginning of the first-year physics course, $26.2 \pm 5.9\%$ of the students surveyed were using significant aspects of deep approaches and at the end of the year there were only $8.3 \pm 5.9\%$. In contrast the students in our study were in the middle of their second year and a higher proportion ($37.5\% \pm 12.7\%$) were using significant aspects of deep approaches. Biggs (1987, p.8) goes on to say that "Those students continuing with postgraduate study, however, show a marked rise in deep approach." The students in Prosser, Walker and Millar's study were from a prestigious, major metropolitan university where students would be encouraged to consider research careers. In contrast, few of our students continue on to postgraduate study. Secondly, students in Prosser, Walker and Millar's study would have had university entrance scores considerably higher than those of our students. The Bendigo campus of La Trobe University is in a rural area and takes in students with a much broader range of university entrance scores than do metropolitan universities. Therefore, we may have been even more successful in improving our students' approaches to learning when these factors are taken into account.

We believe we have successfully begun the task of establishing the best ways to teach and learn about IT. A relational perspective on learning and the framework of learning context and activity factors we developed are worth pursuing as foundations for improvement. Learning contexts and learning activities grounded in this perspective and framework are better ways to teach and learn about IT. So what do we do next?

Insight can be gained from considering why our efforts have not been more successful. Our evaluation method involved investigating how students approached their learning. While providing insight into the overall effectiveness of our interventions, this method does not tell us why the majority of students continue to use surface learning approaches and, hence, how we can improve matters further. From a relational perspective on learning, students using surface learning approaches are not perceiving the learning contexts as we intended. Identifying which factors need further manipulation is critical to continuing our efforts to establishing the best ways to teach and learn about IT.

We have some evidence from the data collected from the course, Information Systems Development, to suggest that students do not perceive their workload as being manageable (1d.). This evidence is described in detail in Staehr and Cope (1999) and comes from further statistical analysis of the Likert scale questions on our measuring instrument (Appendices A and B). This is despite the fact that we have decreased the number of contact hours and content we cover and included two weeks of consolidation where we do not cover new content. We concluded that the problem could well lie in the workload in other courses the students were undertaking concurrently with Information Systems Development and the fact that full-time students are increasingly having to take on part-time work to pay for their education. Our research indicates that we need to begin to try to influence these broader contexts in a structured, evaluated way. We need to talk to other lecturers in our department and at our university and inform them of our commitment to, enjoyment in and strategies for improving our teaching and our students' learning. We need to communicate the encouraging results of our quantitative and qualitative evaluations. We need to negotiate our students' workloads at a department and university level.

We have no evidence of which other factors in our framework are being perceived inappropriately by our students. Research into students' perceptions of our learning contexts is needed to isolate the IT-specific learning context and activity factors we need to manipulate further. Further research will involve using the Course Experience Questionnaire (Ramsden, 1991) which has sub-scales for the factors known to encourage surface and deep approaches. In addition in-depth interviews with small groups of students about perceptions of their learning situations are necessary to provide us with a more complete picture.

Given the myriad of factors which make up the learning contexts we provide for our students, we conclude our chapter with a call to arms. Our research has shown that the task of establishing the best ways to teach and learn about IT is clearly incomplete, is a complex one and is an important challenge for IT education in the 21st century. The task is beyond the efforts of a small research group. A global, collegial approach to IT education research is called for to take into account global variations in culture, history and location of teaching and learning contexts. There is a need on a global scale to design and implement new IT learning contexts and activities as improvements to those already evaluated and reported in the literature. It follows that there is a need to make ourselves aware of what has already been done through reference to the literature and to make relevant, justified changes that are grounded in an accepted perspective on student learning. Reported evaluations of interventions to teaching strategies are critical. The evaluations need to be considered, structured and grounded in theory.

The time to establish the best ways to teach and learn about IT is now. Any present and future view of our world indicates the growing importance of IT and hence IT education. We must actively seek to make our teaching of IT effective. The task is beyond an individual. The challenge is a global one. The global communication means are available in terms of relevant electronic journals and international conferences. The call is for published, structured research grounded in the existing literature and contemporary views of student learning and teaching.

APPENDIX A

Short answer questionnaire items used to investigate approach to learning in IS Development in 1997 (lecture/tutorial strategy)

1. Describe what **you** do during lectures in IS development.
2. How does what you do in the lectures assist you to learn?
3. Describe what **you** do during tutorials.
4. How does what you do in the tutorials assist you to learn?
5. Describe how you have studied for the assignments in IS development.
6. Describe any ways in which the assignments in IS development have assisted you to learn.
7. Describe any additional study you have done at home that has contributed to your learning in IS development.
8. How has this study assisted you to learn?
9. Describe in words or pictures what '*learning*' means to you.

APPENDIX B

Questionnaire items used to investigate approach to learning in IS Development in 1998, 1999 and 2000 (small student group strategy)

Likert scale questions (5 - True all of the time, 4 - True most of the time, 3 - True half of the time, 2 - True little of the time, 1 - True none of the time)

1. The best way for me to understand technical terms in this subject is to memorize definitions.

2. I find I have to concentrate on memorizing a good deal of what we have to learn in this subject.
3. I try to relate ideas in this subject to those in others, wherever possible.
4. I find it helpful to 'map out' a new topic in this subject by seeing how the ideas fit together.
5. In this subject, I generally put a lot of effort into trying to understand things which initially seem difficult.
6. I usually set out to understand thoroughly the meaning of what I am asked to read in this subject.
7. Often I find I have read things in this subject without having a chance to really understand them.
8. In trying to understand new ideas, this subject encouraged me to relate them to real-life situations.
9. I usually don't have time to think about the implications of what I have read in this subject.

Open-ended questions

1. Why do you think your lecturers chose to teach ISD in the way they did (i.e., having workshops rather than lectures and expecting you to read about each topic beforehand)?
2. How have you gone about learning in ISD? Say what you actually did rather than what you think you should have done.
3. Why did you go about learning in this way?
4. Describe what you did in the workshops in Information Systems Development. Say what you actually did rather than what you think you should have done.
5. How did your activities in the workshops contribute to your learning in the subject Information Systems Development?
6. Describe any work related to Information Systems Development that you did outside of class time. Say what you actually did rather than what you think you should have done.
7. How did your work outside of class time contribute to your learning in the subject Information Systems Development?

ACKNOWLEDGMENTS

The teaching initiative in the course, Information Systems Development, was supported financially by the La Trobe University, Bendigo Teaching Committee and by the School of Management, Technology and Environment Research Advisory Group.

Dr. Graeme Byrne, Division of Mathematics, La Trobe University, Bendigo, for assistance with the statistics in the project.

REFERENCES

Athey, S., & Wickham, M. (1995). Required skills for information systems jobs in Australia. *Journal of Computer Information Systems*, 36(2), 60-63.

Avison, D.E. (1991). Action programmes for teaching and researching information systems. *The Australian Computer Journal*, 23(2), 66-72.

Biggs, J. (1987). *Study Process Questionnaire Manual*. Melbourne: Australian Council for Educational Research.

Biggs, J. (1993). From theory to practice: A cognitive systems approach. *Higher Education Research and Development*, 12, 73-85.

Biggs, J. (1999). *Teaching for Quality Learning at University: What the Student Does*. Buckingham: Society for Research into Higher Education & Open University Press.

Checkland, P. (1981). *Systems Thinking, Systems Practice*. Chichester: Wiley.

Cohen, E. (Ed.) (2000). Curriculum Model 2000 of the Information resource management Association and the Data Administration Managers Association. [On-line]. Available: http://gise.org/IRMA-DAMA-2000.pdf.

Cope, C.J. (1997). Learning about information systems: A relational perspective. *Proceedings of HERDSA '97*, Adelaide, July 8-11.

Cope, C.J. (2000). Educationally critical aspects of the experience of learning about the concept of an IS. Unpublished PhD thesis. La Trobe University, Australia. [On-line]. Available: http://ironbark.bendigo.latrobe.edu.au/~cope/cope-thesis.pdf.

Cope, C. J., & Horan, P. (1994). An alternative curriculum for introductory information system students. *Proceedings of the Eleventh Information Systems Education Conference*, Louisville, U.S., October 28-30, pp. 167-173.

Cope, C. J. & Horan, P. (1996). The role played case: An experiential approach to teaching introductory information systems development, *Journal of Information Systems Education*, 8 (2&3), 33-39.

Cope, C. J. & Horan, P. (1998). Toward an understanding of teaching and learning about information systems. *Proceedings of the Third Australasian Computer Science Education Conference*, Brisbane, July 8-10th, pp. 188-197.

Cope, C. J., Horan, P. & Garner, M. (1997). Conceptions of information systems and their use in teaching about IS. *Journal of Informing Science*, 1(1), 8-22.

Couger, J., Davis, G.B., Dologite, D.G., Feinstein, D.L., Gorgone, J.T., Jenkins, A.M., Kasper, G.M., Little, J.C., Longenecker, Jr., H.E., & Valacich, J.S. (1995). IS'95: Guidelines of undergraduate IS curriculum. *MIS Quarterly*, 19, 341-359.

Crawford, K., Gordon, S., Nicholas, J., & Prosser, M. (1994). Conceptions of mathematics and how it is learned: The perspectives of students entering university. *Learning and Instruction*, 4, 331-345.

Crow, G.B., & Rariden, R.L. (1992). Strengthening the computer information systems curriculum through cooperative education. *Journal of Computer Information Systems*, 32(3), 52-55.

Davis, G.B., Gorgone, J.T., Couger, J.D., Feinstein, D.L., & Longenecker, H.E. Jr. (1997). IS'97: Model curriculum and guidelines for undergraduate degree programs in information systems. *Joint Report of the Association for Computing Machinery (ACM), Association for Information Systems (AIS) and Association of Information Technology Professional (AITP)*. Available from ACM and AITP.

Doke, E., & Williams, S. (1999). Knowledge and skill requirements for information systems professionals: An exploratory study. *Journal of IS Education*, 10(1), 10-18.

Entwistle, N. J. (1998). Improving teaching through research on student learning. In Forest, J. F. F., (Ed.), *University Teaching: International Perspectives*. New York: Garland Publishing.

Entwistle, N. J., & Ramsden, P. (1983). *Understanding Student Learning*. London: Croom Helm.

Fritz, J. (1987). A pragmatic approach to systems analysis and design. *SIGCSE Bulletin*, 19(1), 127-131.

Gibbs, G. (1992). *Improving the Quality of Student Learning*, Bristol: Technical and Educational Services.

Godfrey, R.M. (1995). Students as end-users: Participative design of the I/S learning experience. *Journal of Computer Information Systems*, 36(1), 17-22.

Hawforth, D.A., & Van Wetering, F.J. (1994). Determining underlying corporate viewpoints on information systems education curricula. *Journal of Education for Business*, 69, 292-295.

Hazel, E., Prosser, M., & Trigwell, K. (1996). Student learning of biology concepts in different university contexts. *Research and Development in Higher Education*, 19, 323-326.

Horan, P. (1996). Teaching information systems analysis and design using case studies. *Proceedings of PRIISM '96*, Hawaii, January, pp. 39-46.

Horan, P. (2000). Using rich pictures in information systems teaching. *Proceedings of the first International Conference on Systems Thinking in Management*, Geelong, November, pp. 257-262.

Jackson, M.W., & Prosser, M.T. (1989). Less lecturing, more learning, *Studies in Higher Education*, 14(1), 55-68.

Johansson, B., Marton, F., & Svensson, L. (1985). An approach to describing learning as change between qualitatively different conceptions. In Pines, A. L., & West, L. H. T., (Eds.), *Cognitive Structure and Conceptual Change* (pp. 233-258). New York: Academic Press.

Lee, D. M. S., Trauth, E.M., & Farwell, D. (1995). Critical skills and knowledge requirements of IS professionals: A joint academic/industry investigation. *MIS Quarterly*, 19, 313-340.

Little, E., & Margetson, D.B. (1989). A project-based approach to information systems design for undergraduates. *The Australian Computer Journal*, 21(2), 130-136.

Longenecker, H.E. Jr., Feinstein, D. L., Couger, J. D., Davis, G.G., & Gorgone, J.T. (1995). Information Systems '95: A summary of the collaborative IS curriculum specification of the joint DPMA, ACM, AIS task force. *Journal of Information Systems Education*, 6(4), 174-186.

Lu, H. (1994). A preliminary study of student responses to different CIS course teaching strategies. *Journal of Computer Information Systems*, 34(4), 31-36.

Lybeck, L., Marton, F., Stromdahl, H., & Tullberg, A. (1988). The phenomenography of the "Mole Concept" in chemistry. In Ramsden, P., (Ed.), *Improving Learning. New Perspectives* (pp. 81-108). London: Kogan Page.

Mantelaers, P.A.H.M., & Creusen, M.W.F.J. (1990). Teaching information systems design: Mission impossible? In Richardson, J., (Ed.), *Computers in Education: Conference Abstracts. IFIP Fifth World Conference on Computers in Education (WCEC90)*. Australian Council for Computers in Education.

Martin, E., Prosser, M., Trigwell, K., Leuckenhausen, G., & Ramsden, P. (In press). Using phenomenography and metaphor to explore academics' understanding of subject matter and teaching. In Rust, C., (Ed.), *Improving Student Learning*. Oxford: Oxford Centre for Staff Development.

Marton, F. (1998). Towards a theory of quality in higher education. In Dart, B., & Boulton-Lewis, G., (Eds.), *Teaching and Learning in Higher Education* (pp. 177-200). Camberwell, Victoria, Australia: Australian Council for Educational Research.

Marton, F., & Booth, S. (1996). The learner's experience of learning. In Olson, D. R., & Torrance, N., (Eds.), *The Handbook of Education and Human Development: New Models of Learning, Teaching and Schooling* (pp.534-564). Oxford: Blackwell.

Marton, F., & Booth, S. (1997). *Learning and Awareness*. Mahwah, NJ: Erlbaum.

Marton, F., & Saljo, R. (1976). On qualitative differences in learning. I. Outcome and process. *British Journal of Educational Psychology*, 46, 4-11.

Marton, F., & Saljo, R. (1997). Approaches to learning. In Marton, F., Hounsell, D., & Entwistle, N. J., (Eds.), *The Experience of Learning: Implications for Teaching and Studying in Higher Education* (2nd Ed.) (pp. 39-58). Edinburgh: Scottish Academic Press.

Misic, M., & Russo, N. (1996). Educating systems analysts: A comparison of educators' and practitioners' opinions concerning the relative importance of systems analyst tasks and skills. *Journal of Computer Information Systems*, 36(4), 86-91.

Mitri, M. (1993). The role-play exercise for an introductory computer information systems course. *Interface*, 15(2), 39-43.

Mowete, R.G. (1993). Enhancing conceptual learning in the systems analysis course. *Interface*, 14(4), 2-6.

Mukherjee, A., & Cox, J.L. (1998). Effective use of mastery-based experiential learning in a project course to improve skills in systems analysis and design. *Journal of Computer Information Systems*, 38(4), 46-50.

Mulder, F. & van Weert, T. (2000). Informatics Curriculum Framework 2000 for higher education. Publication of the International Federation for Information processing (IFIP). Available: http://Poe.netlab.csc.villanova.edu/ifip32/ICF2000.htm.

Nunamaker, J.F., Cougar, J.D., & Davis, G.B. (1982). Information systems curriculum recommendations for the 80s. *Communications of the ACM*, 25(11), 781-805.

Osborne, M. (1992). APPGEN: A tool for teaching systems analysis and design. *SIGCSE Bulletin*, 24(1), 259-263.

Prosser, M., & Millar, R. (1989). The how and what of learning physics. *European Journal of Psychology in Education*, 4, 513-528.

Prosser, M., & Trigwell, K. (1999). *Understanding Learning and Teaching: The Experience in Higher Education*. Philadelphia, PA: Society for Research into Higher Education & Open University Press.

Prosser, M., Trigwell, K., & Taylor, P.T. (1994). A phenomenographic study of academics' conceptions of science learning and teaching. *Learning and Instruction*, 4, 217-231.

Prosser, M., Walker, P. & Millar, R. (1994). Differences in students' perceptions of learning physics. *Research and Development in Higher Education*, 17.

Ramsden, P. (1979). Student learning and perceptions of the academic environment. *Higher Education*, 8, 411-428.

Ramsden, P. (1987). Improving teaching and learning in higher education: The case for a relational perspective. *Studies in Higher Education*, 12, 275-286.

Ramsden, P. (1988). Studying learning: Improving teaching. In Ramsden, P., (Ed.), *Improving Learning. New Perspectives* (pp. 13-31). London: Kogan Page.

Ramsden, P. (1991). A performance indicator of teaching quality in higher education: The Course Experience Questionnaire. *Studies in Higher Education*, 16, 129-150.

Ramsden, P. (1992). *Learning to Teach in Higher Education*. London: Routledge.

Ramsden, P. (1997). *Using Aims and Objectives*. Research Working Paper 89.4, University of Melbourne.

Ramsden, P., Prosser, M., Trigwell, K. & Martin, E. (1997). Perceptions of academic leadership and the effectiveness of university teaching. Paper presented at the *Annual Conference of the Australian Association for Research in Education*, Brisbane, Australia.

Richards, M., & Pelley, L. (1994). The 10 most valuable components of an information systems education. *Information and Management*, 27, 59-68.

Richards, T., Yellen, R., Kappelman, L., & Guymes, S. (1998). Information systems manager's perceptions of IS job skills. *Journal of Computer Information Systems*, 38(3), 53-57.

Roth, M.K., & Ducloss, L.K. (1995). Meeting entry-level job requirements: The impact on the IS component of business undergraduate curricula. *Journal of Computer Information Systems*, 35(4), 50-54.

Schuldt, B.A. (1991). Real-world versus "Simulated" projects in database instruction. *Journal of Education for Business*, 61(1), 35-39.

Staehr, L. (1999). Teaching ethics to computing students. *Proceedings of the First AICE International Conference*, Ed. Simpson, C. R., Melbourne, Australia, July 14-16, pp. 347-355. Full paper available online: http://www.aice.swin.edu.au/events/AICEC99/webabstracts.html#STAEHR.

Staehr, L., & Cope, C. J. (1999). A new model for teaching information systems? *Proceedings of the 3rd World Multiconference on Systemics, Cybernetics and Informatics and the 5th International Conference on Information Systems Analysis and Synthesis,* Callaos, N. et al., (Eds.). Vol. 1, Orlando, FL., USA, July 31-August 4, pp. 357-362.

Sullivan, S. L. (1993). A software project management course role-play team-project approach emphasizing written and oral communication skills. *SIGCSE Bulletin,* 25(1), 283-287.

Svensson, L. (1984). Skill in learning. In Marton, F., Hounsell, D. and Entwistle, N. J. (Eds.), *The Experience of Learning,* 56-70. Edinburgh: Scottish Academic Press.

Thomson, N.S. (1994). Using TQM principles to teach current topics in information systems. *Journal of Information Systems Education,* 6(2), 65-72.

Trauth, E.M., Farwell, D.W., & Lee, D. (1993). The IS expectation gap: Industry expectations versus academic preparation. *MIS Quarterly,* 17(3), 293-307.

Trigwell, K., & Prosser, M. (1991). Improving the quality of student learning: The influence of learning context and student approaches to learning on learning outcomes. *Higher Education,* 22, 251-266.

Trigwell, K., & Prosser, M. (1996). Changing approaches to teaching: A relational perspective. *Studies in Higher Education,* 21, 275-284.

Wagner, W. P. (1997). Teaching information systems concepts using World Wide Web-based content. *Journal of Computer Information Systems,* 38(2), 76-81.

Yaverbaum, G.J. (1987). An evaluation of a realistic approach to MIS. *SIGCSE Bulletin,* 19(1), 36-39.

Chapter 22

Bridging the Industry-University Gap: An Action Research Study of a Web-Enabled Course Partnership

Ned Kock
Temple University, USA

Camille Auspitz and Brad King
Day & Zimmermann, Inc., USA

This chapter discusses a course partnership involving Day & Zimmermann, Inc. (DZI), a large engineering and professional services company, and Temple University. The course's main goal was to teach students business process redesign concepts and techniques. These concepts and techniques were used to redesign five business processes from DZI's information technology organization. DZI's CIO and a senior manager, who played the role of project manager, championed the course partnership. A Web site with bulletin boards, multimedia components and static content was used to support the partnership. The chapter investigates the use of Web-based collaboration technologies in combination with communication behavior norms and face-to-face meetings, and its effect on the success of the partnership.

Previously Published in *Challenges of Information Technology Education in the 21st Century* edited by Eli Cohen, Copyright © 2002, Idea Group Publishing.

INTRODUCTION

Industry-university partnerships, particularly those involving research universities, are commonplace and on the rise (Burnham, 1997). They allow industry access to quality research services at subsidized costs, as well as to potential future employees while still in their formative years. Universities benefit from such partnerships through research grants that complement dwindling government funding, and student exposure to current "real-world" problems and issues.

Some sectors of the economy are more active than others in research involving industry-university collaboration. The manufacturing sector is arguably the most active. In 1998, the National Coalition for Advanced Manufacturing, based in Washington, DC, released a report on the topic covering a wide range of industries. The vast majority of the companies surveyed for the report praised the concept and highlighted the crucial importance of industry-university partnerships for competitiveness improvement. One association of manufacturers in particular, Sematech, made up of companies in the U.S. semiconductor industry, stated that a considerable portion of its membership had been literally rescued from their competitiveness downslide by industry-university research partnerships (Wheaton, 1998).

Irrespective of economic sector or industry, the vast majority of industry-university partnerships are of the *research partnership* type, which predominantly involves applied firm-specific research. In this type of partnership, funding from the industry partner is received in exchange for "intellectual horsepower" in the form of research services and technology transfer (Hollingsworth, 1998). In science-based fields, universities focus on basic research, and the main interest of industry partners is in the commercial and industrial implications of a scientific project and how they can be taken advantage of by internal research and development departments. In less science-based fields, the solution of technical problems is a major concern of industry. In all fields, the exchange of knowledge in techno-scientific communities is a crucial element of interaction in research partnerships (Meyer-Krahmer, 1998).

A much less common type of industry-university partnership is what we refer here to as a *course partnership*, which gravitates around a regular university course (or set of courses) rather than a research project or program. In these types of partnerships, the industry partner agrees to sponsor one or more courses in which the students are expected to apply concepts and theory learned in class to the solution of some of the industry partner's key problems. Students benefit from the direct contact with the industry they are likely to join after they graduate as well as professional relationships they are able to establish during the course.

This chapter discusses a *course partnership* involving a large engineering and professional services company, and a public university, both headquartered in Philadelphia. An action research study of the course partnership conducted between May and July of 1999 is used as a basis. The main goal of the course was to teach students business process redesign concepts and techniques, which were used to redesign several real processes at the industry partner. One salient aspect of this action research study is the role played by a Web-based collaboration system as a communication hub and information repository during the course partnership, which is investigated in light of previous empirical research and key theories. Like typical action research studies (Checkland, 1991; Lau, 1997; Peters and Robinson, 1984; Winter, 1989; Wood-Harper, 1985), ours aimed at providing a service to the research clients (Jonsonn, 1991; Rapoport, 1970; Sommer, 1994), while at the same time performing an exploratory investigation of the effect of Web-based collaboration technologies on course partnerships. The research clients in question were the students and the industry partner. Also, in line with a subclass of action research, namely participatory action research (Greenwood et al., 1993; Elden and Chisholm, 1993; McTaggart, 1991; Whyte, 1991), one of the research clients, the industry partner, participated actively in the compilation and analysis of the exploratory research data, as well as in the interpretation of the findings, including the writing of this chapter.

OBSTACLES TO COURSE PARTNERSHIPS

The wide proliferation of research partnerships in the U.S. and several other countries (Cabral, 1998; Jones-Evans, 1999; Saegusa, 1997; Wong, 1999) can be explained by the incentives to those who directly participate in the partnership. The benefits for industry partners, faculty and students involved range from knowledge acquisition to financial incentives. Often, research partnerships reward research and development department members with workload reduction, increased productivity and knowledge acquisition. Faculty and students are rewarded with funds to support their research and exposure to industry-specific problems and issues outside the scope of university education.

Course partnerships, on the other hand, often fail to benefit a key group of players – the faculty developing and teaching the courses. Most course partnerships involve the adaptation of existing university programs or the creation of new programs to address the needs of a particular industry or company (Mengoni, 1998). In these "wholesale partnerships," the industry benefits from a university program better tailored to its needs, and the university as a whole from an increase in enrollments. The faculty who teach those courses, however, are rarely provided with any direct incentive to participate in such partnerships, in spite of the extra work required to develop new or adapt existing courses to the new program.

A possible alternative to overcome the barrier above is for universities to stimulate and provide the necessary infrastructure for faculty to lead the development of course partnerships on a course-by-course basis, which could potentially lead to better aggregate results in terms of tailoring courses to industry needs. This new approach could be implemented by supporting the development and teaching of specific courses in close collaboration with industry partners, who would provide funding to compensate faculty for their participation and cover other expenses such as specific equipment and software needed to implement the partnership. Key potential benefits of course partnerships for students and industry partners are listed in Table 1:

Assuming that the problem of lack of direct incentives for faculty is solved, key obstacles to course partnerships still remain. Some of these stem from difficulties in the communication and coordination between industry and university participants. Industry and universities often have different organizational cultures, languages and values, which pose communication difficulties. Their members follow different work schedules, are rarely co-located, and have different and sometimes conflicting goals (Brannock, 1998), which create coordination difficulties.

Table 1: Potential Benefits of Course Partnerships

Benefits for students	**Benefits for industry partners**
Putting concepts and theories learned in class in practice, which adds a new and valuable "real-world" dimension to the learning process.	Hiring selected students with top potential, and whose behavior and values match the firm's internal culture, customer orientation and mission.
Experiencing first-hand professional issues in their chosen fields.	Creating the appropriate climate for change due to the infusion of new ideas.
Establishing company contacts that may lead to future employment.	Absorbing new concepts and ideas that may be used to boost competitiveness.

In addition to communication and coordination difficulties, a key obstacle to course partnerships is the extra time commitment required from both industry as well as university participants. It can be inferred from careful inspection of Table 1 that the more company members are directly involved in the partnership, the better. For example, the more company members observe students in action during the course partnership, the more accurate will be the identification of future "stellar" employees. However, work pressures may make it difficult to motivate a critical mass of employees to participate actively. Also, faculty teaching such courses must to be willing to take on heavy project management responsibilities in addition to normal teaching duties (Lee, 1998).

THE ROLE OF WEB-BASED COLLABORATION TECHNOLOGIES

The deployment of standard Web-based technologies in organizations opened up new opportunities for the development of Web-based systems to support inter-organizational collaboration. Since course partnerships are, by definition, inter-organizational initiatives involving at least two different entities, i.e., an industry partner and a university, they are prime candidates for the use of Web-based collaboration technologies. The availability of a common infrastructure, the Internet, allows for fast implementation of low-cost Web sites with effective communication support and data centralization features. Such Web sites can potentially be used to overcome several of the obstacles outlined in the previous section in the context of the course partnership discussed in this chapter.

As stated earlier, the course partnership described here involved the establishment of teams whose main goal was to improve several business processes of the industry partner. For this to happen effectively, both industry partner members and students had to agree on the basic concepts, techniques and language used in process improvement initiatives. In this context, Web-based bulletin boards were seen as likely to be useful complements to face-to-face meetings by allowing participants to conduct part of their interaction in an asynchronous and distribute manner, using standard Web browsers. Previous research suggests that the use of electronic bulletin boards is likely to decrease the amount of time required from each individual member of a process improvement team, without any loss of quality, provided that Web-based interaction is used in combination with face-to-face meetings (Kock, 1999; Kock and McQueen, 1998).

Most process improvement initiatives involve the subsequent phases of process selection, modeling, analysis and redesign (Davenport, 1993; Davenport and Short, 1990; Hammer and Champy, 1993; Harrington, 1991). Given that progressing through these phases generates a large amount of documentation, another useful function of a Web site would be that of providing a central repository for the documentation generated by process improvement teams. The documentation of a given team could also be made available to all teams, so opportunities for integration of the outcomes from different teams could be identified and taken advantage of.

Finally, the combined use of a Web site for communication and centralized data storage would likely improve coordination of the work of different process improvement teams and reduce the amount of time and effort required for that coordination. The project manager would be able to monitor the progress of each team vis-à-vis the progress of the other teams through the Web site, without having to rely only on time-consuming face-to-face meetings, and take action when needed. General project instructions and guidelines could be provided once for everyone through a specific area of the Web site, rather than repetitively to each team. The sharing of data among teams would likely enable some teams to avoid mistakes made by other teams, as well as reuse interesting process designs and related ideas.

ACTION RESEARCH STUDY: DAY & ZIMMERMAN, INC. AND TEMPLE UNIVERSITY

This section describes the course partnership and discusses the key role that a Web site has played in the success of the partnership. While this chapter has three co-authors, including the instructor who was one of the investigators, this section was written in most part by industry partner co-investigators. It reflects their perceptions of the partnership, which the instructor validated through participant observation and research data analysis (this is mentioned so the reader can better appreciate the narrative). It is clear from this section that several of the expected technology benefits above were realized, but some were not. The next section summarizes and discusses both types of effects as "lessons learned" from the action research study.

Initial Contacts and Meetings:
Do We Really Want to do This?

In late April of 1999, the CIO of Day & Zimmermann, Inc. (DZI) received a letter from the instructor (first author of this chapter) inquiring if DZI was interested in partnering with Temple University for a graduate-level course in business process redesign with applications of Internet collaboration technologies. From the outset, the CIO seemed to believe that this project would benefit DZI's enterprise IT organization (eIT). A meeting was arranged and the instructor went to DZI's headquarters in Philadelphia to meet with the CIO and his management team. At the meeting the instructor presented his ideas about the course partnership and proposed an implementation plan. eIT's management found the idea intriguing. The consensus was that a collaboration of this order presented a number of opportunities as well as a number of obstacles.

eIT had recently gone through a major transformation, which included a Capability Design project. This project involved many eIT employees in various teams that evaluated high-level processes and designed new processes as a foundation for the newly reorganized unit. The proposed partnership with Temple University was seen as likely to enable eIT to leverage some of the momentum created by the Capability Design project. In addition to gaining valuable process design experience, the eIT employees involved in the Temple project would, working with the student team members, be able to identify real process improvements that could be applied once the course was completed. Temple's offer of evaluating and redesigning tactical-level processes was seen as a good complement to the high-level process redesign of the earlier Capability Design project.

The most significant obstacles faced by eIT to the implementation of the course partnership were related to time and resource constraints. In addition, there was some concern about whether the redesigned processes would actually be implemented once the course was over. eIT's management and staff were fully engaged and had little or no spare time in which to fulfill the obligations of this type of project. In response to this concern, the instructor proposed that a Web site be used to support the project as a data repository and communication tool. And since the course was being taught both online and in lectures, and the entire course material was to be posted online (including streamed video-clips of lectures); any eIT employee would be able to take the course online, even if he or she was not able to sit in the face-to-face class meetings. An additional, albeit less tangible benefit was the opportunity for the company to observe and evaluate young talent for potential hire into eIT or DZI. It was determined that the benefits outweighed the drawbacks even when taking into consideration that the redesigned processes may not be implemented. The course partnership was formed.

Selecting Projects and Defining Their Scope:
Managing Expectations

Several processes within eIT were identified for the project. The following processes were selected jointly by eIT and the instructor: Asset Management,

Help Desk Call Response, SLA (Service Level Agreement) Development, New Employee Account Set-Up and Key Person University (KPU). A process owner from within eIT was assigned to each of the selected processes. Each process was then assigned a team of students, who were expected to work closely with the process owner. A key element of this project was the working relationship between the process owners and the student teams. Everyone involved was forced to stretch intellectually, organizationally and socially to coordinate multiple schedules and skills. It was evident from the beginning that some groups would perform at a higher level than others. The instructor cautioned eIT management about setting expectations too high. The goal for the university was to teach the students about process redesign and collaborative work methods. eIT had to understand that even though the project very closely resembled a consulting project, the actual redesign results might not be functional or feasible.

eIT strongly believed that this partnership and the project as a whole would have a higher success rate if the focus remained inside eIT and thus limited the amount of involvement required from other DZI businesses and staff units. eIT also assigned one of its senior managers as a full-time project manager for the course partnership. This level of commitment on the part of the sponsoring company, as well as the decision to fund the partnership through a cash grant, clearly signaled the significance of the project for both the process owners and the student teams. Temple University provided two technical support specialists who were available to assist both eIT and the student teams with various technical issues that arose during the course.

The overall scope of the course was clearly defined in the course outline. Three reports were to be developed. Report 1 included a contextualized description, model and list of problems associated with the current process, as well as desired achievements of the redesign. Report 2 included the redesign guidelines used and how they were used, and the redesigned process model. Report 3 consisted of an analysis of three different IT solutions to implement the redesigned process, as well as a cost/benefit analysis and an implementation plan for each solution. Specific requirements for the individual processes varied. Of the five selected processes, all were existing processes within eIT with the exception of the KPU. Therefore, development of the first report for the KPU process team was more complicated because they first had to develop a process that they could then redesign. Some of the processes such as the Help Desk and New Employee Account Set-up required greater involvement from extended team members and eIT customers.

Creating a Web Site: Not Only a Communication Tool

The development of a Web site to support the partnership was a key selling point to eIT from the outset. The instructor created a Web site as the hub of information and collaboration for the course. The Web site contained all the course material, lecture slides, course outline, contact information, pictures and video clips of student teams, discussion threads for each of the processes and a "tools" area that provided detailed tutorials that explained how to create a Web site with similar functionality. It was through this Web site that eIT employees could "attend" the course and all the process team members communicated asynchronously (see Figure 1).

The team members used the discussion threads available on the Web site to post and resolve many issues while working on various draft reports. The process teams met regularly to discuss and review these reports. The Web site enabled all parties involved to access and review draft documents prior to a meeting. Meeting time was therefore maximized and used to discuss modifications to the document content as opposed to being wasted while all present familiarized themselves with a revised document.

Figure 1: Main Page of the Web Site

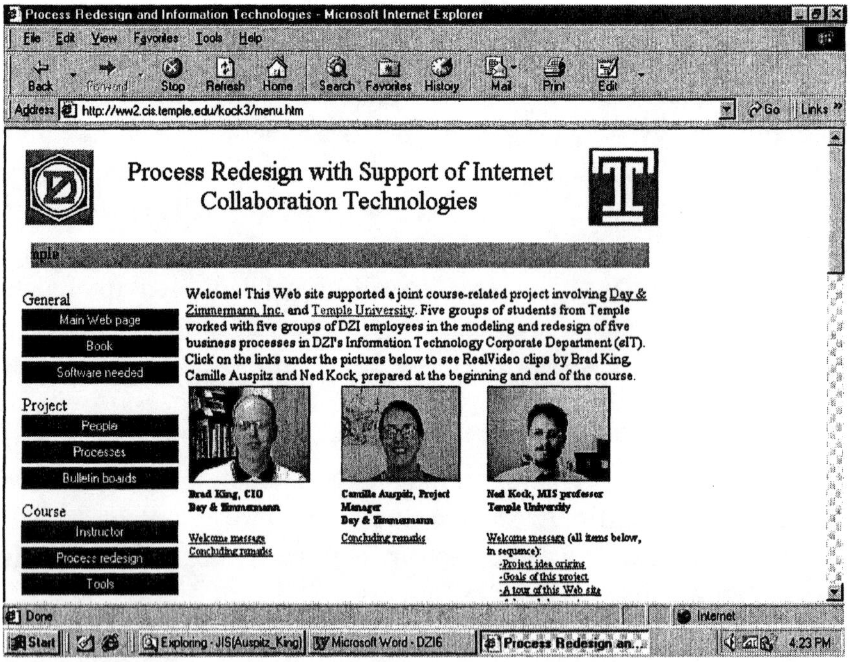

It was essential that the skills needed to take advantage of the Web site were developed quickly, which was facilitated by the fact that all features of the Web site required only a standard Web browser and some free players to be fully utilized. DZI's project manager strongly encouraged all the process owners to access the Web site and review their discussion threads at least twice a day; the instructor did the same for the students. Process owners and student team members were asked to review the progress of the other process teams as well. Each process team developed their own schedule and style to accomplish the requirements of the course. Some teams met weekly; others twice-weekly; others still met only every other week; all with more or less the same level of success in regards to completing the reports.

The Web site was also made available to all eIT employees throughout DZI (over 100 people). While interest and participation from employees not directly involved in the course partnership fell below expected levels, there was enough interest in the technology behind the site to initiate conversations about applying similar technology within the organization. It is essential that diverse IT organizations, such as eIT, share information and collaborate on enterprise issues. Today, well after the course partnership was concluded, eIT has a very active discussion site that addresses numerous topics and issues throughout the organization. While the underlying technology is different, using Lotus Notes and Domino instead of Microsoft FrontPage and Internet Information Server (IIS), the capability is very similar and mirrors that of the Web site developed to support the course partnership.

Electronic Versus Face-to-Face Meetings:
Which One to Choose and When?

There were advantages and disadvantages to using Web-based collaboration technologies to address and resolve issues and interact with project team members. The teams were very diverse. Utilizing the online electronic discussions (see Figure 2) was often seen as an effective way to overcome language barriers by formally defining process-specific terms and to clarify issues not properly addressed in face-to-face meetings. In addition, as stated earlier, the ability to maximize precious face-to-face time by enabling all team members to have access to documentation and discussion topics prior to a meeting was seen as essential. In order to accomplish the objectives of the course, the electronic collaboration capability also enabled team members who were not able to attend a meeting to contribute as well.

However, most participants felt that it was necessary to complement the Web site interaction with face-to-face meetings. From a project management perspective, the face-to-face meetings were seen as particularly effective for

Figure 2: General Discussion Board for the Course Partnership (each process team had its specific discussion board)

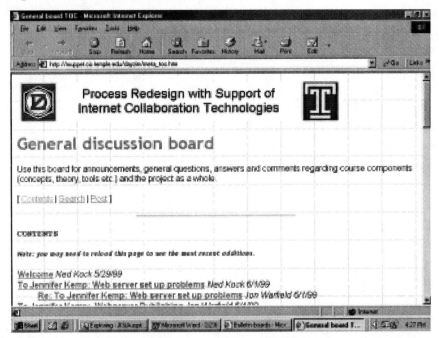

building and ensuring consensus. From a corporate standpoint, it was during the face-to-face meetings that the "stellar performers," both students and process owners, could be identified. The same was true for student evaluation from an academic standpoint. While the reports were collaborative efforts and discussions often involved many team members, it was in the meetings and final presentations that the natural leaders and above-average achievers became evident.

Going the Extra Mile: Project Review, Pizza Party and Final Presentations

Throughout the five weeks of the course, DZI's project manager provided eIT management with regular status reports summarizing the progress of the various teams. This enabled DZI's CIO to remain up to date as the course progressed. However, the CIO was also interested in the technology used to support the project, the general subject of process redesign, the participation of his staff in the project and what they had learned about their specific processes. In order to provide him with a clearer perspective of his staff's experience, a project review was scheduled in which the eIT process owners would offer the CIO and an external consultant from the Concours Group a presentation detailing the teams' progress.

The review took place on June 22, 1999 just three days before final reports and final student team presentations were due. Student team members were asked to be present for the review as well. This allowed each presentation to be followed by a dynamic discussion between the process owner, the student team members, the CIO and the external consultant. These discussions ranged from delving deeper into process descriptions and redesigns to lively forays into technologies' future. A fair amount of time was spent discussing how technology affects business processes and the growing role technology will continue to play in strategic business planning initiatives.

DZI's eIT organization was very satisfied with the progress and outcomes of this collaborative project and was able to demonstrate that enthusiasm by hosting a party following the project review presentations. All the students, process owners, extended team members and eIT management sponsors enjoyed a casual party at a local pizza restaurant. This setting was conducive to informal and lively conversations and made the CIO, the instructor and the external consultant available to many of the project participants. Given that the course had been very intense for all the participants, the gathering also allowed for sharing of personal stories and interests, and seemed to have created a relaxed atmosphere and an engaging and satisfying note on which to end the project.

The final presentations took place on the last day of the course and were held in DZI's boardroom. Each of the student teams prepared a PowerPoint presentation that summarized Reports 1 and 2 and focused on the content of Report 3, which, as mentioned before, consisted of an analysis of IT implementation solutions for the redesigned process, as well as a cost/benefit analysis and implementation plan for each IT implementation solution.

In many of the final presentations the IT solutions in conjunction with the redesigned process were viable when considered independent from one another. What came to light essentially during these presentations was the fact that since all the processes were within the domain of eIT, they were all in some way related. However, the teams had proceeded in an insular manner. Had the connections been identified early on in the project, the teams may have worked together and produced very different findings and recommendations.

Nevertheless, a number of the process evaluations and redesigns were seen as having provided important contributions for eIT's organizational development efforts. In addition, the skills developed during this project were significant for both the students and eIT professionals. Remaining true to the course topic, the most significant benefit for eIT as an organization was the ability to develop collaborative skills. These skills fall into two categories: collaboration with academia and effective collaboration on a decentralized project team. Overall DZI and Temple University viewed this collaboration between industry and academia as a success.

THE OUTCOMES OF THE PARTNERSHIP IN THE EYES OF THE PARTICIPANTS

When asked to rate their agreement with the statement, "Overall, this is one of the best courses I have had at Temple," 58% of the students responded "Strongly agree" (the highest level of agreement); all the remaining students responded "Agree somewhat." The average rating for this question was 3.52 out of 4 (0 = strongly disagree, 4 = strongly agree). Several students pointed out that the course had required much more time and effort from them than traditional courses, which was the reason some students did not rate the course as their "best ever" in the "Strongly agree" category.

A survey was sent to all the eIT project participants and received a 50% return. The results were interesting and suggested a variance in satisfaction between eIT management and eIT staff. While the CIO and DZI's project manager clearly felt that the project was successful as a whole, the eIT staff members differentiated between the content outcomes and the intangible outcomes. Overall the intangible outcomes of exposure to new talent, gaining process design skills, focusing attention on eIT's processes, etc., were ranked high. There was, however, expectation by the process owners that the redesigns would be applied to the processes during the course partnership, which was impossible due to the nature and scope of the process changes, requiring several additional months to be implemented. After all, the process owners had to spend a considerable amount of time and effort in order to participate, and the combination of this with the fact that the process redesigns were not implemented during the course was a source of mild dissatisfaction.

LESSONS LEARNED
Information Sharing Among Teams
Does Not Ensure Integration

One of the key lessons learned regarding the use of the Web site is that, even though all the documentation generated by each team was available to all the other teams, process redesign and implementation proposals were developed in relative isolation.

The evidence gathered during the action research study strongly suggests that most teams monitored the work of the other teams through the Web site, by reading team-specific bulletin boards and documents, and even posting comments and suggestions for other teams. However, it seems that the use of that information was restricted to monitoring purposes, so teams would know, for example, if what they were doing was "as good as" what other teams were doing.

This result is in some ways similar to that of an experimental study conducted by Dennis (1996), which found that even though some collaboration technologies may lead users to more information, they may not ensure that the users effectively use the information available. This may be due to information overload (Casey, 1982; Chervany and Dickson, 1974; Kock, 1999a; Meyer et al., 1997; O'Reilly, 1980). That is, even though enough information about the work of each team was available to all teams, their members were not able to effectively process it, probably due to time constraints. This may also explain the fact that even though DZI's CIO had full access to the Web site, he preferred to be briefed about the main outcomes through a face-to-face project review meeting.

The Combined Use of Online and Face-to-Face Interaction Modes is Better Than Having Either Only One or the Other Mode of Communication

The evidence from the action research study suggests that the online interaction is preferable for certain communication and coordination activities than face-to-face interaction, and vice-versa. The combined used of the two modes of communication was seen as a major factor in ensuring the success of the course partnership. The following quote, from a manager directly involved in the partnership, illustrates many of the participants' views regarding this:

> It was fantastic how effectively the combination of online discussion and in-person meetings and reviews melded to create a truly collaborative experience...the success of this type of project seems dependent on a blend of both the online and face-to-face interaction. Too much of either would result in a need to extend the schedule, in the case of doing all the work face-to-face, or risking a lack of consensus or true teamwork/team spirit, in the case of a fully electronic experience.

This lesson is aligned with previous research findings (Kock, 1999; Kock and McQueen, 1998). However, the search for optimal combinations of communication modes suggested as relevant by this study is in stark contrast with most of the academic research on collaboration technologies in the 1980s and 1990s, which have focused on experimental comparisons between computer-mediated and face-to-face communication (Kock, 1999).

The Combined Use of Commercial Web Technologies and Interaction Norms Can Remove Computer-Mediated Communication Obstacles

Our study suggests that appropriate use of commercial Web-based technologies can compensate for some of the difficulties inherent in computer-mediated communication. Several empirical studies, particularly those related to media richness theory (Daft and Lengel, 1986; Daft et al., 1987; Kock, 1998; Markus, 1994; Rice, 1992), have shown beyond much doubt that users see certain communication media other than face-to-face interaction as less appropriate for tasks as complex as process improvement. For example, computer-mediated communication is seen as depersonalizing ideas, removing non-verbal cues and preventing immediate feedback, all of which are perceived as having a negative impact on the process and outcomes of teamwork.

On the other hand, prior research findings also suggest that social and organizational norms, such as project guidelines set by management, may compensate for difficulties associated with computer-mediated communication (Markus, 1994). The action research study provides confirmation for this hypothesis. Feedback immediacy, for example, was increased by both the instructor and project manager at DZI directing the participants to check the bulletin boards available from the Web site twice a day and use them as much as possible for interaction regarding the project. As a result, over 300 postings were exchanged within a four-week period, all of which were about tasks related to the course partnership.

In addition to face-to-face meetings and communication behavior guidelines, two commercial Web-based technologies, Internet streaming and image processing, were used to mitigate the depersonalizing effect of computer-mediated communication. Video clips of the CIO, project manager and instructor addressing important issues regarding the partnership were prepared and posted on the Web site along with video clips with team members' introductions. Pictures of the team members, with names added to them, where also posted together with contact information (see Figure 3).

The amount of interaction during the course and the familiarity with which participants from Temple and eIT behaved toward each other during the pizza party is indicative of the "virtual community" sense fostered in part by behavioral norms, electronic interaction and the multimedia components of the Web site.

CONCLUSION

This chapter discussed a course partnership involving Day and Zimmermann, Inc. (DZI), a large engineering and professional services company headquartered in Philadelphia, and Temple University, a public university with its main campus located also in Philadelphia. The course was taught in the First Summer Session of 1999, between the months of May and July. The main goal of the course was to teach students business process redesign concepts and techniques, which were used to redesign five business processes from DZI's information technology organization. DZI's CIO and a senior manager, who played the key role of project manager, championed the course partnership within DZI. A Web site with bulletin boards, multimedia components and static content was used to support the partnership.

Our experience indicates that, given the communication and coordination difficulties associated with such partnerships, the development of a Web site with the features of the one described here is likely to be a key success factor in similar initiatives. Even though the research literature suggests a number of difficulties associated with conducting projects with the characteristics described, it has been our experience that the combined use of Web-based collaboration technologies with appropriate communication behavior norms

Figure 3: Images and Video Clips Were Used to Mitigate the Depersonalizing Effect of Computer-Mediated Communication

and face-to-face interaction is likely to contribute to the success of such projects.

Overall, we believe that the benefits of course partnerships such as the one described here far outweigh their costs. However, we also identified some difficulties that are likely to be faced in similar initiatives. The work of different teams, even when shared among all the participants of the partnership, may not be easy to integrate if synergy is not set as a key goal of the project. Moreover, even though course partnerships may offer several benefits in the eyes of upper management, they may place undesirable pressure on staff who interact directly with students. These problems can be addressed by setting integration of the outcomes of different teams as a key goal of the partnership, as well as building special rewards into the project for the staff involved and those who are able to demonstrate high levels of synergy.

REFERENCES

Brannock, J.C. (1998). Basic guidelines for university-industry research relationships. *SRA Journal*, 30(1/2), 57-63.

Burnham, J.B. (1997). Evaluating industry-university research linkages. *Research Technology Management*, 40(1), 52-56.

Cabral, R. (1998). From university-industry interfaces to the making of a science park: Florianopolis, Southern Brazil, *International Journal of Technology Management*, 15(8), 778-800.

Casey, C.J. (1982). Coping with information overload: The need for empirical research. *Cost and Management*, 56(4), 31-38.

Checkland, P. (1991). From framework through experience to learning: The essential nature of action research. In Nissen, H., Klein, H. K., and Hirschheim, R. (Eds.), *Information Systems Research: Contemporary Approaches and Emergent Traditions*. New York, NY: North-Holland, pp. 397-403.

Chervany, N. and Dickson, G. (1974). An experimental evaluation of information overload in a production environment. *Management Science*, 20(10), 1335-44.

Daft, R.L. and Lengel, R.H. (1986). Organizational information requirements, media richness and structural design. *Management Science*, 32(5), 554-571.

Daft, R.L., Lengel, R.H. and Trevino, L.K. (1987). Message equivocality, media selection and manager performance: Implications for information systems. *MIS Quarterly*, 11(3), 355-366.

Davenport, T.H. (1993). *Process Innovation*. Boston, MA: Harvard Business Press.

Davenport, T.H. and Short, J.E. (1990). The new industrial engineering: Information technology and business process redesign. *Sloan Management Review*, 31(4), 11-27.

Dennis, A.R. (1996). Information exchange and use in group decision making: You can lead a group to information, but you can't make it think. *MIS Quarterly*, 20(4), December, 433-55.

Elden, M. and Chisholm, R.F. (1993). Emerging varieties of action research. *Human Relations*, 46(2), 121-41.

Greenwood, D.J., Whyte, W. F., and Harkavy, I. (1993). Participatory action research as a process and as a goal. *Human Relations*, 46(2), 175-91.

Hammer, M. and Champy, J. (1993). *Reengineering the Corporation*. New York, NY: Harper Business.

Harrington, H.J. (1991). *Business Process Improvement*. New York, NY: McGraw-Hill.

Hollingsworth, P. (1998). Economic reality drives industry-university alliances. *Food Technology*, 52(7), 58-62.

Jones-Evans, D. (1999). Creating a bridge between university and industry in small European countries: The role of the industrial liaison office, *R&D Management*, 29(1), 47-57.

Jonsonn, S. (1991). Action research. In Nissen, H., Klein, H. K., and Hirschheim, R. (Eds.), *Information Systems Research: Contemporary Approaches and Emergent Traditions*. New York, NY: North-Holland, pp. 371-396.

Kock, N. (1998). Can communication medium limitations foster better group outcomes? An action research study, *Information & Management*, 34(5), 295-305.

Kock, N. (1999). *Process Improvement and Organizational Learning: The Role of Collaboration Technologies*. Hershey, PA: Idea Group Publishing.

Kock, N. (1999a). Information overload in organizational processes: A study of managers and professionals' perceptions. In Khosrowpour, M. (Ed.), *Proceedings of the 10th Information Resources Management International Conference*. Hershey, PA: Idea Group Publishing, pp. 313-320.

Kock, N. and McQueen, R.J. (1998). An action research study of effects of asynchronous groupware support on productivity and outcome quality of process redesign groups. *Journal of Organizational Computing and Electronic Commerce*, 8(2), 149-68.

Lau, F. (1997). A review on the use of action research in information systems studies. In Lee, A. S., Liebenau, J., and DeGross, J. I. (Eds.), *Information Systems and Qualitative Research*. London, England: Chapman & Hall, pp. 31-68.

Lee, Y.S. (1998). University-industry collaboration on technology transfer: Views from the Ivory Tower. *Policy Studies Journal*, 26(1), 69-85.

Markus, M.L. (1994). Electronic mail as the medium of managerial choice. *Organization Science*, 5(4), 502-527.

McTaggart, R. (1991). Principles for participatory action research. *Adult Education Quarterly*, 41(3), 168-87.

Mengoni, L. (1998). Cooperation between university and industries in organizing a 'Diploma Universitario' curriculum: The Politecnico di Milano-Assolombarda experience. *European Journal of Engineering Education*, 23(4), 423-30.

Meyer, M.E., Sonoda, K.T. and Gudykunst, W.B. (1997). The effect of time pressure and type of information on decision quality. *The Southern Communication Journal*, 62(4), 280-92.

Meyer-Krahmer, F. (1998). Science-based technologies: University-industry interactions in four fields. *Research Policy*, 27(8), 835-52.

O'Reilly, C. A. (1980). Individuals and information overload in organizations: Is more necessarily better? *Academy of Management Journal*, 23(4), 684-96.

Peters, M. and Robinson, V. (1984). The origins and status of action research. *The Journal of Applied Behavioral Science,* 20(2), 113-24.

Rapoport, R.N. (1970). Three dilemmas in action research. *Human Relations*, 23(6), 499-513.

Rice, R.E. (1992). Task analyzability, use of new media, and effectiveness: A multi-site exploration of media richness. *Organization Science*, 3(4), 475-500.

Saegusa, A. (1997). Japan ties the industry-university knot. *Nature*, 390(6656), 105.

Sommer, R. (1994). Serving two masters. *The Journal of Consumer Affairs*, 28, (1), 170-87.

Wheaton, Q. (1998). Government-university-industry cooperation: Does it work? *Quality*, 37(5), 20-24.

Whyte, W.F. (Ed.) (1991). *Participatory Action Research*. Newbury Park, CA: Sage.

Winter, R. (1989). *Learning from Experience: Principles and Practice in Action-Research*. New York, NY: The Falmer Press.

Wong, P. (1999). University-industry technological collaborations in Singapore: Emerging patterns and industry concerns. *International Journal of Technology Management*, 18(3), 270-85.

Wood-Harper, A.T. (1985). Research methods in information systems: Using action research. In Mumford, E., Hirschheim, R., Fitzgerald, G., and Wood-Harper, A. T. (Eds.), *Research Methods in Information Systems*. North-Holland, Amsterdam, The Netherlands, pp. 169-191.

Chapter 23

Data Modeling: A Vehicle
for Teaching Creative Problem
Solving and
Critical Appraisal Skills

Clare Atkins
Nelson Marlborough Institute of Technology, New Zealand

INTRODUCTION

Despite extensive changes in technology and methodology, anecdotal and empirical evidence (e.g., Davis et al., 1997) consistently suggests that communication and problem-solving skills are fundamental to the success of an IT professional. As two of the most valued skills in an IT graduate, they should be essential components of an effective education program, regardless of changes in student population or delivery mechanisms. While most educators would concur with this view, significantly more emphasis is generally placed on teaching the tools and techniques that students will require in their future careers, and a corresponding amount of energy is expended in attempting to identify what those tools and techniques might be. In contrast, successful problem solving is often seen either as an inherent capability that some students already possess or as a skill that some will magically acquire during the course of their studies.

Data modeling as an activity, by which we mean the gathering and analysis of users' information needs and their representation in an implementable design, is largely one of communication and problem solving and, consequently, provides an excellent opportunity for explicitly teaching these skills. Data modeling is generally considered to be one of the more difficult skills to teach (e.g., Hitchman, 1995; Pletch, 1989), particularly if the student has no previous understanding of physical data structures (de Carteret & Vidgen, 1995). The essential constructs, such as entities, attributes or objects, may be elegant in their powerful simplicity, but their combination into a useful design is a complex process of categorization in which there is "considerable room for choice and creativity in selecting the most useful classification" (Simsion, 1994 p.82). Data modeling requires not only the ability to communicate about and to solve a problem, but also to create possible solutions and then choose between them. Herein lies the difficulty. It is not enough to learn what the different constructs are, or even to study simple textbook examples of how to put them together. The student must really understand the problem, be able to create and recognize a number of possible ways in which the problem can be solved, and then exercise considerable critical skills in choosing between them.

This chapter examines these issues and describes various ways in which final-year undergraduate students, taking a specialist module in data modeling, have been encouraged to develop, and have confidence in, their creative and critical ability to solve problems in a disciplined and systematic way.

BACKGROUND

In many respects the entire systems development lifecycle (SDLC) can be considered as a complex problem-solving activity. The need to communicate effectively with all levels of users, with technical personnel and with management has long been accepted as an integral part of the process. Texts on systems analysis and design generally include at least one chapter on the topic, including basic skills of interviewing, report writing and presentations. These texts will often use the language of problem solving to describe the activities and context of the SDLC, for example referring to the system environment as the 'problem domain,' the need to 'identify the problem' and 'seeking solutions.'

In their exemplary text, Satzinger et al. (2000) speak specifically of the "Analyst as a Business Problem Solver," commenting that analysts must have both "a fundamental curiosity to explore how things are done and the determination to make them work better" (p.4). However, while they diagrammatically describe the SDLC in problem-solving terms, the book is primarily focused on detailed and clear explanations of tools, techniques, methods and methodologies, with little indication of the thinking skills that are required to synthesize information, to extract the problems and to create alternative solutions. Yet it is precisely these skills that are required to transform a novice into a competent analyst or designer.

Clearly, learning the tools of the trade is an important and necessary requirement of an IT student's education but this alone is not sufficient. It can be argued that it is the remaining work that a student engages in, particularly assignments, that provides these necessary skills but is this really the case? In the 'real world' there are no model answers, no completely right or wrong solutions. However, there is a limit to the amount of subjectivity we can allow our students in a modeling, analysis or even programming assignment if we are to have any chance of providing fair and timely feedback. This conundrum is highlighted by Simsion and Shanks' (1993) experiment where each of 51 modelers, with varying experience, provided a different data model solution to a given scenario, and only three were more than superficially similar. Consequently, it seems far more effective, and certainly easier, to provide students with a limited and tightly focused case study that provides only limited opportunity for interpretation and creativity but which, by focusing primarily on the correct use of tool or technique, can be graded with some confidence. However, we need to question whether this approach is providing students with the best possible skill set.

The debate about which programming languages or development methodologies should be taught in depth are only likely to become more complex and more protracted as the IT profession continues to diversify. It is no longer possible to second-guess whether a student will be best served by learning Java or C++, Rational or ORACLE; any choice is likely to be outdated within a short time. Different institutions or instructors will make different decisions on these matters, based on a number of factors, but underlying any of these choices must be a commitment to developing the students' ability to ultimately identify the problems, find the solutions and choose for themselves. Communication studies and, less often, problem-solving skills may be taught as discrete modules in some programs but all modules need to acknowledge these skills and integrate them with the more technically specific teaching topics. In this way, students not only increase their opportunity to practice these skills but also to see how relevant they are to all subject areas.

As a specific teaching area, data modeling has some inherent difficulties of its own and many of them are related to the wider problems of teaching any design technique. As Batra and Zanakis (1994) point out, there is not a "precise set of rules and heuristics to develop an E-R diagram" (p.228) because "most design methods are informal in the way in which the task of identifying candidate objects is achieved" (Eaglestone and Ridley, 1998). This can result in the phenomenon that Pletch (1989) observed where modeling students often display the same characteristics of high school math students who "sit and look at the words in the text for some time waiting for the required equation to be miraculously revealed to them" (p.74). In order to make any move towards a useful design, a novice modeler has to come to a clear understanding of the 'problem' situation, has to test out a number of possibilities, often by trial and error, and then use some ill-defined set of criteria to choose between them. Even then the choice may not be straightforward. As Simsion and Witt (2001) emphasize, there is definitely "more than one workable answer in most practical situations" (p6).

Given the difficulty of recognizing the 'best' solution for anything other than trivial examples, together with the obvious problem of determining what criteria a student has used for classification, and consequently how a student has arrived at a solution, it is difficult for an educator to provide any objective assessment or feedback. Once again the easier option of restricting the assessed scenario and focusing the grading on the 'correct' use of constructs and notation can seem very attractive and more impartial. However, once again, it is at the expense of encouraging the development of the very skills that the expert modeler needs. Indeed, it can be counter-productive, encouraging students to concentrate on discovering the (assessor's) expected solution rather than experimenting with different and possibly innovative solutions (Postman and Weingartner, 1969).

In order to address some of the issues, a specialized data modeling module was developed in 1994 for use with final-year undergraduate Information Systems and Computer Science students at Massey University in Aotearoa/ New Zealand. The students had received standard tuition in systems analysis and database design, and were very familiar with the constructs of entity-relationship (ER) and relational data modeling. However, they had had little opportunity to experiment with using these techniques in scenarios of their own choice. The module was designed specifically to redress this lack and to provide a wide variety of opportunities to try out a number of techniques that could potentially assist them to improve their thinking, critical appraisal and communication skills and, above all, to bolster their confidence in these abilities.

DATA MODELING TECHNIQUES–A TAUGHT MODULE

Module Overview

The module, named Data Modeling Techniques, was developed as a single-semester elective module consisting of approximately 160 hours of student learning of which a third was timetabled contact time with the teacher (i.e., lectures and tutorials). The module was described as "the study and application of techniques commonly used in the business world for formalizing information needs and data structures, together with an investigation into the importance of data modeling as a means of communication and understanding." Between 1995 and 2000, the average number of students taking the module was 40, which represented about 40% of the students graduating with a major in Information Systems.

Module Objectives

The objectives as laid out in the module documentation were:

- to appreciate the value and purpose of data modeling as a business technique,
- to appreciate several aspects of the problem-solving process,
- to thoroughly understand the techniques of entity-relationship/relational modeling as commonly used in business situations,
- to gain a holistic view of the data modeling process,
- to experiment with ways of applying the techniques, and
- to successfully apply all the above to a problem domain of interest to the student.

In addition, it was also explained to students that expertise in data modeling could not come from study alone and that none of them would be 'experts' at the conclusion of the module. Instead, it was emphasized that expertise comes largely from experience, from exposure to a wide range of modeling applications and situations, and from the ability to think creatively 'outside the square.' It was also explained that it was not possible to gain this kind of expertise without making mistakes and that a failed exercise was often a positive learning opportunity. Consequently, the module had a strong emphasis on rewarding demonstrated experiential learning rather than 'right' answers. In addition, the module explicitly explored the kinds of mistakes, which research suggests, are made by novice modelers and focused on strategies for avoiding them.

Module Structure

The module ran in four hours of timetabled contact time with the instructor per week. Of these, one hour was used for the delivery of lecture material, one hour for the presentation of student seminars and two hours for interactive tutorial activities. Students were also expected to spend eight hours each week either on work set as part of the summative assessments or in reading and class preparation. The schedule of assignments is shown at Table 1. For most of the module, students were encouraged to work in pairs as 'buddies' and one assignment had to be completed with the buddy. All other work, except for the examination, could be completed alone, but the majority of students found it

Table 1: Assessment Schedule

Assignment	Weight	Purpose
Problem Solving: You will be asked to solve up to five problems requiring the use of imagination, lateral thinking and advanced problem solving strategies.	15%	To encourage you to think creatively about problems and how to solve them.
Data Model: Working in pairs, you will identify your own set of data and construct an entity-relationship/relational model (30%). You will keep a journal of your modeling (10%) and write evaluations of both your final model (30%) and the process that you followed to construct it (30%).	35%	To demonstrate your ability to create a model that captures and describes the data of a specific problem domain at the implementation (relational) level, document the process by which the model was created, and critically assess both your model and the process by which it was created.
Peer Assessment: A grade is awarded to you by the person you are buddying. Staff may also have some input into this mark based on their own observations.	5%	To provide peer support and encouragement and to reinforce the essentially cooperative nature of the modeling activity.
Class Contribution: You are expected to contribute in class on the basis of your reading and practical experiences. Working in randomly assigned groups, you will also be asked to prepare a seminar on a relevant topic. These should be imaginative, creative and interesting.	10%	To encourage lively debate on relevant issues and encourage you to try out new ideas and explore new concepts.
3-Hour Open-Book Examination: There will be two sections in the examination. You will be asked to answer one question in Section 1 (30 minutes) and one question from Section 2.	35%	To provide an opportunity for you to reflect on and apply your learning in this course to situations you may well meet in your early working life. The emphasis will be on your understanding, thinking and application of experiences and not on factual learning.

beneficial to work cooperatively, either with their buddy or a small group of students.

Module Content

Using *Data Modeling Essentials: Analysis, Design and Innovation* (Simsion, 1994) as a required textbook, the module focused on standard data modeling issues with a practical rather than a theoretical emphasis. The module was arranged around five broad themes set out in Table 2. The first two themes not only provided the context for the module but also introduced and developed the underlying themes of self-appraisal, critical thinking and problem solving. It is these aspects of these themes that are described here.

SELF-AWARENESS

The first theme encouraged students to become aware of the kinds of activities data modeling entails, and how they, and their peers, approach these tasks. Some time was given to discussing the differing requirements of analysis and design, in particular the different kinds of thinking that they require, for example analytical, scientific thinking and intuitive, creative thinking "that

Table 2: Data Modeling Techniques – Broad Themes

Data Modeling – the process	Observing the process of modeling Modeling as analysis or design Modeling as a creative activity
Improving modeling behavior	Common errors of novice modelers – 7 habits of highly effective modelers Problem solving and thinking strategies Interacting with users
Advanced modeling techniques	Advanced normalization Generalization and specialization etc
Evaluation and communicating data models	What is a 'good' model – Understanding the semantics of a model Presenting a model to other people Getting user validation
Data modeling and the real world	The time dimension Generic and enterprise models Business constraints Modeling a data warehouse

reaches out beyond what is now known into what could be" (Kepner, 1996). Having established that data modeling (at least in the way it was approached in the module) is primarily a design activity, some time was spent in exploring ways of encouraging creative thinking. When the module was first offered, this exploration was mainly confined to common techniques such as brainstorming and mind-mapping, but as the module matured this initial discussion of creativity was linked far more closely to problem solving and thinking strategies as described in the next section. The concept of 'problems,' as having agreed formulations but arguable solutions, as opposed to 'puzzles' and 'messes' (Pidd, 1996), was also discussed.

This theme also incorporated the idea of becoming aware of how an individual actually approaches a modeling exercise. While there has been little academic research in this area, the findings of Srinivasan and Te'eni (1995) were discussed, particularly the suggestion that more experienced modelers are less likely to spend concentrated periods of time focusing on low-level detail. One tutorial was given over to an exercise in which students worked in small groups to complete a number of simple modeling tasks. For each task, a different student played the role of observer and recorded in broad terms the approaches that the group was taking. At the end of the session, the groups looked through these observations and discussed the different approaches that had been used and identified the elements of the approach that either helped or hindered the creation of a model. A number of useful observations often resulted from this exercise, including the effect that a very confident and vocal group member could have on a group's success, that time is often wasted because no strategy for developing the solution has been decided, the way in which different individuals may interpret a problem domain and, of course, the difficulty of finding consensus, particularly when there are deadlines looming! Many of the students came away from this tutorial with a much improved understanding of their own modeling behavior, its strengths and its weaknesses, and began to appreciate the value of having a buddy to both exchange viewpoints with and to use as an observer of their own behavior.

Building on these initial explorations, the second theme developed them further by examining, through discussion and examples, a number of common errors made by novice modelers. This work was based primarily on the errors identified by Batra and Antony (1994), particularly those related to 'anchoring' which they describe as the novice modeler's unwillingness to move away from their initial design. Various strategies, based largely on Moody (1996) and De Bono (1985, 1993) were suggested for overcoming some of these errors, and students were asked to consider their own strengths and weaknesses, and identify ways in which they would address their weaknesses during the course of their data modeling assignment. Many students recognized their problems with anchoring and the difficulty they found in generating alternative designs, and were thus alerted early on in the module to the need to pay attention to the creation of alternative designs. At this point, the first assignment was introduced, usually to the bemusement of a number of the students.

CREATIVE PROBLEM SOLVING

The first assignment was concerned with finding solutions to problems that were deliberately unrelated to data modeling. The students could choose to provide a solution or solutions to one or more of five problems. If all five problems were attempted, then 20 marks were available for each one, and were graded on the understanding of the problem, the seriousness of the attempt(s) to solve it, and the effectiveness and originality of the proposed solutions. If a student decided to solve less than five problems, the remaining marks were distributed evenly among the attempted questions and awarded for creativity. As another variation, a student could choose to provide a new problem as a substitute for providing two solutions.

The problems had been carefully chosen to illustrate various aspects of creative thinking. The students were told at the beginning that the problems did not have any specifically correct answers, although a reasonable and satisfying answer could be provided to all of them. They were also told that the only way that they would find answers was by using their imagination, thinking laterally and working through a number of possible interpretations of the problems.

The first problem asked the student to construct a grammatically correct and meaningful English sentence that had the word 'and' repeated five times with no other words in between; punctuation between the five 'ands' was allowed. The original intention was that the student would need to recognize the difference between 'and' as a part of a sentence and 'and' as a symbol. For example, one expected solution was "…a sign-writer completed a sign saying 'FishandChips.' Unfortunately, he forgot to put a space between 'Fish' and 'and' and 'and' and Chips…"

In practice, the range of solutions offered each year was astonishing and ranged from re-interpretations of the problem, by, for example, placing numbers between the 'ands' as in "The conductor counted us in by saying 'and 1 and 2 and 3 and 4 and…'," to a clever turn of the tables with "what does putting and and and and and into a sentence have to do with data modeling." The initial reaction to the problem was usually one of disbelief in the possibility of any reasonable solution. However, the majority of students found several possible solutions to the problem and surprised themselves with their ability to produce several alternatives.

For the second problem, students were given a 'mystery object,' asked to study the various design features of the object and then to suggest and justify a possible use for it. It was made clear that the actual use of the object was irrelevant and that discovering the real purpose was not the point of the exercise. In order to score well, the students needed to consider each design aspect of the object – e.g., its bright orange coloring, the small dimples in the lid, the sprung steel closing mechanism, the half-moon shape – and attempt to describe the object that it was designed to hold. There was a generally positive response to this question. The object was difficult to identify and students' curiosity was immediately engaged, and the range of solutions offered showed varying degrees of imagination and problem understanding. High on the popularity list every year are banana or jelly bean container, suggested by the shape, although some of the more adventurous have included "The Ultimate Pet Accessory food bowl, toy box and poop-scoop in one" and "a fine example of an early aboriginal Survival Boomerang." The latter managed to address all the obvious design elements while ignoring the question of how a primitive population was able to source orange plastic and steel springs.

The third problem asked students to identify three things that English does not appear to have a word for but which perhaps it should. Some students became fascinated with the process of looking for things that they didn't have a word to describe and several have remarked on the changes they had noticed in their own perception following this exercise. Probably the most interesting answer to this solution came from a student who commented, "I confess that at the beginning I thought this would be easy and straightforward. What started as an hour or two in the library turned into many hours of interesting discovery and enlightenment. The library is a mine of information regarding words. They provided me with dictionaries and encyclopedias of dictionaries...." This student went on to suggest the word *fempallas* to describe female intuition based on a detailed etymology of 'feminine' and Athena Pallas, the Greek goddess of wisdom, by way of 'philosophy,' 'insight' and 'wise.' The student concluded, "The process of searching, discovering, evaluation, searching again and the eventual decision of a 'new' word was interesting. It was difficult to detail the process because an idea or direction would sometimes just appear. I find it to be a real problem-solving exercise. I am not 100% sure about the new word but I learned a lot about searching and evaluation of alternatives. There were two questions that kept reappearing for me: how do you know which path to follow and how do you know when to stop searching? I do not profess to having discovered the answers, but this exercise made me very conscious of the problem-solving process."

The problem that presented most difficulties was the fourth, where students were asked to construct an English sentence, which is correct and meaningful when spoken but which cannot be written down and remain correct. Solutions generally fell into two categories: statements which use slang expressions which are acceptable when spoken but are not grammatically correct when written, and statements which are logically incorrect when written, e.g., I can't write; This page is blank; This sentence is four words long. Occasionally a student will identify a sentence such as, "There are three (twos) in the English language, two, too and to," having realized that without resorting to phonetics, the sentence cannot be written.

In the final question students were asked to make sense of the expression HOCUS + POCUS = PRESTO and this proved popular among those who decided to treat it as a mathematical equation. Many found mathematical solutions of varying degrees of reasonableness while others used it as a metaphor for the idea that the whole is greater than the sum of its parts. On two occasions, students constructed purely graphical solutions by incorporating the shapes of the letters into a drawing or a painting.

The overall purpose of the assignment gradually became apparent to most of the students as the module progressed. While their initial reaction was often confusion and exasperation, occasionally accompanied by hostility and fear, as they entered into the spirit of discovery, many commented on how they continued to work on and think about the problems long after the assignment had been handed in and graded. Others shared the problems with family or roommates and were surprised by the very different approaches that other people took to solving the same problems. Following the grading of the assignment, a two-hour tutorial session was spent talking about the range of solutions that the class had provided. For many students this was one of the most enlightening aspects of the exercise as they became aware of the variety of solutions that their classmates created. However, it was a question in the final examination, which asked them to comment on what they saw as the purpose of this assignment, which provided some of the most interesting insights into the learning process that had taken place in the preceding three months. Although the question was optional, almost all the students chose to answer it and it was gratifying to see them reflect on their growing awareness of the legitimate existence of differing viewpoints, the possibility of different solutions and their own creativity ability. In addition, most of the students had no difficulty in relating the importance of this to their data modeling (or other design) work. Almost all of the students came to appreciate the limitations in looking only for a 'right' answer, and a significant number of them commented on their increased self-confidence when tackling design problems.

CRITICAL SELF-APPRAISAL

In general, textbooks on data modeling concentrate on the process of constructing a data model and pay little attention to the means by which a data model can be 'read.' One useful exercise is to ask students to exchange a model that they have been working on with another student and ask them to describe what the model appears to be 'saying.' While they are used to interpreting the classic and simplified textbook models, it is often the first time that they have been asked to interpret a complex, incomplete and possibly misleading model. Both sets of students, those whose work is being read and those doing the reading, comment on both the difficulty and the value of this exercise. A technique that can assist them in this work, NaLER (Natural Language for Entity-Relationship Models) by Atkins and Patrick (2000), is taught to students in preference to SERFER (Batra and Sein, 1994) once they have experienced the problem described above. Although the technique can be rather tedious to undertake, it does provide a means for students to appraise the meanings inherent in their own models as they are being constructed. This helps to address the problem of 'outcome-irrelevant learning' noted by Batra and Antony (1994). The technique is straightforward to learn, and some students have remarked that it provides a structure for which they had intuitively recognized a need. Once the NaLER technique had been introduced, the exercise of 'reading' another's model was repeated – this time with the draft version that has been constructed for the second assignment. Students were generally enthusiastic about completing this, partly because they could see the value in having someone else 'proof-read' their model and partly because it offered a sneak preview of what other groups were doing. It was always difficult to restrain students from trying to correct errors that they believed they had identified in another's model. However, when they received back their own set of sentences, they were almost always surprised by the amount of correction their own model required!

The second assignment required the students, working in pairs, to identify a suitable set of data to model, preferably from a real environment, and it was made clear that the primary objective of the assignment was to provide an opportunity to explore, investigate and experiment with ideas and methods of modeling. The assignment description stated that 'how much you learn is more important than the quality of the final model that you produce...To do well in this assignment, it is not sufficient to just produce a model that solves a problem…you will be expected to be able to describe both the faults in your model and in the process by which you created it.…" The grading scheme reflected this emphasis by giving 30% of the marks to the model itself and 60% to a critical appraisal of the model and the process (see Table 1).

This scheme was initially driven by two concerns: the difficulty of both fully understanding and objectively assessing more than 20 models from a wide variety of problem domains, and from the belief that once in the workplace, the students would be expected to be aware of the limitations of their own work. By placing significant emphasis on the evaluations, both these concerns were addressed. When grading the model, the marker was not required to fully understand, often with minimal contextual documentation, the problem domain addressed by the model, but could focus on the correct use of constructs, notation and normalization. It thus became the responsibility of the student to describe both the strong and the weak aspects of the model, to identify where further work was required and to, in effect, audit the process that had been followed to create it. This proved to be beneficial to both the students and to the marker, and resulted in any number of very fruitful discussions between them on the reasons for, or the implications of, specific design decisions.

THE CHALLENGE

As an instructor of students who will make their IT careers in the 21st century, one thing is certain - the technologies, the methodologies and the applications that they will learn, use and implement in the course of their careers are likely to be more complex, more sophisticated and very different from those they learned as students. However, the ability to identify, analyze and solve problems, the need to be innovative and creative in their thinking and the ability to step back from their work and appraise it critically, are skills that they will rely on, develop and use throughout their working lives (Sawyer, 1999). As educators we have a responsibility both to our students and to their future employers to provide a sound framework on which these skills can be founded. This is a challenge that we have found difficult to meet in the 20th century, but one which we cannot afford to avoid, for it is these skills, more than any others, which will ensure that today's students become competent and expert practitioners and academics. If we fail, we are severely limiting their chances of successfully meeting the challenges that they will face in realizing the potential of Information Technology in the century ahead.

REFERENCES

Atkins, C. F. & Patrick, J. D. (2000). NaLER: A natural language method for interpreting entity-relationship models. *Campus-Wide Information Systems, 17*(3), 85-93. Available online at www.emerald-library.com.

Batra, D. & Antony, S.R. (1994). Novice errors in conceptual database design. *European Journal of Information Systems, 3*(1), 57-69.

Batra, D., & Sein, M. K. (1994). Improving conceptual database design through feedback. *International Journal of Human-Computer Studies, 40*, 653-676.

Batra, D., & Zanakis, S.H. (1994). A conceptual database design approach based on rules and heuristics. *European Journal of Information Systems, 3*(3), 228-239.

Davis, G. B., Gorgone, J. T., Couger, J. D., Feinstein D. L., and Longenecker, H. E. (1997). *IS'97 Model Curriculum and Guidelines for Undergraduate Degree Programs in Information Systems*. Association of Information Technology Professionals.

de Bono, E. (1985). *Six Thinking Hats*. London: Penguin Books Ltd.

de Bono, E. (1993). *Parallel Thinking*. London: Penguin Books Ltd.

de Carteret, C., and Vidgen, R. (1995). *Data Modeling for Information Systems*. London: Pitman Publishing.

Eaglestone, B., and Ridley, M. (1998). *Object Databases: An Introduction*. London: McGraw-Hill.

Hitchman, S. (1995). Practitioner perceptions on the use of some semantic concepts in the entity-relationship model. *European Journal of Information Systems*, 4, 31-40.

Kepner, C. H. (1996). Calling all thinkers. *H R Focus, 73*(10), 3.

Moody, D. (1996). The seven habits of highly effective data modelers. *Database Programming and Design*, October, 57-64.

Pidd, M. (1996). *Tools for Thinking – Modelling in Management Science*. Chichester, John Wiley & Sons.

Pletch, A. (1989). Conceptual modeling in the classroom. *SIGMOD RECORD*, 18(1), 74-80.

Postman, N., & Weingartner, C. (1969). *Teaching as a Subversive Activity*. New York, Dell Publishing.

Satzinger, J. W., Jackson, R. B., & Burd, S. D. (2000). *Systems Analysis and Design in a Changing World*. Cambridge, MA: Thompson Learning.

Sawyer, D. (1999). *Getting it Right: Avoiding the High Cost of Wrong Decisions*. Boca Raton, FL: St Lucie Press.

Simsion, G. (1994). *Data Modeling Essentials: Analysis, Design and Innovation*. Boston: Van Nostrand Reinhold.

Simsion, G., & Shanks G. (1993). *Choosing Entity Types: A Study of 51 Data Modellers*. Department of Information Systems, Monash University, Working Paper Series 17/93. Melbourne, Australia.

Simsion, G., & Witt, G. (2001). *Data Modeling Essentials Analysis, Design and Innovation, 2nd Edition*. Arizona: Coriolis.

Srinivasan, A. & Te'eni, D. (1995). Modeling as constrained problem solving: An empirical study of the data modeling process. *Management Science*, 41(3): 419-434.

Chapter 24

Information Systems Curriculum Development as an Ecological Process

Arthur Tatnall
Victoria University of Technology, Australia

Bill Davey
RMIT University, Australia

INTRODUCTION

The discipline of Information Systems (IS), in common with the other major branches of computing, is subject to constant and continuing change as new technologies appear and new methodologies and development techniques are devised. IS professionals working in the computer industry need to keep abreast of these changes to remain useful and, of necessity, curriculum in information systems must also undergo frequent revisions and changes.

To those of us involved in research and teaching in information systems, it is clear that curriculum innovation and change in this area is complex, and anything but straightforward (Longenecker & Feinstein, 1990). Of course, all curriculum innovation is complex (Boomer, Lester, Onore, & Cook, 1992; Fullan, 1993; Fullan & Hargreaves, 1992; Kemmis & Stake, 1988) due to the involvement of a large number of human actors, but in information systems curriculum change, this is particularly so, due to the need also to consider the part played by such non-human actors (Latour, 1996) as the technology itself.

We will argue that if you want to understand *how* IS curriculum is built, and how both the human and non-human interactions involved contribute to the final product, then you need to use approaches that allow the complexity to be traced, and not diminished by categorisations (Law, 1999) or assumptions about intrinsic attributes of humans and non-humans. One way that this can be achieved is by using models and metaphors that relate to how people interact with each other, with the environment, and with non-human artefacts. One such approach is provided by the ecological metaphor described in this chapter.

MODELS CURRICULUM DEVELOPMENT

Curriculum change can be modelled in many different ways, and we will here consider just a few of those we consider most relevant. Models of change based upon a process of Research, Development, and Dissemination (RDD) are a common way of attempting an explanation of the process of curriculum development (Nordvall, 1982). In models like this, a rational and orderly transition is posited from research to development to dissemination to adoption.

Although much of the literature relates to the use of these models to explain curriculum change in *schools*, they are also commonly applied to the development of higher education curriculum – the subject of this chapter. Models of this sort suggest that curriculum development follows a logical process of working out the objectives of a particular program, matching these to curriculum elements, developing materials, and then spreading the good word among educators so that the new curriculum will be speedily adopted. We will argue, however, that curriculum change involves a much more complex process than this, and although this approach is one commonly cited in the literature, other models should also be considered. We will now look at four other such models.

An approach that is related to RDD models suggests that many curriculum statements result from the conscious or unconscious copying of 'authoritative' existing statements, rather than from any new thought (Clements, Grimison, & Ellerton, 1989). Although this approach, sometimes known in Australia as the 'Colonial Echo Model,' may have some credence in consideration of curriculum areas such as school mathematics or history, it has been shown to have less relevance in information systems curricula (Tatnall, 1993) at the university level. In most industrialised countries, information systems curriculum was developed primarily in response to local needs (Tatnall, 1993), at least up until the mid-1980s.

Figure 1: Research, Development, Diffusion and Dissemination models

Research ▸▸ Development ▸▸ Production ▸▸ Dissemination ▸▸ Adoption

Since that time, however, well-accepted curriculum documents from groups like IFIP, ACM, DPMA, and IEEE have tended to act as 'authoritative' statements, giving use of this approach more credence today.

A quite different approach makes use of Rapid Application Development (RAD) techniques, adapted from IS systems development. RAD techniques have also been incorporated into a model of IS curriculum development (Davey & Tatnall, 2000). One of the useful ideas to arise from RAD is the concept of a directed process involving 'users' through meetings with very specific agenda, and this can offer advantages in moving forward a curriculum process that has become stalled by directionless debate. The RAD curriculum approach makes use of directed processes involving academics and other stakeholders through a series of meetings with specific agendas.

Information systems curriculum development in a university takes place in the environment of an educational institution containing both academic and industrial elements, and also artefacts such as computers, peripherals, development tools, and methodologies. Any process of curriculum development in such an environment involves a set of complex negotiations between those writing the details of the curriculum. Tatnall (2000) proposes that higher education information systems curriculum can usefully be seen as an actor-network (Callon, 1999; Latour, 1996; Law, 1991) involving the contributions of both human and non-human actors. Approaches such as this see the interactions of individuals and artefacts acting within a system or environment as important, as does the next model we will consider.

This chapter offers the metaphor of an ecological model to help explain how curriculum change occurs within university courses in information systems. Writing about the development of school mathematics curriculum in Australia, Truran (1997) offers what he calls a 'Broad Spectrum Ecological Model' to illustrate curriculum change and to explain the divergence between programs. Truran proposes that systems of education may be seen as ecosystems containing interacting individuals and groups of individuals. The interactions between these parties will sometimes involve cooperation and sometimes competition, and may be interpreted in terms of these interacting forces along with mechanisms for minimising energy expenditure. In this chapter we will examine the application of this metaphor to curriculum change in information systems.

METAPHORS AND MODELS

Before proceeding, however, we need to caution the reader on the limitations and appropriate uses of models and metaphors. A model is an abstraction that is intended as a *representation* of some idea or thing. A model is not itself reality, but just a representation intended to fulfill some explanatory purpose; models thus always have limitations. The dictionary describes a metaphor as a term "applied to something to which it is not literally applicable, in order to suggest a resemblance" (Macquarie Library, 1981:1096).

When a young man says that his girlfriend's eyes glow like diamonds, he is not suggesting that they are made of the hardest material he can think of, but something entirely different. A metaphor is useful, not in giving a literal interpretation, but in providing a viewpoint that allows us to relate to certain aspects of a complex system. In a recent issue of *New Scientist* magazine, James Lovelock, devisor of the Gaia hypothesis, remarked that: "You've got to use metaphor to explain science, it's part of the process of giving people a feel for the subject" (Bond, 2000).

When curriculum developers use the Colonial Echo Model (Clements et al., 1989) of curriculum development, they are using a metaphor that asks us to look for connections between the current curriculum and curricula of the past, or of a 'mother country,' in order to understand the components of the curriculum statement or of the development process. We would contend that most curriculum models and metaphors are too simplistic to allow a useful view of a curriculum, and its development, as a complex system involving human and non-human interactions. An ecological model offers two main advantages:

- A way of allowing for the inclusion of complexity.
- A new language and set of analytical and descriptive tools from the ecological sciences.

AN ECOLOGICAL MODEL
OF CURRICULUM CHANGE

In ecology, organisms are seen to operate within a competitive environment which ensures that only the most efficient of them will survive. In order to survive, they behave in ways that optimise the balance between their energy expenditure and the satisfaction they obtain from this effort. These two key principles underlie the discipline of ecology, which is concerned with the relationship of one organism to another and to their common physical environment (Case, 2000; Townsend, Harper, & Begon, 2000). In particular, ecology is concerned with the way that organisms respond to the various forces that operate within the environment.

An ecosystem can be considered to contain producers, consumers, and decomposers. A classical definition is "a natural unit of living and non-living parts that interact to produce a stable system in which the exchange of materials between the living and non-living parts follows a circular path" (Ville, 1962:89). The idea that organisms may be controlled by the weakest link in the ecological chain of requirements, also known as Liebig's Law or the law of the minimum, has been around for some time (Odum, 1963). Under Leibig's Law the rate of growth of an organism is dependent on the nutrient conditions present in the *minimum* quantity in terms of availability and of need.

Habitat, ecological niches, and the exploitation of resources in predator-prey interactions, competition, and multi-species communities (Case, 2000) are all important considerations in ecology. Many different individuals and species typically occupy any given ecosystem, and they can be considered to interact in the following ways:

- When two individuals or species are in **competition** with each other, they are each striving for the same thing, which is typically food, space, or some other physical need. When the thing they are striving for is not in adequate supply for both of them, the result is that both are hampered, or adversely affected, in some manner (Odum, 1963).
- **Proto-cooperation** is the situation in which each population is benefited by the presence of the other, but can survive in its absence.
- **Mutualism** occurs when each population is benefited by the presence of the other, but cannot survive in nature without it (Ville, 1962).
- **Commensalism** occurs when two species habitually live together, and one species is benefited by this arrangement, and the second is unharmed (or not affected) by it.
- The situation in which two species live in close proximity and one species is inhibited by this, but the second is unaffected by the presence of the first, is called **amensalism**.
- When one species adversely affects the second but cannot live without it in the relationship, the result is either **parasitism** or **predation**. These types of interaction are closely related and form a continuum. A small number of predators can have a marked effect on the size of specific prey populations as the energy flow of predators is relatively small.
- The situation in which there is no interaction between two individuals or species is called **neutralism**.

Truran (1997) suggests that these ideas correspond to the process of curriculum development by arguing that an educational system may be seen as an ecosystem, and that the interactions within this ecosystem can be analysed in terms of ecological concepts such as competition models, cooperative behaviour, predator-prey relationships, and niche-development. He argues that curriculum change can be interpreted in terms of interacting forces, mechanisms for minimising energy expenditure, and decisions that individuals make about whether to cooperate or to compete, and goes on to discuss the evolution of high school mathematics curricula in Australia in terms of three ecological principles:

1. **Criteria for behaviour optimisation**. Biological behaviour that requires the least effort to obtain adequate food and shelter is considered optimal. This tendency can be seen in IS curriculum development in examples such as: 'How do we devise a suitable new curriculum in the simplest possible way? Let's just use the material developed by XXXX University.'

2. **Proximate and ultimate behaviour factors.** An ecological example of this is in animal breeding which is seen to be affected by proximate, or short-term, factors such as changes in the hours of daylight, but also by ultimate, or long-term, factors like the need to produce young when food and shelter are most readily available. In relation to IS curriculum, while the need to keep courses relevant and up-to-date with industry developments might be the ultimate aim, proximate factors such as lack of funds to purchase equipment may interfere.

3. **The principle of convergence.** Unrelated families of animals living in the same area are often similar in appearance despite their quite different genetic makeup. This is due to environmental factors. While similarities in curriculum in different countries or locations may seem to suggest that one example has been copied from the other, it is quite possible that they have developed independently due to the similarity in educational environments.

In information systems curriculum development, we should thus look at all the factors, both human and artefact, to see which could be expected to compete, and which cooperate to become part of the surviving outcome. A non-human stakeholder such as a development tool or methodology must cooperate with the environment, compete successfully, or die out. This may mean a new curriculum element becomes incompatible with an old element and so replaces it. Alternatively it may mean that two new design tools can be used together, or that a particular curriculum element is compatible, or perhaps incompatible, with the desires and interests of a particular faculty member.

Ecological metaphors can, however, be used in areas other than just in biology and curriculum change. This type of ecological framework has also been used quite successfully in several other areas including a study of the effects of violence on children (Mohr & Tulman, 2000). Ecology as a framework tells us to expect progress of a task through cooperative or competitive behaviours of the animate and inanimate factors in the environment. A factor that cannot compete or cooperate is inevitably discarded.

CURRICULUM CHANGE AND THE ECOLOGICAL METAPHOR

Many factors influence how an information systems curriculum is developed, and Sandman (1993) outlines these below.

This model provides a good starting point to define the nature of the information systems curriculum ecosystem, and to identify the ecological factors involved in determining how it can be changed.

Ecosystems and Complexity

An ecosystem contains a high degree of complexity due to the large number of creatures and species living in it, and to the variety of interactions possible between each of these. The 'ecosystem' represented by the curriculum in a university information systems department contains (at least) the following 'species': lecturers, researchers, students, professional bodies, university administrators, Course Advisory Board members, and representatives of the computer industry. The 'environment' also contains many inanimate objects relevant to the formation of the curriculum, including: computers, programming languages, textbooks, lecture rooms, analysis and design methodologies, networks, laboratories, programming manuals, and so on.

When using an ecological metaphor, curriculum development can be seen as attempting to introduce change within an ecosystem. The problem of course is the large number of interested parties that must be contended with before this change can be implemented. Curriculum development is more complex than resolving the conflicting needs of students, employers, academics, and the academy. There is ongoing conflict between many things such as educational philosophies, pedagogical preferences, perceived resource constraints, and personal issues. Consider the following example of an attempt to introduce a new course in data communications and networking into an undergraduate degree. This would involve many factors and interactions in the ecosystem, including:

- A perception that many job advertisements include the word 'networking' in their text.

Figure 2: Influences on IS Curriculum (adapted from Sandman, 1993

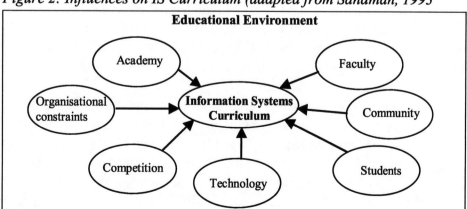

- A set of curriculum standards using the word 'networks' to describe a content area.
- A careers adviser who has been asked, by employers, to provide students with more knowledge of networks.
- Several textbooks with the word 'networks' in the title.
- Some students who have expressed an interest in learning about networks.
- An expert teacher who has industrial experience as a network installer.
- An expert teacher who has industrial experience as a network administrator.
- A researcher who has been studying network topologies.
- A researcher who has been studying network software.
- A researcher who has studied the effects of networks on work practices in organisations.
- An Advisory Board member who works for a large bank.
- Another Advisory Board member who works for an IT engineering firm.
- A university facilities manager whose performance is measured by total size of budget and percentage of room usage.
- A curriculum statement aimed at implementing a program that is flexible, and that meets future needs of business.
- A curriculum statement that attempts to give students skills that will be immediately applicable in business.
- A program coordinator who has selected courses that are regarded as essential for an undergraduate education.
- A university ruling that sets the maximum content for a degree.
- Some students who have complained that their program is too technical.
- Some students who have complained that their program is not technical enough.

These are only some of the ecological factors involved in the curriculum development process, and the interactions between these factors will depend upon the power and influence of each factor. We could now ask: Given these factors what will the affect be? Will a networks course be included in the curriculum? If so, will this course involve practical electronics, topological architecture, network administration, or networks in organisations? How long will the course be? Who will be involved with teaching the course? How will the course be assessed? Who will be involved in evaluation of the course?

The answers to these questions, and the progress of the curriculum development, will depend on the complex nature of the ecosystem and the interactions between each of these factors – between the individuals and species in the ecosystem. We will now look at each of the different types of interaction that, apart from neutralism where there is no interaction, can be summarised as: competition, and the various different types of cooperation (proto-cooperation, mutualism, commensalism, and amensalism).

Competition

Competition in nature can occur both within and between species. In many species the males compete with each other for mates, while different species of fish compete for the best feeding areas. In IS curriculum we see many examples of competition, some of which are useful in determining the 'fittest' topics and techniques best suited for survival (Darwin, 1958) in the curriculum, while others involve time-wasting clashes of personality between academics.

One example of competition seen in recent years in many IS Departments is between the programming languages Pascal and Visual Basic. The advocates of Pascal contend that, as a highly structured language, it is still the best vehicle for introducing students to the concepts of programming. Visual Basic advocates, however, argue that while this may be so, Visual Basic is easier to use and moreover is used to a much greater extent in industry. The result of this competition is, most likely, that one language will survive in the curriculum and the other will die out. Similar examples can often be seen in competition between different methodologies and between software products. Most university courses now make use of Microsoft Office rather than Lotus, Work Perfect, and the like, as Microsoft has clearly won the competition and has become dominant in this area.

Sometimes competition can be seen between two teachers with different philosophies or approaches to the teaching of a particular topic area. This can result in the topic being taught twice. Competition between academic departments within a university sometimes results in a topic area being taught in an inappropriate department in order to preserve academic jobs or to retain a balance between the size and importance of these departments. Competition between universities can, unfortunately, result in 'flavour of the month' curriculum development designed with the express purpose of attracting students.

One would hope that predation and parasitism do not have parallels in university IS curriculum development, but most of us know better and could cite an example or two that would fit here also. We will, however, not pursue this line of inquiry here.

Cooperation

There are many examples of unexpected cooperation between organisms in nature: the oxpecker bird that lives with a rhinoceros (commensalism), sharks and suckerfish, barnacles that attach themselves to whales, and dogs and cats living in close proximity with people. It is also possible to think of an organism living in cooperation with its environment: something the native peoples of many countries speak about.

In an educational program such as an information systems degree, some courses rely on earlier courses, i.e., they have prerequisites. This can be seen as a form of cooperation in which each course benefits from the existence of the other (mutualism). Another similar example is in software and programming languages where, for instance, the use of Visual Basic in a computer laboratory requires the presence (and cooperation) of Microsoft Windows. Likewise subject material that relies on the use of a specific textbook could also be seen as an example of cooperation.

Team teaching is an obvious example of cooperation from which all parties benefit. Two teachers working together to develop teaching materials may represent proto-cooperation where both parties benefit, but where either party could get along perfectly well working alone. In many information systems departments, cooperation between teaching and research interests of individual academics results in an improved curriculum.

Ecological Niches

An ecological niche is a place where a particular species that is well suited to this environment is able to thrive, where other species may not. A curriculum example of this is in the teaching of the PICK operating system by a university in Australia. Some years ago PICK was a serious challenger to UNIX for the 'universal operating system' in business, but PICK has now decreased in importance. Despite the fact that no other university in the region now teaches it, and its place being challenged by more recent operating systems, PICK has remained in the curriculum of this university. It has remained largely because an academic involved in its teaching was able to argue convincingly (Tatnall, 2000) that learning PICK allowed students to take up jobs in the small number of prominent local industries using this system – that it filled an important ecological niche.

Other examples include one Australian university that has a close relationship with IBM so that its students work principally with IBM equipment, operating systems, languages, and software. This gives these students an edge in applying for jobs in an IBM environment. Several other universities are working closely with SAP and integrating this product into their courses so that their students gain a better understanding of enterprise resource planning systems and will be able to easily take up jobs in this field.

In each of these cases, the course at the university concerned is aimed at filling a niche – perhaps a small one, perhaps a large one, but a niche nevertheless. The implication is that rather than trying to produce students who know something of the complete field of computing, they will turn out graduates who have specialised in just one or two aspects of it.

IS Curriculum and Other Ecological Processes

Other aspects of ecology can also be related to IS curriculum. Optimisation of behaviour, or minimisation of energy expenditure, is an important principle in ecology as mentioned earlier. It is easy to find examples of this in curriculum development in the use of curriculum templates, and the copying of curriculum from other institutions or countries (Clements et al., 1989). A related example is seen in choosing curriculum elements so that they fit in with existing university resources.

Any factor that tends to slow down potential growth in an ecosystem can be considered as a limiting, or regulatory, factor. The concept of organisms being controlled by the 'weakest link in an ecological chain of requirements' comes from early in the 1800s in Leibig's 'law of the minimum' (Odum, 1963). When any condition approaches or exceeds the limit of tolerance for the organism in question, that is there is too little or too much of this factor, then this will act to limit growth. Many examples of this can be found in IS curriculum change. For example, too little laboratory space or too many students may reduce the quality of learning. Conversely, the availability of a large amount of money for industry-based research may also reduce the amount of academic time spent in preparation for teaching and curriculum development.

Finally, we invite our readers to consider whether they can find curriculum parallels for some of the following ecological situations: island-based examples of evolution such as Australia's specialisation in marsupials, terra-forming by rabbits, herds and pack instincts, and the link between man's introduction of pigs and rats to Mauritius and the extinction of the Dodo.

METAPHORICAL OUTCOMES

To ignore complexity in the curriculum development process will not make it go away, it will just give you less control over this process. We need to decide how to handle complexity and there are different ways that this can be achieved. It would be useful to see how the ecological metaphor might be applied to the process of developing an information systems curriculum, and we will now look at three different ways of thinking about IS curriculum development from the view of this metaphor and from the perspective of three different groups of people. We will call them industrialists, farmers, and biologists.

The curriculum developer who is acting as an *industrialist* works to achieve total control of the educational environment towards the single-minded end of building a curriculum product. In a general context the industrialist has a clear view of what the required outcome is and how it should be manufactured. This may be achieved by activities such as bulldozing the area to be developed, laying concrete, building a factory, and stamping out plastic food. The situation created by the industrialist is a forced one and will only remain in place as long as the industrialist continues to exert his will. In the curriculum context this could be seen to relate to centralised curriculum development and dissemination.

A farmer seeks to exert some control over growing and living things in order to fill some need. He has a clear view of the nature of the crop that is being produced and will seek to exert some control over those parts of the ecology that will lead to a good yield. A farmer will plough the ground and burn the stubble in an attempt to reduce complexity and diversity so that nothing gets in the way of achieving the desired yield. Presuming that he knows what the 'right' crop to grow is, and how to grow it, it will be possible for this crop to remain right over time. A curriculum developer acting as a *farmer* might act, for example, to restrict membership of the curriculum committee to keep out the 'trouble makers,' and to reward cooperative behaviour between groups of academics.

A biologist observes, records patterns, and categorises the behaviour of plants and animals. Standing amidst the complexity of the ecology, the biologist looks for patterns in the interactions between the actors so that useful advice can then be given to the participants. The biologist does not force change, but merely observes it. From her observations she may advise, for instance, that if lions and zebras are allowed to remain in too close proximity, the zebras may not survive. A curriculum developer acting as a *biologist* might advise that if a very strong personality is allowed to dominate curriculum development meetings, then the curriculum is likely to have reduced diversity.

To make use of an ecological metaphor in considering curriculum change, it is first necessary to think of the way you want to view the curriculum development process. We have here offered three ways, but there are no doubt others that could also have been considered. In our example you need to decide if you want to view curriculum as being developed by someone acting like an industrialist, a farmer, or a biologist. When the desired view has been determined, fitting relevant aspects of the metaphor to this view is not a difficult exercise.

CONCLUSION: BENEFITS OF USING AN ECOLOGICAL METAPHOR

Researchers investigating curriculum development, or any other field, must use language in framing their research questions. The language used often reflects a general viewpoint of the field being investigated and will always embody some metaphor for the principle components of the field. The metaphor is not useful in *proving* relationships but can be used to convey meaning once relationships are discovered, and an appropriate metaphor can lead the researcher towards or away from useful possible conclusions. Many of the metaphors for curriculum development are simple ones from areas such as manufacturing or the physical sciences. Any investigation of real development processes in rapidly changing areas such as information systems shows that a common factor is complexity. This leads the search for a suitable metaphor to those disciplines that have accommodated complexity. One such area is that of ecology, and we have shown how ecological principles appear to provide good descriptions of common curriculum development activities. The ease with which the metaphor can be used to describe actions within IS curriculum development shows that it can be useful as a set of language elements that might lead the researcher to framing useful questions that do not trivialise the complexity of the field.

The advantages of the ecological metaphor include the presumption of complexity and interaction. We are not suggesting that the curriculum development process *is* a biological system, but that concepts taken from the field can be seen to be applicable to IS curriculum development. This gives a framework in which researchers can attempt to develop and test models of curriculum development that include the obvious complexity of the real processes.

Many people nowadays tend to use the word 'Web' most often in relation to the Internet, but Darwin (1958) first used it to refer to the set of complex relationships by which plants and animals are bound together, and to their environment in nature. We have argued that this can also be a useful way in which to view information systems curriculum development. Use of an ecological metaphor provides access to a range of concepts and tools with which to understand the complexities of IS curriculum development and the processes by which this development occurs.

IS curriculum development involves a complex process of negotiation between actors, and one that cannot be simply explained by reference to a set process of referring new ideas to a series of university committees. The choices of individual academics, or groups of academics, to adopt or ignore a new concept or technology, and to compete or cooperate, must also be considered. This inevitably involves a negotiation process between many different actors. We have argued that this negotiation process can be analysed in terms of ecological behaviour, and have utilised an ecological metaphor to assist in visualising the curriculum development process. We have stressed the value of using models and metaphors to describe or illustrate complex activities, and we remind the reader of Lovelock's remark (Bond, 2000) that the value inherent in the use of a metaphor is to give people a 'feel for the subject.' We have argued that use of an ecological metaphor can give people a *better feel* for IS curriculum development.

REFERENCES

Bond, M. (2000). Father Earth. *New Scientist,* 167, 44-47.

Boomer, G., Lester, N., Onore, C., & Cook, J. (1992). *Negotiating the Curriculum: Educating for the 21ˢᵗ Century.* London: The Falmer Press.

Callon, M. (1999). Actor-network theory - The market test. In Law, J. & Hassard, J. (Eds.), *Actor Network Theory and After* (pp. 181-195). Oxford: Blackwell Publishers.

Case, T. J. (2000). *An Illustrated Guide to Theoretical Ecology.* New York: Oxford University Press.

Clements, M. A., Grimison, L. A., & Ellerton, N. F. (1989). *Colonialism and School Mathematics in Australia 1788-1988.* Paper presented at the School Mathematics Conference: The Challenge to Change Geelong, Geelong, Australia.

Darwin, C. (1958). *The Origin of Species.* (Mentor edition.). New York: The New American Library. (Obviously the first edition was published much earlier than this!)

Davey, B., & Tatnall, A. (2000). *Rapid Curriculum Development: A RAD Approach to MIS Curriculum Development.* Paper presented at the Information Systems Education Conference (ISECON 2000), Philadelphia, PA.

Fullan, M. (1993). *Change Forces: Probing the Depths of Educational Reform.* London: The Falmer Press.

Fullan, M., & Hargreaves, A. (1992). Teacher development and educational change. In Fullan, M. & Hargreaves, A. (Eds.), *Teacher Development and Educational Change.* London: The Falmer Press.

Kemmis, S., & Stake, R. (1988). *Evaluating Curriculum.* Geelong: Deakin University Press.

Latour, B. (1996). *Aramis or the Love of Technology.* Cambridge, MA: Harvard University Press.

Law, J. (Ed.). (1991). *A Sociology of Monsters. Essays on Power, Technology and Domination.* London: Routledge.

Law, J. (1999). After ANT: Complexity, naming and topology. In Law, J. & Hassard, J. (Eds.), *Actor Network Theory and After* (pp. 1-14). Oxford: Blackwell Publishers.

Longenecker, H. E. Jr., & Feinstein, D. L. (1990). *Information Systems (IS'90) DRAFT Report: The DPMA Model Curriculum for a Four-Year Undergraduate Degree.* USA: DPMA (CTF-90).

Macquarie Library. (1981). *The Macquarie Dictionary.* Sydney: Macquarie Library.

Mohr, W. K., & Tulman, L. J. (2000). Children exposed to violence: Measurement considerations within an ecological framework. *Advances in Nursing Science, 23*(1), 59-67.

Nordvall, R. C. (1982). *The Process of Change in Higher Education Institutions.* (ERIC/AAHE Research Report 7). Washington DC: American Association for Higher Education.

Odum, E. P. (1963). *Ecology.* USA: Holt, Rinehart and Winston.

Sandman, T. E. (1993). A framework for adapting a MS/MIS curriculum to a changing environment. *Journal of Computer Information Systems, 34*(2), 69-73.

Tatnall, A. (1993). *A Curriculum History of Business Computing in Victorian Tertiary Institutions from 1960-1985.* Geelong, Deakin University.

Tatnall, A. (2000). *Innovation and Change in the Information Systems Curriculum of an Australian University: A Socio-Technical Perspective.* Rockhampton, Central Queensland University.

Townsend, C. R., Harper, J. L., & Begon, M. (2000). *Essentials of Ecology.* Massachusetts: Blackwell Science.

Truran, J. M. (1997). *Reinterpreting Australian Mathematics Curriculum Development Using a Broad-Spectrum Ecological Model.* Paper presented at Old Boundaries and New Frontiers in Histories of Education: Australian and New Zealand History of Education Society Conference, Newcastle, Australia, December 7-10.

Ville, C. A. (1962). *Biology.* Philadelphia, PA: W. B. Saunders Company.

Chapter 25

Teaching or Technology: Who's Driving the Bandwagon?

Geoffrey C. Mitchell
Victoria University of Wellington, New Zealand

Beverley G. Hope
Victoria University of Wellington, New Zealand
and City University of Hong Kong, China

Fuelled by the increasing connectivity afforded by the Internet and the flexibility offered by Web technologies, the use of technology in education has become increasingly common. However, despite claims that the Web will revolutionise education, many attempts at Web-based education simply reinforce current 'poor' teaching practices or present more of the same disguised in updated packaging. We argue that this occurs because of differing pedagogical assumptions and a limited understanding of how flexible learning differs from traditional approaches. In particular, we argue that flexible learning demands an increased focus on constructivism and the sociological aspects of teaching and learning. This chapter presents two frameworks that situate our approach to flexible learning with respect to more traditional offerings and discusses the implications for educational technology design.

INTRODUCTION

Advances in information and communication technologies (ICT) in the last 20 years have had a significant social and economic impact (Adams & Warf, 1997). The diffusion of ICT includes not only the ubiquitousness of computers, but also increases in computing power, multi-media capability, and interconnectedness. The

Previously Published in *Challenges of Information Technology Education in the 21st Century* edited by Eli Cohen, Copyright © 2002, Idea Group Publishing.

education sector has not been immune to the impact of these developments. While moves from purely synchronous to asynchronous delivery modes preceded the ascendance of ICT, ICT has been a major enabling factor in more recent shifts from broadcast (1-m) to interactive (m-m) interaction modes and from linear (textbook) to network (hypertext) information presentation.

The new technologies have both 'pull' and 'push' impacts on trends in flexible education. That is, they provide a solution to demands for more flexible forms of education and, because of their capabilities, also serve to increase demand. Informed, motivated students in the new competitive educational environment are demanding modes of learning that suit their individual needs.

Life-long education and global course offerings have led to increasingly diverse student populations at the higher education level. This diversity is apparent in demographic characteristics such as age, culture, prior education, work and life experience, and learning style. Meeting the needs of this diverse population requires greater flexibility in course delivery. This is difficult to achieve in a traditional, large-class, same-time/same-place teaching environment. Increased availability of computers and greater connectivity can overcome these difficulties. Regrettably, many Web-based educational implementations reinforce rather than replace inflexible teaching practices.

In this chapter, we argue that to maximise the benefits of educational technology, greater attention must given to the motives and planning behind the adoption of educational technology. We first discuss some of the underlying pedagogical assumptions of instructional choices from three perspectives: technological determinism, psychological determinism, and sociological determinism. This forms the background to the development of a framework comparing 'emergent' teaching and learning practices with more traditional practices. Emergent, flexible forms of education are discussed in terms of their implications for educational technology design. We conclude by presenting some simple guidelines for the design of educational technology to support both teaching and learning practices.

BACKGROUND

Underlying the debate about the role of ICT in education are some basic pedagogical assumptions (Berman, 1992; Cowley, Scragg, & Baldwin, 1993; Harsim, 1990; Kozma & Johnston, 1991; Miller & Miller, 1999) and some theories about the relationship between technology and organizations (Eason 1988, 1993; Hirschheim, 1985; Keen, 1981; Leonard-Barton, 1988; Markus & Robey, 1988; Sproull & Goodman, 1990). Differing assumptions influence expectations and implementations. These assumptions can be grouped and summarised as three perspectives:

1.   technological determinism,
2.   psychological determinism, and
3.   social interactionism

Our review of these three perspectives is necessarily brief, and to that end simplified. However, an understanding of the underlying assumptions is essential for understanding approaches to and pitfalls of educational technology implementations.

Technological Determinism

Technological determinism assumes an intrinsic worth of technology and is optimistic about the effect ICT will have on education. Opportunities for adding value are considered to depend on the features and quality of the technology and on users' ability to recognize them (Campbell, 1996). In this respect, technological determinism takes a utopian view of technology.

The view discounts the impact of the context into which technology is introduced. Issues such as power and politics are ignored because teachers and students are considered rational beings, following logical decision-making processes toward shared goals (Markus & Robey, 1988). Technology is an "exogenous force which determines or strongly constrains the behaviour of individuals" (Markus & Robey, 1988, p.585). Consequently, the technology rather than the educational environment, the teacher, or the learner determines the success of an educational technology implementation.

Technological determinism in educational technology design results in an over-emphasis on hardware and technical capability and an under-emphasis on student needs and characteristics. The focus is on the technology in the confident belief that "If we build it, they will come."

Psychological Determinism

This pedagogical perspective is founded in cognitive processing theories of the 1970s and 80s. These theories focused attention on internal mental processes of learners and provided an alternative to the behaviourist approaches which had motivated earlier programmed instruction and computer-assisted instruction (Miller & Miller, 1999). However, like behaviourism, cognitive processing theories follow an objectivist paradigm in assuming that knowledge is independent of and external to the learner.

A belief in objective and external knowledge leads to teaching strategies in which the instructor (knowledge expert) structures and presents knowledge in such a way that the learner can accurately acquire it. The educational objective is to transmit knowledge. Successful learning is evidenced by the learner's ability to correctly reproduce this knowledge (Cronin, 1997; Jonassen, Davidson, Collins, Campbell, & Haag, 1995).

Educational technology design under this perspective focuses on the structure and presentation of knowledge. Information structure is likely to be strongly hierarchical, mirroring the reality of the external knowledge. Presentation considerations include giving attention to such issues as font size, use of colour, and use of images in the belief that these will aid attention and foster knowledge retention. Web-based instruction founded in this perspective can result in the placement of traditional course material onto static Web sites.

Social Interactionism

Social interactionism is founded in the constructivist paradigm. In contrast to psychological determinism, constructivism does not view knowledge as external to the learner. Rather, knowledge is internally constructed as the learner attributes meaning to experiences within their environment (Bereiter, 1990; Cronin, 1997; Jonassen et al., 1995). Purists under this view may hold that knowledge has no objective reality, while moderates may acknowledge an objective reality but one which can only be subjectively known (Miller & Miller, 1999).

Whatever the degree of a constructionist's belief, society cannot function on purely individualistic conceptualisations of knowledge. Some consensus of meaning must be obtained and this is achieved through social interaction with others (Heylighen, 1997). This social aspect of knowledge construction is often termed 'social interactionism,' because it necessitates interaction and collaboration.

The social interactionism perspective offers no prescriptions for educational success, since requirements depend on the particular skills, abilities, and needs of individuals. Nevertheless, several authors have produced lists of implications of constructivist theories for learning and teaching. Murphy (1997) reviews some of the major theorists and summarises the implications as:

1. Multiple perspectives and representations of concepts and content are presented.
2. Goals and objectives are derived by the learner or in negotiation with the teacher.
3. Teachers serve as guides, monitors, coaches, tutors, and facilitators.
4. Activities, tools, and environments encourage metacognition, self-analysis, self-regulation, self-reflection, and self-awareness.
5. The learner plays a central role in mediating and controlling learning.
6. Learning environments, content, and tasks are relevant, realistic, and represent the natural complexities of the 'real world.'
7. Primary sources of data are used to provide authenticity and real-world complexity.

8. Knowledge construction and not reproduction is emphasized.
9. Knowledge construction takes place in individual contexts and through social negotiation, collaboration, and experience.
10. The learner's previous knowledge constructions, beliefs, and attitudes are considered in the knowledge construction process.
11. Problem-solving, higher-order thinking skills, and deep understanding are emphasized.
12. Errors provide opportunities for insight into learners' previous knowledge constructions.
13. Exploration is a favoured approach to encourage learners to seek knowledge independently and to manage the pursuit of their goals.
14. Learners are provided with the opportunity for apprenticeship learning in which there is an increasing complexity of tasks, skills, and knowledge acquisition.
15. Knowledge complexity is reflected in an emphasis on conceptual interrelatedness and interdisciplinary learning.
16. Collaborative and cooperative learning are favoured in order to expose the learner to alternative viewpoints.
17. Scaffolding is facilitated to help students perform just beyond the limits of their ability.
18. Assessment is authentic and interwoven with teaching.

These tactics can be difficult to achieve with large undergraduate classes. However the use of ICTs, and in particular Web technologies, can greatly facilitate their successful implementation.

The three perspectives outlined – technological determinism, psychological determinism, and social interactionism – show how differing assumptions affect education and educational technology design and implementation. Each perspective contributes something to our understanding, but given the prevalence of technological determinism and the entrenched practices derived from psychological determinism, it is important in our efforts to develop flexible education that we give consideration to the tactics arising from a social interactionism perspective.

TRADITIONAL AND EMERGENT FORMS OF EDUCATION

According to Willis (1995), traditional education is characterised by the following:
• learning process is sequential and linear;
• planning is top down and systematic;

- course objectives guide all learning activities;
- teachers are perceived as experts with special knowledge;
- careful sequencing of teaching activities is important to learning predefined skill sets;
- the main goal is delivery of pre-selected knowledge;
- summative evaluation forms the basis of assessment; and
- objective results are critical.

Traditional education revolves around the group lecture, supplemented by tutorials or workshops designed to reinforce the material 'delivered' by the lecturer. Courses are often modularised with each week covering a new area of knowledge or skill set. Learning objectives are carefully spelled out in course outlines and clearly linked to the various pieces of assessment. Courses emphasize parity and are readily accepted by faculty steering committees and external moderators.

While well accepted and often successfully executed, this form of learning generally fails to engage students in deeper learning (Mills-Jones, 1999) or to deliver the problem-solving skills favored by employers (Bentley, Lowry, & Sandy, 1999). Some instructors, departments, or disciplines have adopted problem-based learning and active learning strategies to address these concerns. However, until recently the logistics of dealing with large student numbers have limited the opportunities in these areas.

To date, economic issues have commonly been the driving force behind flexible learning and educational technology initiatives. The drive to attract more students and the associated funding at least cost has seen schools and universities adopt Web-based systems which merely deliver traditional mail-based distance courses over the Internet. Under the banner of 'flexible education,' instructors have provided online access to lecture notes and in some cases streamed lectures using Web-based audio and video technology. Unfortunately, there has been limited evidence that this newer approach to material delivery has added any real value to students' learning experiences (Riddle, Nott, & Pearce, 1995; Vargo & Cragg, 1999). The nature of the course and the assumptions of student learning are fundamentally the same as those of traditional education. It has been argued that to achieve real added value, the use of educational technology must be adopted in conjunction with a more fundamental change in the nature of student learning activities (Lamp & Goodwin, 1999; Mak, 1995; Ramsden, 1992; Vargo & Cragg, 1999). This is true flexible learning.

Situating Flexible Learning

Sociological theory has for many years recognised the essentially dualistic nature of human activity systems. Parsons and Bales (1955) labelled these dimensions task and socio-emotional, reflecting the difference between the technical aspects of work-related structures and the social concerns of the human actors operating within those structures. The theory suggests that these activity dimensions are central to individual and group development of values and beliefs (Pfeffer, 1981), a perspective in keeping with the notion of education as developing new value and belief structures or schemata. Consequently, an argument can be made for the view that because education is an important context for personal interaction – second only to 'work' – it is central to the social creation of meaning.

Student development of shared knowledge and meaning can be described within the context of the two dimensions. Students interact at many levels to create, confirm, and recreate shared meanings. This shared meaning construction covers a much larger knowledge domain than has traditionally been considered in the context of academic learning. The broader definition is consistent with Brown's (1994) examination of outside school learning, Fensham's (1992) work on commonsense knowledge, and Resnick's (1987) exploration of learning and reasoning outside school. However, educational research has often identified these knowledge construction activities as separate functions taking place (1) inside and (2) outside of school. This view denies the role of social interaction within school in constructing shared meaning.

We situate approaches to education within this two-dimensional framework to highlight the differing perspectives and assumptions of teachers. Assumptions regarding the appropriate structure for education (task) can be thought of in terms of a uniformity-diversity dimension, while assumptions regarding appropriate student relations (socio-emotional) may be represented in a competition-collaboration dimension (Figure 1).

Figure 1: Socio-Technical Domains of the Educational Context

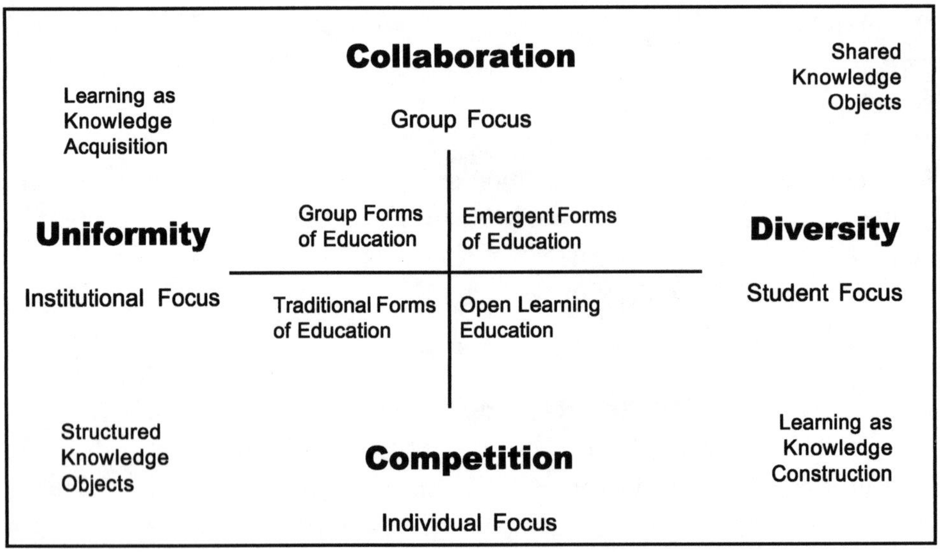

Uniformity-Diversity Dimension

The uniformity-diversity dimension distinguishes between those approaches to curriculum design that concentrate on singular notions of subject design, course delivery, and assessment, and those which emphasize flexible approaches. Uniformity of task is institutionally focused, that is, it concentrates on meeting university-wide standards or norms by offering the 'same' experience and assessment to all. Such programmes are readily accepted by boards of studies and external moderators. By contrast, diversity of task is student focused, offering different learning experiences for individual students. Diversity is often accepted in principle but less frequently practiced and less readily accepted. The uniformity-diversity distinction has received a great deal of attention in recent research into effective teaching and learning practices (Ramsden, 1992; Ramsden, Margetson, Martin, & Clarke, 1995).

Behind the current calls for more flexible teaching and learning practices lies the belief that teaching, particularly in higher education, needs to adopt a stronger student focus (Boyer, 1990; Brown, 1994). While academics who adopt a uniform approach talk about the 'right' teaching strategy, those interested in diversity deny the existence of any single 'right' way to teach (Bentley, Lowry, & Sandy, 1999; Mak, 1995; Mills-Jones, 1999). They argue instead that 'best' practices can only be based on an understanding of particular student learning needs. Thus uniformity is grounded in psychological determinism, while diversity is grounded in social interactionism. The growing pressure for diversity stems from a number of factors, including the diverse nature of the student population, the diverse needs of employers, the diversity of educational intentions, and the need to provide greater levels of teacher satisfaction with the educational process.

Competition-Collaboration Dimension

The competition-collaboration dimension reflects differing perceptions concerning the complex social interactions between students which are so important in developing shared knowledge objects. The extremes of this dimension are somewhat multi-faceted in that they deal with the distinction between an individual focus (competition) and a group focus (collaboration), as well as dealing with the underlying assumptions regarding student attitudes to both their peers and teaching staff (Johnson & Johnson, 1989).

At the simplest level, the competitive aspect of the socio-economic dimension views students as a large collection of individual units (Bereiter, 1990), a perspective strongly evident in traditional educational activities. This view assumes students are motivated primarily by assessments, and that it is through assessments that students can be manipulated to receive planned educational objectives. By contrast, the collaborative end of the dimension views students as active constructors, rather than passive recipients of knowledge (Brown, 1994). The view assumes that learning is best facilitated through shared learning experiences among students as well as between students and teachers (Kushan, 1994). These views are often represented in notions like communities of learners (Brown, 1994), cooperative learning (Johnson & Johnson, 1989), and professional communities (Lieberman, 1992). Such views of the learning context and student interaction have strong implications for the appropriateness of current assessment tactics and the role students should play in them.

The intersection of these two dimensions results in four domains representing traditional education (uniformity/competition), group education (uniformity/collaboration), open learning (diversity/competition), and emergent forms of education (diversity/collaboration). The focus of this chapter is on the emergent forms of education resulting from an increased focus on diversity and collaboration.

Traditional Education

The uniformity-competition domain is strongly indicative of traditional forms of education. Within this domain, teaching is highly structured, singular in nature, and focused on rational teaching strategies in line with deterministic psychological theory. It is concerned with institutional procedures and practices and treats learning as a process of knowledge acquisition. Improvements in teaching strategies in this domain focus on finding better ways to deliver information or to motivate students to perform better in assessment exercises.

Group Education

The uniformity-collaboration domain is characterised by highly structured group forms of education. Learning is a process of knowledge acquisition, and the value of group interaction lies in the opportunity to reinforce the acquisition process. There is some conflict between the assumptions of the uniformity dimension and those of the collaborative dimension, evidenced by oft-repeated concerns regarding group assessments. These conflicts are responsible for a decrease in the popularity of group assessment activities in higher education.

Open Learning

The diversity-competition domain includes some current open learning activities. Students are still viewed as individual units, but more flexible teaching tactics are used. More recent open learning practices tend to treat learning as a process of knowledge construction rather than knowledge acquisition (Mayer, 1992), leading to emergent forms of education.

Emergent Forms of Education

We give the diversity-collaboration domain particular attention because we argue that this domain contains much of the current thinking regarding emergent forms of education. While the other three domains are largely representative of current teaching practice, this fourth domain is largely untested. We label this domain 'emergent forms of education.'

Our thinking behind labelling the diversity-collaboration domain 'emergent forms of education' is based on the definition of emergent as newly independent or becoming known as a result of inquiry (Sykes, 1982). Such a definition fits well with new conceptions of learning which focus on notions of inquiry and increased student responsibility for learning (Ramsden, 1992).

The domain views learning as shared knowledge construction, in keeping with notions of scholarship which emphasise a broad conception of knowledge gathering and dissemination as part of academic learning. The domain holds that the development of shared knowledge is best facilitated through collaborative student interaction (Staehr, 1993). There is also a strong focus on contextualising learning in the environment in which it finds its applicability (Friedman & Kahn, 1994). There is a focus on frequent interaction with students and an emphasis on students "organising the content and sequence of the teaching-learning process" (Riding & Cheema, 1991, p. 198). There is also a greater focus on encouraging divergent thinking and encouraging students to develop independence and responsibility for their learning engagement (Ramsden, 1992).

Overall, the domain is based on the assumption of education as a participative process in which there are very few absolutes and where both the content and the context of the learning process are open for negotiation between students and teachers. The underlying assumptions of this domain inform emergent educational practices and student expectations.

Characteristics of Emergent Forms of Teaching and Learning

Emergent forms of education will expand educational technology beyond current conceptions of flexible delivery. We envisage a three-stage model that highlights the maturity of flexible learning initiatives, from flexible delivery through flexible interaction to flexible exploration (Figure 2). The majority of current educational technology implementations fit into the first stage and very few reach the third stage. Consequently, we represent the three levels as a pyramid, highlighting the present focus on lower level activities and the need to progress to higher level activities.

The *first stage*, flexible delivery, embraces the majority of current Web-based delivery efforts. The *second stage*, flexible interaction, supports a more cooperative form of flexible delivery by using Web and Internet technologies to enable students to interact outside traditional boundaries. Many course Web sites already utilise bulletin board and chat facilities. However, this is often an adjunct to the learning process and simply continues the information delivery notion. Movement from the first level to the second implies a more conscious utilization of synchronous and asynchronous communication devices to engage students in both lecturer-to-student and peer-to-peer investigations of problems being explored. The *third stage* is characterised by student exploration of concepts using Web and Internet technologies. At this stage, students can explore concepts in a non-linear, student-directed fashion. They can, in effect, design their own learning experiences. For the most part, little effort has been expended at this level.

The emergent forms of education, situated in the diversity/collaboration quadrant, encompass the flexible interaction and flexible exploration stages. These are summarised next.

Flexible Interaction

If we accept that effective teaching and learning involve a process of developing and changing individuals' values and beliefs, enabling them to see the world from a different perspective, then it is appropriate to view the educational process as complicated layers of social interaction. But, no matter which definition of teaching and learning we subscribe to, a high level of student-student or student-teacher interaction is inevitable. The Web and the Internet offer a wide array of opportunities to support student interaction. The facilities range from the simple bulletin board, ICQ, IRC, and other generic chat facilities to the more sophisticated

Figure 2: A Maturity Model of Flexible Learning Facilities

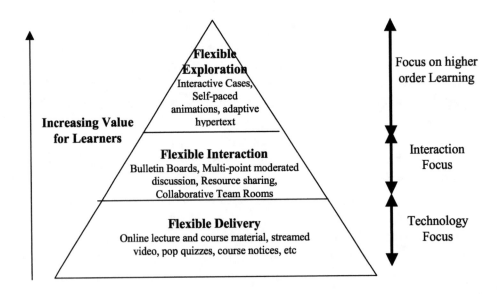

online tutorial facilities like Net Meeting, White Pine's Meeting Point and Class Point, and Lotus's Learning Space. Web-based courseware products like Web CT, TopClass, eCollege, and Blackboard's Course Site, which offer interactive facilities, are increasingly being used. However, recent surveys have shown that communication facilities alone will not deliver increased value to students or academics (Parry, Cockroft, Breton, Abernethy, & Gillies, 1999; Vargo & Cragg 1999). It is not the technology itself, but the way it is integrated into the learning process that creates value for students.

An example of an integrated learning process using Web and Internet technologies is the virtual collaborative team room. Traditional project groups often base themselves around a team room—a physical location where material related to the project can be grouped together in a work environment. As a collaboration tool, the physical team room is often highly effective. Group members are able to enter the room and begin working by themselves on a particular piece of the project, and then easily adapt themselves to working in groups should another member arrive. Further, due to its ability to develop project memory, the physical team room facilitates group members to pick up where another member left off on a particular task, thereby allowing for time-diverse collaboration. But the physical team room requires the co-location of all members of the project group. An alternative is to create a virtual team room utilising groupware applications. By locating the team room within an Internet-connected computer system, group members are able to participate in the project, and obtain many of the advantages of the physical team room even if they are in geographically diverse locations (Davis, Motteram, Crock & Mitchell, 1999).

Flexible Exploration

Flexible exploration focuses on students as active constructors of knowledge (Brown, 1994). Practically this is reflected in the widespread adoption of case-based and problem-based learning approaches to student learning (Bentley, Lowry & Sandy, 1999; Prawat, 1993). One of the perceived advantages of these methods is that they allow students to deal with complex but realistic situations, to gain experience in practical decision-making, and to develop their own models and approaches for dealing with unstructured problems (Bentley, Lowry, & Sandy, 1999). It is claimed that student recall and understanding of key concepts is improved when they are actively engaged in such realistic learning activities (Mills-Jones, 1999).

However, too often case and problem situations become overly sanitized and artificially abbreviated. The loss of richness in the material is commonly a product of tight teaching schedules or attempts to highlight the lecturer's perception of the important aspects of the case. As a result, students tend to approach the case as an exercise in re-organising the material to find the answer. This reduces both the experiential and realism aspects of the learning exercise (Bentley, Lowry & Sandy, 1999; Friedman & Kahn, 1994; Gallagher, 1994). The Internet and the Web offer a range of opportunities to address these concerns, particularly in terms of increased realism, improved student motivation, and an increased emphasis on self-directed student exploration of the material. At the simplest level multimedia facilities can enhance the visual aspect of case material. Audio and video tools can be used to upgrade case exhibits and break up the written components of the material. This is often enough to improve student motivation to explore the case material on their own or with peer groups.

In teaching cases specifically developed to take advantage of new technologies, communications tools and simple artificial intelligence agents can be used to encourage student interaction with the virtual actors in the case. Controlled interaction with artificial organisational units like steering committees or management groups can be supported allowing students to explore the material in ways not originally conceived by the lecturer. The student experience can also be enhanced by the ability to contextualise the case material within the wider context of resources available on the Web. These features all add to the complexity and realism of the problem being explored.

Another initiative that supports student-centered, self-paced learning is the use of adaptive hypertext. Technologies like XML and knowledge mapping concepts like Walden's Paths can allow students to direct their own exploration of the course material (Shipman, Furuta, Brenner, Chung, & Hsieh, 1998). By mapping all the concepts covered in online course material using XML, it is possible to allow students to retrieve information based on search criteria they establish rather than the week-by-week delivery that currently defines information retrieval.

Use of online feedback can address an often-cited criticism of flexible exploration, namely, a lack of feedback and direction provided to students. For example, results of online quizzes can provide a nominal value that represents how well a student understands particular concepts. Based on this feedback, course material relevant to identified 'problem' areas can be collected by meta-crawler programs and delivered to the student. Given that many university undergraduate courses are reaching class sizes of over 300 students, and that tutorial classes often do not benefit shy or less self-assured students, adaptive hypertext as a supplement to traditional methods can potentially offer a more effective feedback mechanism than traditional learning environments can offer alone.

IMPLICATIONS FOR EDUCATIONAL TECHNOLOGY DESIGN

Ramsden (1992) suggests six key principles for effective teaching in higher education, many of which are in keeping with the emergent forms of education.

- raising student interest and providing clear explanation of concepts;
- having genuine concern and respect for students and student learning;
- providing appropriate assessment mechanisms and useful feedback;
- setting a clear goal and providing an intellectual challenge;
- encouraging student independence and control over learning engagement; and
- learning from students.

These principles all have a strong student focus and imply the need for a flexible approach to subject design and execution. In addition, the principles depend on a strong collaborative interaction among students and between students and teachers.

Brophy and Alleman (1991) pose a series of relevant comments for curriculum developers that are also important in the development of educational technology. They state that curriculum developers should pay attention to some very fundamental questions:

- What are the intended functions of activities within various types of curricula, and what is known about the mechanisms through which they perform these functions (if they do)?
- What is it about ideal activities that make them so good?
- What are some common faults that limit the value of less ideal activities?
- What principles should be followed by curriculum developers in designing activities and by teachers in implementing them with students?
  (Brophy & Alleman, 1991, p. 10)

By adapting similar principles, and by taking into consideration the issues outlined in the previous discussion on emergent teaching practices, it is possible to outline a number of educational technology design principles. The following may be considered good principles for the design and development of effective educational technology systems to support emergent teaching practices.

1. Support appropriate curriculum goals and objectives

Educational technology needs to be developed to support educationally derived objectives and goals. This necessitates detailed exploration of how each technological mechanism supports learning in specific higher education contexts. Well-designed educational technology should allow multiple teaching goals to be realised. For a system to be widely useful and broadly accepted, it needs to fulfill a variety of educational objectives and student needs. The most important design question for educational technology is probably whether the system should be developed at all.

2. Contextualise learning

The use of new technologies offers the opportunity to contextualise learning in ways not previously possible. The use of on-line systems and simulators allow for student exploration of knowledge domains within a framework resembling actual practice. It is particularly important that technology does not de-contextualise learning by conveying mixed messages.

3. Create communities of self-directed learners

Interactive communication facilities are of value only when they create communities of learners and not when they simply provide additional avenues of information delivery. Well-designed technology-based systems also ensure that students progress in their learning activities, while allowing them to broaden their understanding and explore tangents if they wish. One of the strengths of emergent educational technology is its ability to broaden students' conceptions of the world. Pop quizzes are useful tools, animations can engage, and discussion forums can support communication, but none of these by themselves will promote learning. Good educational technology should not promote rote learning but encourage exploration, thinking, and problem solving.

4. Encourage and facilitate open discourse

Many existing technology-based educational systems are designed simply to provide a more flexible method for the delivery of existing teaching material. But traditional face-to-face delivery allows students the chance for social learning not automatically present in technology-mediated delivery. In traditional delivery, students meet together in class and in small groups as they walk to or from class. In these groups students may talk about such things as their reactions to material offered, assignments, and workload coping strategies. New educational technology also needs to provide facilities which encourage and allow interaction between students and between students and teachers. This discourse should, where possible, be removed from the limitations of time and locational constraints.

5. Provide appropriate feedback channels

Much of the existing educational technology allows only for one-way communication of material. It is important, in conjunction with the previous principle, that emergent systems allow for teachers to support and monitor student learning through the provision of appropriate feedback. This feedback is an important aspect of any students' performance and perceived self-efficacy (which in turn affects future performance). The feedback should go beyond traditional communication of results and assessment feedback and incorporate more feedback that supports, challenges, and motivates students.

6. **Support teaching and learning needs**

When educational technology is developed from a purely pedagogical perspective, it is likely to support student needs. However, it is important that emergent systems also support teachers' needs. A system's 'success' is highly questionable if it creates extra burdens for teachers or removes those aspects of teaching that are considered enjoyable. A good system should enhance a teacher's participation with students and support other teaching-related issues like satisfaction, motivation, and career concerns.

7. **Engage Students**

Badly designed educational technology can create a gulf between students and teachers, increasing student alienation and reducing their learning capacity. In these circumstances, it is likely that there will be resistance to technology use. It is possible to overcome fear of technology by supporting a variety of learning experiences and by providing choice in learning approaches. Well-designed systems should enhance a student's perception of self-efficacy and not detract from it. Educational technology should highlight a teacher's interest in their students and not create a perception of distance.

8. **Be accurate, adaptable and flexible**

Good educational systems can be costly, complex, and difficult to create and maintain. It is important that anticipated benefits are not negated by poor instructions, simple errors, and technology failings. Systems must be adaptable so that teachers can ensure currency of the material provided. It is also important that they be flexible to allow teachers to adapt the teaching practices to suit different student groupings and learners to adapt them to their individual learning styles. The need for structure in a technology must not remove a student's ability to self-regulate their learning experience.

CONCLUSION

The Web can have a profound effect on course delivery, particularly in relation to developing delivery mechanisms capable of meeting the individual needs of diverse student cohorts. As students become more informed and ICT capabilities develop, there is a need for better-designed educational technology that supports teaching practices rather than acts as a billboard advertising technological wonder.

Our thinking on flexible learning is influenced by our belief in a multi-staged approach to flexible learning, built on the foundations of constructivism and social interactionism. The advantages of constructivism lie in the emphasis on learning as a process of sense-making through experience. Learning under these modes is active and reflective techniques which have been proven to increase understanding and retention. Good ICTs offer many opportunities for students to become active, reflective, self-directed learners. The goals of education technology must be to support truly flexible forms of education, improve opportunities for learning, and cater for different learning styles. Distance learning in disguise will not result in long-term benefits to students and teachers. The key lesson we have learned from our development and assessment of educational technology over the last few years is that educational technology produced without a clear pedagogical foundation rarely results in improved student learning. Finally, the point must be made that educational technology should not be considered a focal point for educational reform but rather a resource to be integrated into a wide repertoire of educational resources.

REFERENCES

Adams, P.C., & Warf. B. (1997). Cyberspace and geographical space. *Geographical Review*, 87(2), 139-145.

Bentley, J. F., Lowry, G.R., & Sandy, G.A. (1999). Towards the compleat information systems graduate: A problem-based learning approach. In Hope, B. G., and Yoong, P., (Eds.), *Proceedings of the 10th Australasian Conference on Information Systems*, 65-75. Wellington, New Zealand, 1-3 December.

Bereiter, C. (1990). Aspects of an educational learning theory. *Review of Educational Research,* 60(4), 603-624.

Berman, A. M. (1992). Class discussion by computer: A case study. *SIGCSE Bulletin,* 24(1), 97-101.

Boyer, E. L. (1990). *Scholarship Reconsidered: Priorities of the Professoriate*. Princeton, NJ: The Carnegie Foundation for the Advancement of Teaching.

Brophy, J., & Alleman, J. (1991). Activities as instructional tools: A framework for analysis and evaluation. *Educational Researcher,* 20(4), 9-23.

Brown, A. L. (1994). The advancement of learning. *Educational Researcher,* 23(8), 4-12.

Campbell, H. (1996). A social interactionist perspective on computer implementation. *Journal of the American Planning Association*, 62(1), 99-107.

Cowley, B., Scragg, G., & Baldwin, D. (1993). Gateway Laboratories: Integrated, interactive learning modules. *SIGCSE Bulletin,* 25(1), 180-183.

Cronin, P. (1997). *Learning and Assessment of Instruction*. Web document. http://ww.cogsci.edu.ac.uk/~paulus/Work/Vranded/litconsa.htm Last accessed on 8 March 2001.

Davis, T. J., Motteram, A., Crock, M., & Mitchell, G. (1999). Recreating a university: New approaches to learning, teaching and technology. *Tenth International Conference on College Teaching and Learning*, Jacksonville, Florida.

Eason, K. D. (1988). *Information Technology and Organisational Change*. London: Taylor and Francis.

Eason, K. D. (1993). Gaining user and organizational acceptance for advance information systems. In Massser, I., and Onsrud, H.J., (Eds.), *Diffusion and Use of Geographic Information Technologies* (pp. 27-44). Dordrecht: Kluwer.

Fensham, P. J. (1992). Commonsense knowledge: A challenge to research. *Australian Educational Researcher,* 20(1), 1-19.

Friedman, B., & Kahn, P.H. (1994). Educating computer scientists: Linking the social and the technical. *Communications of the ACM,* 37(1), 65-70.

Gallagher, J. J. (1994). Teaching and learning: New models. *Annual Review of Psychology,* 45, 171-195.

Harsim, L. M. (1990). Online education: An environment for collaboration and intellectual amplification. In Harrasim, L., and Turoff, M., (Eds.), *Online Education: Perspectives on a New Environment*, 39-64. New York: Praeger Publishers.

Heylighen, F. (1997). *Epistemological Constructivism*. Principia Cybernetica Web Document. http://pespmc1.vub.ac.be/construc.html (last accessed on March 8, 2001).

Hirschheim, R.A. (1985). *Office automation: A Social and Organisational Perspective*. Chichester: John Wiley.

Johnson, D., & Johnson, R. (1989). *Cooperation and Competition: Theory and Research*. Minnesota: Interaction Book Co.

Jonassen, D., Davidson, M., Collins, M., Campbell, J., & Haag, B. (1995). Constructivism and computer-mediated communication in distance education. *The American Journal of Distance Education*, 9(2), 7-26.

Keen, P. G. W. (1981). Information systems and organisational change. *Communications of the ACM,* 24(1), 24-33.

Kozma, R. B., & Johnston, J. (1991). The technological revolution comes to the classroom. *Changes,* 23(1), 10-23.

Kushan, B. (1994). Preparing programming teachers. *SIGCSE Bulletin,* 26(1), 248-252.

Lamp, J., & Goodwin, C. (1999). Using computer-mediated communications to enhance the teaching of team-based project management. In Hope, B. G., and Yoong, P., (Eds.), *Proceedings of the 10th Australasian Conference on*

Information Systems (pp. 484-494). Wellington, New Zealand, 1-3 December.

Leonard-Barton, D. (1988). Implementation characteristics of organizational innovations: Limits and opportunities for management strategies. *Communications Research*, 15(5), 606-31.

Lieberman, A. (1992). The meaning of scholarly activity and the building of community. *Educational Researcher,* 21(6), 5-12.

Mak, S. (1995). Developing a self-access and self-paced learning aid for teaching statistics. *Proceedings of the First Australian World Wide Web Conference,* Ballina, Australia.

Markus, M.L., & Robey, D. (1988). Information technology and organisational change: Causal structure in theory and research. *Management Science*, 34(5), 583-98.

Mayer, R. E. (1992). Cognition and instruction: Their historic meeting within educational psychology. *Journal of Educational Psychology,* 84(4), 405-412.

Miller, S.M., & Miller, K.L. (1999). Using instruction theory to facilitate communication in Web-based courses. *Educational Technology & Society*, 2(3), 106-114.

Mills-Jones, A. (1999). Active learning in IS education: Choosing effective strategies for teaching large classes in higher education. In Hope, B. G., and Yoong, P., (Eds.), *Proceedings of the 10th Australasian Conference on Information Systems*. Wellington, New Zealand, 1-3 December.

Murphy, E. (1997). *Characteristics of Constructivist Learning and Teaching*. Web document. http://ww.stemnet.nt.ca/~elmurphy/emurphy/cle3.html. Last accessed 8 March 2001.

Naisbitt, J. (1984). *Megatrends*. London: McDonald.

Parry, D., Cockroft, S., Breton, A., Abernethy, D., & Gillies, J. (1999). The development of electronic distance learning course in health informatics. In Hope, B. G., and Yoong, P., (Eds.), *Proceedings of the 10th Australasian Conference on Information Systems* (pp. 714-724). Wellington, New Zealand, 1-3 December.

Parsons, T., & Bales, R.F. (1955). *Family, Socialisation and Interaction Process*. Illinios: Free Press.

Pfeffer, J. (1981). Management as symbolic action. *Research in Organisational Behaviour*, 3, 1-52.

Prawat, R. S. (1993). The value of ideas: Problems versus possibilities in learning. *Educational Researcher,* 22(6), 5-16.

Ramsden, P. (1992). *Learning to Teach in Higher Education*. London: Routledge.

Ramsden, P., Margetson, D., Martin, E., & Clarke, J. (1995). *Recognizing and Rewarding Good Teaching in Australian Higher Education.* Canberra: Australian Government Publishing Service.

Resnick, L. B. (1987). Learning in school and out. *Educational Researcher,* 16(9), 13-20.

Riddle, M.D., Nott, M.W., & Pearce, J.M. (1995). The WWW: Opportunities for an integrated approach to teaching and research in science. *Proceedings of the First Australian World Wide Web Conference,* Ballina, NSW, Australia.

Riding, R., & Cheema, I. (1991). Cognitive styles: An overview and integration. *Educational Psychology,* 11(3 & 4), 193-215.

Shipman, F.M., Furuta, R., Brenner, D., Chung, C., & Hsieh, H. (1998). Using paths in the classroom: Experiences and adaptations. *Hypertext 98,* Pittsburgh, PA, USA.

Sproull, L.S., & Goodman, P.S. (1990). Technology and organisations: Integration and opportunities. In Goodman, P. S., Sproull, L. S., et al., (Eds.), *Technology and Organizations* (pp. 254-65). San Francisco: Jossey-Bass.

Staehr, L. (1993). Debating: Its use in teaching social aspects of computing. *SIGCSE Bulletin,* 25(4), 46-49.

Sykes, J.B. (1982). *The Concise Oxford Dictionary of Current English* (7th Ed.). Oxford: Clarendon Press.

Vargo, J., & Cragg, P., (1999). Use of WWW Technologies in IS education. In Hope, B. G., & Yoong, P., (Eds.), *Proceedings of the 10th Australasian Conference on Information Systems,* (pp. 1095-1104), Wellington, New Zealand, 1-3 December.

Willis, J. (1995). Recursive, reflective instructional design model based on constructivist-interpretivist theory. *Educational Technology,* 35(6), 5-23.

About the Editors

Mohammad Dadashzadeh holds a Bachelor's Degree in Electrical Engineering, a Master's Degree in Computer Science, which both were from MIT, an MBA, and a Ph.D. in Computer and Information Science from University of Massachusetts. Since 1989, he has been at Wichita State University where he now serves as the W. Frank Barton Endowed Chair in MIS. He has authored 4 books and more than 40 articles on information systems and has served as the editor-in-chief of *Journal of Database Management*. He has extensive consulting experience and more than 5,000 people have attended his professional training seminars worldwide. Dr. Dadashzadeh has a been a recipient of teaching awards at MIT, at Industrial Management Institute in Iran, and at Wichita State University where he has been recognized by the Board of Trustees' *Excellence in Teaching* as well as *Leadership in the Advancement of Teaching* awards.

Al Saber is a Professor of Management Information Systems and Computer Information Systems at Friends University in Wichita, Kansas. In addition, Dr. Saber is serving as Vice President for Information Technology and Dean of the College of Business and Information Technology. His research interests are in MIS and leadership. He has had a distinguished career as a teacher, administrator and program developer and has developed a number of programs, among them the Master of MIS and Bachelor of CIS that today are the largest programs for graduate and undergraduate students at Friends University. Dr. Saber is a member of various professional organizations, including Information Resources Management Association (IRMA), where he served as Chairman of the Board, American Management Association (AMA) and Association of Computing Machinery (ACM).

Sherry Saber is serving as Assistant Professor of Computer Information Systems at Friends University in Wichita, Kansas. She has 24 years of experience both in public schools and higher education. Her areas of research interest are Management Information Systems and Information Technology in the classroom. She has a talent for program development and was involved in forming the CIS Degree Completion Program at Friends University. Her strength is in teaching, and she has a good reputation among students. She is a member of Information Resources Management Association (IRMA), Midwest Business Administration Association (MBAA) and Decision Sciences Institute (DSI).

Index

NEW from Idea Group Publishing